Autumn C

Autumn Carpentier

authorHOUSE®

AuthorHouse™
1663 Liberty Drive
Bloomington, IN 47403
www.authorhouse.com
Phone: 1 (800) 839-8640

Published by AuthorHouse   02/02/2017

ISBN: 978-1-4969-6564-6 (sc)
ISBN: 978-1-5246-5505-1 (hc)
ISBN: 978-1-4969-6547-9 (e)

Library of Congress Control Number: 2015900943

Print information available on the last page.

Walk on Water

Autumn Carpentier

Just as I thought the world might consume me,
pull me under as if in a stormy sea,
I felt a hand reach out for mine, lifting me up just in time.
I heard the whisper, have faith I am here; there's
nothing to be afraid of, if you'll draw near…
For I will keep you safe from any harm, do not
be distressed…do not be alarmed.
Though you may be tossed, the waters rough,
you feel as if you have had enough,
I'll be your lifeline, the light in the dark; I'll be
your map, the compass of your heart.
I'll guide you through, get you back to shore, no
matter where you are, where you were before.
And if you feel your faith begin to falter, believe
in Me, and you will walk on water.

Dedications

—⁓∿◦◗◦◖◦◗◦∿⁓—

To my daughter, who lovingly believes in me and tells me so. You've always said the right thing at the right time. You are my sunshine.

To my son, for making me laugh when I've felt like crying. I hope you know how amazing and resilient you are! You are a towering mountain of strength.

To my baby brother, who shared much of my journey with both courage and uncanny willpower.

In loving memory of my two younger brothers no longer with us. I hope that somewhere up above they know there is not a day goes by that I do not miss them, or think of them.

Most importantly, this book is dedicated to my Lord and Savior, for those countless times when He has not allowed me to sink into the abyss of life's stormy seas…

Contents

Preface

I have learned that joy and love can sometimes come from the smallest of moments and from the places we least expect, whereas heartache and disappointments seem to flow from every angle of our lives.

Throughout my journey I have frequently said that God has a tremendous sense of humor. Although there have been times I could almost see Him looking at me with a comical smile across His face on the verge of bursting with laughter, there have been other moments I felt as if He must be watching me with a discontented frown, shaking His head and letting me know that I have yet to get it right, letting me know I'll have to do it again until I do get it right.

More times than I can count, I have felt an overwhelming fear of the unknown or the inability to prevail, and it was as if God stretched out His arms to embrace me and softly whisper, "Hang on. This, too, shall pass!"

God has been my compass when I have lost my way, a brilliant light in the midst of every storm both great and small. Through it all I have found that in our weakest moment, when our greatest faith has been tested, there is no finer moment than when we rise above life's stormy seas…and walk on water.

Prologue

January 27, 2010

I aspire to write, but words do not seem to come as easily as they used to. I'm not certain if it is because they have become harder to express or simply harder to unmask. The preceding two years have felt like twenty years, and I have become so weary that I no longer have the motivation to converse with friends, go places, do anything…I certainly do not have the compulsion or energy for tedious writing and emotional dissecting.

Throughout their lives I have lectured the message, "Make the best of the worst" to my children. But as I sit here reflecting, I have one question that holds weight in both my mind and my heart; "What do you do when you continue to put forth the effort to make the best of the worst, and continuously walk away having the worst over and over again?"

For the second time in a year I met with an attorney yesterday in hopes of winning a custody battle for my son, Lucas, who will turn fifteen in four months. Within two years I have been through three attorneys, gotten divorced from my second husband, lost custody of both my children, and moved a total of five times. I have started a new job, had major surgery twice, and moved back into the home I lived in for the past ten years with my second ex-husband. You would probably think that I am an incompetent, psychopathic woman deserving of my experiences, but things are not always what they seem.

Introduction

Autumn is not my real name, nor are the names of the other people in my story. Though I have chosen to change the names along with other identifying elements, the stories behind them are very real.

Overall, if you asked me to sum up childhood I'd have to say it was filled with challenges and moments that prepared me for the life that I would live as an adult. But then I have oftentimes questioned if the life I came to live was a result of that childhood.

While I wasn't cognizant of the things that I didn't have growing up, I can distinctly recall what I dreamed of having one day. With that being said, I have discovered that irrespective of what I may have accomplished since my childhood, when I least expect it something will trigger those familiar emotions experienced in my youth. The heartache and trepidation from being ridiculed, afraid, lonely, incompetent and betrayed rise to haunt me, and can trigger inescapable emotions that take me back in time.

We come into this world an empty slate, and from the moment we take our first breath the slate becomes that which we experience, choose and preordained. The life we live is contingent upon each intricate moment we exist and the soul we create along the way. The outcome is constructed from the spirit in which we contribute, deny, and accept the crossroads taken…the storms braved.

Chapter 1

Memories can warm the soul, protect the past from being forgotten, and remind you from where you've come. They allow us reflection from time to time of our journey.

I was born in Mississippi where my entire family on both my mother's and father's side lived too. We were a fairly large group when we all got together, and those times rendered some of my greatest memories as a child. My mother conjured up a plan to have all of her children born in her home state, and though my parents moved to Texas, they willfully drove back for each of our births.

My childhood wasn't an easy childhood, and I was reared in a home that was anything but typical, maybe even considered abnormal in comparison to the majority of families. My family typically lived in a rundown one- or two-bedroom house, located in unsafe neighborhoods. One of the most dilapidated locations we lived was referred to as the "Projects", which was subsidized housing assistance provided by the government for low-income households. They consisted of one or two concerted blocks of low rise and high-rise apartment buildings, and most were in such poor shape they should have been demolished.

The first house I can remember living in consisted of the standard kitchen and living room, one bedroom and one bath for all of us to share. The bedroom was wall to wall with an upper and lower bunk bed for all four of the kids, and a shabby bed for my parents. Food was scarce, and I remember many times witnessing my father push his plate aside as if he was full, passing what was left on his plate to his children. He would go without so that we could have, and even if what he had wasn't much to give, he gave it with all of his heart.

We did not own a car that we could rely on nine times out of ten, and I remember many winter nights watching my father as he walked down the dark road in the harshest of weather, his head bent downward to fight off the bitter winds as he made his way home to us. My father worked hard to provide for his family which consisted of me, my three brothers, Billy, Corey and Colin, himself and my mother.

Right before I turned nine, my mother left my father after brazenly declaring her love for another man: Tommy. When she told my father, he didn't react in the way men in love would act at such news, but he did act out of love. I remember my father taking my three brothers and me to visit Tommy, waiting outside the music store where he worked until he came out. I'm not sure what Tommy thought would happen when he saw us, but I'm certain he didn't foresee my father insisting that he take care of us if he was going to have a relationship with his wife, then unobtrusively turn to leave.

Afterward, he told my mother that if being with someone else gave her happiness, then that is what he wanted for her. I also remember Tommy coming into my father's home courting my mother while he was at work, never once pretending to be discreet or even acting as if what they were doing was wrong. But each time he came into our home, I wanted to tell him to go away. I wanted to tell him that if my father knew of the things he was doing to my mother that he shouldn't be doing, he'd never let him come back again. I was confused as to why another man was there at all, and why my mother allowed him to be there.

But the answer was divulged when my father walked me home from a neighbor's house one night, like he'd done many times before. I'd spent countless days and evenings at my friend Gloria's house, and even got into mischief a time or two, but it had also supplied me with warmth and food on many occasions when I would have had neither. As I walked beside my father on that icy winter night, he took my hands into his own as if he wanted to take me along a different path, and in my heart I somewhat sensed that this time the walk home was different from the others before.

I can still visualize my father's face as we reached the front door, the intense cold and the combined warmth of the light bulb created an incandescent halo behind him, as his 6'2" frame turned to look down at me. We stood on the front porch hand in hand, but he didn't smile nor did he speak, his eyes conveying more than words ever could. His blue eyes held a deep, troubled sadness that made me wish I could tell him not to worry or be sad concerning whatever was bothering him. But as I was about to relay those thoughts and feelings, he opened the door and we walked into our living room where my mother and brothers sat waiting for us.

The news was swift, and afterward there was an awkward, heavy silence that penetrated the room. We were young and we didn't know how to respond or if it even mattered that we did or didn't. Two weeks later, my mother would move into a two-bedroom house not far from where Tommy worked and we would leave my father behind.

Even as an adolescent I loved to write, and after my mother left my father I began writing the concerns I harbored and my desire to live with my father, profusely disturbed that we left him all alone. When my mother drilled me about what I was writing I told her "Nothing", as she viciously yanked the paper from my hand and began reading my scribble. I knew her anger was growing by the seconds, and I became fearful of what she might do whenever she grabbed me by the arm and hauled me outside, practically throwing me into the front seat of the car. The car had barely come to a stop in front of my father's house when she grabbed my arm again and pulled me from the seat, yelling and cursing at me the entire way to the door. Leaving me standing alone outside in the cold, she got back inside the car and drove off.

My father had a look of compassion at the improbable behavior of my mother when he found me on his doorstep, but when she came to pick me up and take me home later that same night, he did nothing to stop her. My mother didn't say a word the entire drive back, or even when she opened the door of the house and stood aside to let me through. I didn't request dinner or get undressed, but went directly to my bedroom and crawled into bed beside my brothers, who were all sleeping. Colin reached up to place his arms around me pulling me close, sniffling and sporadically gasping for air due to his earlier crying, and didn't let go of me the entire night. For several days afterward my mother was extremely hostile toward me, and spoke to me only if she absolutely had to. As if to guarantee that my father wouldn't get the upper hand, I wasn't allowed to visit him or talk with him for several weeks.

I never understood why my mother left my father, nor did I understand how he let her go. After his talk with Tommy I watched him on numerous nights with his eyes closed and his head bent in prayer, wondering for what and for whom specifically he was praying. Our life with him hadn't been easy, but we never doubted his love.

We didn't realize we were deprived and that going to bed hungry wasn't common in most families, and I'm not sure we ever completely recovered from the meager necessities afforded us while growing up. We'd each eat our food at twice the intake of anyone else, embarrassed by how little we had, especially at school. I once had a lunch of bread and mayonnaise and wanted milk, but didn't have the money to purchase any. The little girl next to me said she would trade her milk for something in my lunch sack and grabbed it, turning it upside down to reveal the single item I had.

I didn't get my milk, and was humiliated at the incident as all the surrounding children laughed at my petty lunch. As an adult, leftovers now have a tendency to remain in the fridge until they've turned a lovely shade of black or green, and groceries are always pulled upfront of the refrigerator and food pantry so that it looks full, never empty.

Retrospectively, being unaware of the deprivation we faced was essentially a blessing at the time we were living in the hideous existence. Through it all, my brothers and I developed a closeness that most siblings did not have, and we were immensely protective of each other. We held onto each other as if a lifeline for each other, and that was pretty much true. Amazingly, when we were together we were mostly happy. We could play together for hours, feeding off of each other's imaginations and creativity, even without toys.

4

Being the oldest child and the only girl of four children, I had considerable responsibilities. Washing clothes ordinarily entailed throwing them into the tub and stomping on them like we were making a fine wine, then hanging them in the backyard to dry. I'd pick up after the boys and do the general cleaning of the house and other various chores, like prepare or help prepare the meals and then usually had to clean the kitchen afterward.

I remember one night standing on a kitchen chair and washing dishes as hundreds of roaches crawled around me, looking out the window, unable to discern anything other than my own reflection staring back at me. What loomed beyond the window didn't frighten me, but being alone in the kitchen where it seemed dark, empty and eerily quiet did. I felt cold and alone, the strange shadows inside the house making me tremor and imposing fear within. I finished the dishes as quickly as I could and then curled up under the covers next to my brothers in bed, seeing the demons even after I closed my eyes to sleep.

Chapter 2

My mother was an unpleasant woman to live with due to her temperament and roller coaster mood swings, you never knew what was in store or where or why her disposition might unexpectedly change. She seemed agitated with my father on a day-to-day basis, and made up for any love lost between them by doting on my three younger brothers. She didn't seem to be too crazy about me, but it didn't bother me because I was my daddy's little girl. Every time he called me princess I felt as though I was a princess, and whenever I crawled onto his lap, I genuinely believed he'd be my knight in shining armor, forever protecting me and saving me from any mishaps, great or small.

As for my mother, hard as I might have tried, I rarely seemed to do anything accurately or satisfactorily according to her: regardless of what I was doing or whom I was doing it for. I can recall how one particular afternoon when I was about five years old, that we were going to visit one of her friends. As we got out of the car she handed me the diaper bag, a glass baby bottle and her purse, telling me to clasp my oldest brother's hand as well.

As I attempted to climb the porch steps with a milk bottle still in hand, I tripped and fell, severely cutting my wrist and upper left eyebrow. At the sound of the shattering glass, my mother yanked my arm and turned me toward her as she began yelling at me for being so clumsy, and ruining the bottle of milk! As my salty tears mixed with the blood from the cut above my eye, she continued yelling at me, instructing me to pick up the pieces of broken glass.

Trying in earnest to stop the blood from going into my eyes so that I could collect the glass on the ground, I did not see my mother's friend walk onto the porch until she bent to take the glass I held in my hand. She removed the diaper bag that was halfway down my arm, and began wiping my face with the bottom of her shirt. My mother stood there apologizing to her about the mess on the porch, but as her friend looked up at her and shouted, "The child is going to need several stitches, she needs to be taken to the hospital!"

My mother didn't speak another word, and I was taken to the hospital for the stitches my wounds required. To this day, I carry the scars from both the glass and my mother's behavior. But that gracious act of kindness from someone I hardly knew taught me that you never know how the most insignificantly virtuous acts can make all the difference in someone's day, in someone's life.

With the exception of going to Mississippi to visit family for Christmas we hardly went anywhere, so whenever we did it was a rare treat. Oddly enough, it was one of those trips for Christmas that I was hopeful I would get the only thing I'd requested from Santa, which was a Barbie doll and case. We had spent Christmas Eve night with my Aunt Dee and her four daughters, staying awake all night giggling in anticipation of the upcoming day.

Waking the following morning before the sun even rose, we all ran into the living room that morning full of excitement! There it sat, my Barbie and doll case! I was downright ecstatic...until I was told that it wasn't mine, but my cousin's. I was tactfully directed to the tall blue plastic cat filled with bubble bath and a package of underwear Santa had brought me. I never did get a Barbie doll.

When I recall Christmases spent with my family as a little girl, those aren't the ones that penetrate my memory. During the holiday season I tend to think back on the last Christmas that we were together as a family, with no foresight that it would be our final. I remember it because we stayed home that year and it was filled with many good things I'll forever hold closest to my heart.

While we may not have eaten well throughout the year, we concocted a well-deserved snack for Santa, to show our appreciation for his labors. Instead of baking cookies that particular year, we baked a cake that had come from the box of food the church had brought us. The smell of chocolate cake in the oven filled the air, and it seemed so appropriate to bake a cake for Jesus's birthday, leaving a slice alongside a glass of milk for Santa Claus. Even though my brothers and I never again made a cake on Christmas Eve, the concept stuck with me, and when my own children were born we made that an ongoing tradition, singing happy birthday to Jesus before leaving a slice for Santa.

In addition to the having cake, that same year we had fruit, which was a rarity! To this day when I smell an orange being peeled, it prompts the memories experienced that Christmas. Not only was having fruit an indulgence for us, a decorated tree was even more of a luxury. I remember the lights that year, and though there were no gifts under the tree, the lights twinkling in the dark that Christmas Eve ignited my spirit. Since we didn't drive eight hundred miles to watch everyone else have a grand Christmas, it made ours seem almost normal.

It was also that same year that my father opened the trunk of his car, and before he could shut it I saw the only gift I had requested from Santa. Intuitively I knew not to utter a word about seeing the doll, but I'd later learn that it broke his heart that morning when I went running into the living room and the same doll was sitting there as if from "Santa". My mother had no idea what had occurred, but as I looked toward my father, bewilderment consumed his face as he quietly stared back at me. My parents could not afford to run to the store and get me another gift, and with nothing else for Santa to leave me, his only option had been to go ahead and set the doll out.

At the time, I did not fully comprehend the significance of that moment, nor did I recognize that a fundamental part of my childhood was gone and could never be recaptured. All I knew was that having the doll in my hand may have been that much more incredible to me by the fact that my daddy had miraculously managed to get me the doll I wanted, over anything else in the world.

With nothing more underneath the tree on that Christmas morning, in the early frosty dawn, my mother and father led us into the backyard to unveil their unbelievable gift to us; a palomino pony my father had traded his carpentry services for. There she stood in all her glory, the prettiest horse I had ever seen, and Daddy placed us individually onto her back and slowly walked us in a circle. As the sun began to rise and shed its light across the yard my mother voiced that it was time to go inside, but I wanted to remain outside and ride. I wanted to ride her faster and farther, fleeing the limitations of our backyard into a world where there were no limits.

And while a little bit of Christmas magic died for me that morning, my love for horses was born. Many years later I rode that same horse in the rodeo, working to take care of other horses by feeding and cleaning their stalls so that I could manage to keep her. I rode and enjoyed her as often as possible, and won several blue ribbons barrel racing with her when I could afford to participate. I never did feel as though I was giving anything up doing the chores to keep her, because she was worth every bit of the hard effort or any sacrifices she may have caused.

Memories, stories…the good and bad still frequently shared when everyone gets together. Being the oldest of three brothers, mine were plentiful! My mother depended on me to take care of my brothers and make sure they stayed out of as much mischief as feasibly possible for three young boys. She referred to it as "keeping an eye" on them. It was during one of our mother's afternoon naps that the house grew mysteriously quiet, and I knew trouble was in the making.

As I investigated my hunch, the only noise I could hear was coming from the bathroom. I knocked on the door to question what was going on, and as Corey hesitantly opened it, I noticed he was holding a wad of toilet paper against his chin. I questioned him about the self-made bandage, urging him to remove it from his chin so that I could see underneath. His rebellious "No, you'll tell momma!" prompted me to reassure him otherwise, once again requesting he show me. His hand was no sooner removed from his chin, than I screamed out for our mother as if a wild beast had attacked.

The story later unfolded of how they were playing on their bunk beds, when Corey made the assumption that he could fly. So fly he did--right across to the opposite side of the room, where his chin struck the bottom bunk rail, and causing him to get three stiches in the emergency room. The scar remained his entire life, and years later would help identify him after he was brutally murdered.

***

Unsurprisingly, my mother married Tommy shortly after she divorced my father. I wish I could say that things improved, but it only worsened with time. While it may have been noticeable that we struggled, just how much we struggled and the disparity by comparison seemed elusive to outsiders. My mother would never acknowledge, and in fact would argue, that the abuse never occurred. But each day bequeathed to us some type of misery and sadness created by both emotional and physical abuse perpetrated by the two of them.

As if the emotional and physical abuse weren't enough at home, shame and ridicule were likewise included in the mix. I recall shortly after we moved to a new town, one particular incident that tainted my spirits and humiliated me to the very core. I was invited to a sleepover, and because I didn't have many friends I was extremely excited to go, if nothing else to get away from home. I took a paper sack and filled it with my only pair of pajamas and my toothbrush, and eagerly headed over to the girl's house after school for the weekend sleepover. Most of the girls had grown up together and had been at the house for some time before I arrived, but it seemed everyone equally welcomed me, and we all spent the evening enjoying fun games, great food, and staying up late into the night to tell ghost stories.

Early the next morning before breakfast, one of the girls became rattled. It seemed she had placed some money in her travel suitcase and couldn't find it anywhere around the house. The mom was informed of the dilemma, and the decision was made for each of us to empty out our bags and display what was inside. Surely, none of us had taken the money! But there seemed to be no other choice but to check, "just in case." I was secure in the knowledge that I had not taken it and did not hesitate to grant access to my folded brown sack. The mother had already gone through two of the other girl's items when she selected mine and turned it upside-down. Out fell the money. I had no money, and my intuition told me the money that was now lying there with my things was the money they had been looking for.

As my face turned red and I denied taking the money, everyone was distracted by a knock on the front door. It was my mother coming to get me and take me home so that I could stay with the boys while she went to bail Tommy out of jail--for stealing. That was her frenzied and fanatically loud explanation when came to the door that morning, and everyone on the other side of me heard every disgraceful word. With my belongings in hand, I walked past the girls and headed outside to leave with my mother.

Not a word was spoken, but every eye was on me as if I should be in jail myself, and at that moment I felt that's exactly where I was. I sat beside my mother in the car disheartened, halfway listening to her telling me how Tommy had been incarcerated for stealing from the part-time sales job he had taken. Tuning out her voice I distracted myself, thinking it ironic that Tommy unnecessarily ridiculed and depicted my father as a loser, while he was the one who sat in jail.

As children, it was hard to observe our father openly derided each time he arrived for his visitations, just so he could spend time with us. Upon his arrival Tommy would instantly begin badgering and belittling him, or yelling and cursing at him without any provocation. Attempting to deter his visitations, they deliberately moved us further from the town he lived in. It played on our emotions and it played on our father's emotions, and somewhere along the way my father came to the conclusion it would be best if he were entirely removed from the situation.

He eventually relocated to Mississippi and never found his way back, leaving us behind with a stepfather who emotionally and physically abused us, and a mother who closed her eyes to it. Even though I wrote to our father religiously, begging him to come, we never heard from him, and he later claimed that he didn't receive my letters. In fact, we seldom saw him as the years passed, and ultimately the time would come when we didn't see or hear from him at all.

I continued to write to him in hopes of getting a response of some kind, wishful that he would come back if nothing else than to protect us. Paradoxically, considering our everyday plight, there were frequently times when we visited our father that we needed shelter from him as well, though not for the same reasons we needed protection from Tommy and mother. Our father did not inflict his wrath or abuse on us, but simply liked to drown his misery in beer, whisky and rum. Habitually, he'd start with beer and work his way to the hard liquor, playing the saddest music as loud as he could. The blinds were kept shut to keep the house dark during the day, as his moods became even darker throughout the day.

There were times he would rant and rave as if he was directing his wrath at someone, throwing whatever was within reach across the room in the direction of his anger. It was during those times that our father became a dangerous stranger to us. I did what I could to divert the boys away from him, by having them play outside or in their room if possible. The majority of the time we'd end up in the bedroom behind a locked door without having had dinner, fearfully waiting for the episode to pass. There was nothing we could do to drown out the torturous sounds that filled the house as he drank more and more.

Our mother leaving our father marred him dramatically, and the manner in which she did it seemed to taunt him every waking hour. In addition to his avid drinking, we watched him go through women almost as incessantly as his consumption of liquor. After he got a much younger woman pregnant and moved her in, our time with him was preponderantly strained, whether he was drinking or not. Their relationship was volatile, which provoked increasing terror at times when they yelled and threw things at each other. She finally packed her things and left around the time she was due to have the baby and he never heard from her again whatsoever, not even about the baby.

A short time afterward, he married a girl only six years older than me after she became pregnant with his child. They later had four children together, three girls and a boy, and remained married for many years. Never once did he abandon them. It was bittersweet that he was there for them, loving and taking care of them, whereas it was emphatically opposite for us. He'd call here and there, making excuses that so much time had passed because he'd lost his little black book, which of course contained our phone number. But with the invention of cell phones, the little black book was no longer a plausible excuse when we didn't hear from him.

While our father was supporting his other four children, Tommy was supporting us…if you could call it that. He had everyone convinced that he was such an incredible man taking on four children that were not his own, and rendering the role of fatherhood. But Tommy was an arrogant bully, whose quest each day he woke was to demoralize and oppress us any way possible, by using inconceivable tactics. He'd attend church on Sundays singing and playing his guitar in praise, and afterward go home and burn the boys with cigarettes, or strike them wherever his hand or belt happened to land. He was more discreet with my abuse, but nonetheless left his mark on the innermost core of my being. Time would never efface or diminish the abuse we sustained.

In addition to the food and other various items donated by friends through the church, we also obtained food stamps. Canned foods were delivered to us in boxes, the labels torn off of the cans with no way of knowing what was in them. We called those "surprise dinners", because until we opened the cans, we wouldn't know what were having for dinner. Canned beets and spinach aren't the tastiest of dinner combinations even when there is nothing else on the table, and especially enjoyable to have that combination by candlelight due to unpaid electric bills and disconnected service.

Our hunger was never satisfied from the portions of food provided at mealtime, and the meals weren't even plausibly nutritious. When we did not get the canned goods or meals from someone else, meals primarily consisted of cookies and milk or biscuits and gravy for dinner. Unlike my father, Tommy never let the boys have the last of anything on the table, indifferent to their hunger pains, he'd force them to remain at the dinner table until he had consumed the last of the food.

Our clothes and shoes came from garage sales and second hand shops: the clothes never the right size, the soles of the shoes virtually falling apart at the seams sometimes. I can vividly recall my brother Billy, walking up the school sidewalk as the bitter wind penetrated his frail body because he didn't have a coat, the soles of his shoes flopping with each step he took allowing the cold to spread even further. I watched as they pointed to him, insensitively laughing at his discomfort.

The electricity was turned off on a regular basis, so washing ourselves required heating the water on a gas stove--if the gas wasn't turned off as well, staying warm at night by sleeping together and sharing any covers that we had. Even the most basic toiletry items were sparse or not available, including menstrual pads when I started my period. I had to fold toilet paper several times over to insert inside my panties in place of a pad the first time I started my cycle, and numerous times afterward, praying that I didn't bleed through.

Unfortunately, my worst nightmare came true when I got home from school one afternoon, and discovered blood on the crotch of my pants all the way up to my backside, realizing it was there when I got off the bus and walked across the street. I was mortified and cried the entire night from the humiliation, remaining home the next two days from school.

Alarmingly, I began my menstrual cycle at ten years old and was petrified that I had something terribly wrong with me, or even worse, that I was dying. The only reason I learned I wasn't dying, was by offhandedly saying something about my lower back hurting to my mother while sweeping the floor, and mentioning that I had gone to the bathroom several times in my panties. She instructed me to pull my panties down to show her, and a strange smile crossed her face when she saw the brownish discharge, flippantly informing me that I had started my menstrual cycle and was on the verge of entering my womanhood! My mother had never discussed the facts of life with me so I was extremely embarrassed and self-conscious with the entire incident.

I was especially uncomfortable when she took it upon herself to make a personal announcement about it to Tommy later that day, going into every detail with me there. He leered at me as if turning into a "woman" implied I was waiting and ready for sexual action, creating a terrible awkwardness for me whenever he was near. If I even insinuated there was inappropriate behavior from Tommy, I received retaliation and additional anger and resentment from both of them. Strangely enough, my mother's actions came across as if letting me know that he was incapable of such unthinkable behavior, and that I was crazy for my feelings and thoughts.

But the more she sought to entertain the development of a father-daughter relationship between us, I was increasingly convinced that the relationship Tommy had in mind was not of a platonic nature. As time passed, it was even more unsettling and bewildering that she would become angry and annoyed with me when I didn't want to be around him, then in the next moment acting as if I had become her adversary in some strange way, plotting against her while scheming to get attention from her husband.

She discredited my fears as if they were a childish malady in my head, but the discovery that Tommy's malicious intent was not in my mind but a legitimate fear, was imminent. The first time he inappropriately touched me occurred one night when the boys and I had contracted a stomach virus, and we were all in bed running a high fever. Even though I had my own room at the time, my mother had placed me in the boy's bedroom on their bottom bunk bed, with Corey and Billy on the upper bunk. Colin was the only one of us who wasn't sick, so after she checked our fever, had him in bed with her for the night.

I'm not certain how long I'd been asleep, when I felt hands repeatedly moving across my chest, and turned to find Tommy instead of my mother. His voice was shushing me and telling me that he was checking my fever, but as his hands lingered and began moving downward, I knew it was more than that. As one hand gradually began sliding in the direction between my legs, the other hand was drawing me against him. He had removed my panties almost down to my knees, when I heard him unbuckling his belt, confining me as he did. I wanted to scream, but froze in fear, and just as he moved closer my mother yelled across the house to him. He franticly stood, pulling at his pants and buckling his belt before he walked over to open the door. The light from the hallway was just enough that I could see the penetrating stare he turned to give me before leaving, the look that told me it wouldn't be the last time. He then walked out of the room leaving me alone in the dark, the tears falling silently down my cheeks as I tried to contain my wretched sobs. Shaking vehemently, I knew it was no longer due to the fever but from nothing less than absolute fear.

When morning came he acted as if nothing out of the ordinary had occurred, but I knew that it had. Confiding in my mother wasn't an option, and I didn't know who else to talk with or what to do. Every time she wanted to send me somewhere with him I would beg her not to make me, finding any plausible pretext not to go. Going to the store or errands in broad daylight was one thing, but there was one night that he wanted me to ride with him to a secluded dumpsite. It was located miles from the house off an isolated road, and with the exception of the truck lights, there were no other lights. The road would have horrified anyone, even under normal circumstances.

I knew I couldn't make that ride alone with him, frightened that he would have his way with me one last time and then leave me for dead on the side of the road, claiming I had run away. I had heard too many stories with just that scenario, and I had no cause to believe I couldn't become another statistic. With those thoughts flashing before me I began to cry, telling my mother I didn't want to go. She instantly became angry, shouting at me and telling me that I had to go, shrieking the question "Why not?" To my dismay I was unable to find the words rationalizing my apprehension, positive that she would dismiss my allegations and insist I go regardless.

That ride was the longest ride I had ever been on in my life, sitting as close to the car door as I could while gripping its handle the entire time. I was prepared to jump from my seat even if it killed me, but to my surprise he never laid a hand on me that night. I was never sure if it was because he had gotten enough thrills from my distress, or if he'd just wanted to witness my articulation of anguish and fear expressed to my mother, having already arrived at the conclusion that she'd never condone such accusations. Whatever the reasons, it became clear to me that I had to take care of myself, because my mother wasn't going to.

I wasn't aware anyone else even suspected what was occurring, until a couple of years later when my father arrived at my grandmother's during one of our visits with her. He stood at the bathroom door as I brushed my hair and in a discreet, even toned voice said to me; "If Tommy ever touches you in a way that makes you feel uncomfortable, I want you to tell me." He didn't linger for a reply, but turned and walked away, and the subject was never approached or further discussed between us.

For some strange reason, I didn't want to tell him that Tommy already had. I think maybe I feared being subjected to the same humiliation on a much higher level once it was publicized. What if people thought I'd done something to entice his behavior? At the end of the day it would be Tommy and my mother's word against mine, and after everyone moved on with their lives, I'd be left alone with them... with him.

A short time after my father approached me that day, my aunt witnessed a hug exchanged between my father and me, and took me aside to explain that my behavior was inappropriate for a young lady with a man. I looked at her bewildered, uncertain what it was that she was implying. I was not just a lady with any man--he was my father, who wanted to protect me. I said nothing in response, but in my mind questioned why the abuse from Tommy went unnoticed by her and everyone else, yet she was lecturing me about my own father who had never once laid a hand on me with nothing less than love and respect? It did not seem fair, and I resented that she impugned my father's character by implying that he would hurt me, while they all seemed to look the other way from the man that actually was.

Chapter 3

I guess being the oldest of the boys made Billy extremely protective of his siblings and mother, or maybe that's just who he was. He hated Tommy, and the war between them was as powerful as between any two grown men. Even though Tommy was the head of the home, Billy was the man of the family: at twelve years old. Strong in mind and heart, there was such a spirit surrounding him that you couldn't overlook it or not sense it whenever he was near, and made you miss him when he wasn't. He was kindhearted, thoughtful and generous, with a soul that was wise and exceptionally mature for his young age.

He routinely worked at the same little convenience store that I worked at on the weekends to help contribute toward buying food and whatever else we needed at the time. Unbeknownst to us, his goal was to buy something special for each of us Christmas of 1976. He swept the parking lot, cleaned around the building, replenished the shelves and any other miscellaneous chores the storeowners needed. He gave some of the money he earned to our mother, while managing to keep enough to buy each of us a gift. Mine was a lovely granite necklace, and his entire face lit up when I opened it and squealed with delight. I had never been given such a lovely gift, and the look of joy across his face at my happiness, meant as much to me as the gift itself.

It was the following May that I came home from school to find a note on the kitchen table from my mother briefly explaining she had taken Billy to the doctor due to a debilitating migraine so severe, he had begun throwing up. I didn't really know much else, but a nagging, sad feeling was in the pit of my stomach. I started my chores to keep me occupied, and then finished his so that when he returned home he wouldn't have to. I kept reflecting on the previous week when he'd gone on a Boy's Scout camping trip and how we had all missed him so much. None of us had ever gotten to do anything like that, but his Boy Scout troop and the other families pitched in enough money so that he could go, and he had been so excited when he headed off on his adventure.

The week he was on his excursion, our electricity was off, and the 'surprise dinners' were at their worst. I remember sitting around the kitchen table watching the candlelight flickering across the walls and across the faces of my two younger brothers, thankful that at least one of us was in a better place. While we missed our brother, we were glad he was instead somewhere having a happy, ordinary life that every child should have. It was a week of his life that we lost, and a mere prelude to the emptiness that we would soon experience.

It was the week after returning home from his Boy Scout trip that Billy's headaches seemed noticeably closer together, causing him to miss several days of school. As I was leaving to catch the morning school bus I quietly peeked into his bedroom to check on him, and found him lying on his side with both hands holding his head, his eyes closed. It looked as if he were sleeping, so I softly closed the door trying not to disturb him and hurried to the bus stop. When I got home from school that afternoon I ran inside to check on him, only to find his bed empty and beside it the note my mother had left behind. It was later that same evening she came home without Billy, and sat us all together to explain that he was extremely sick and the doctors were running tests probing for the reason why. He would never come back home again.

***

As a little girl I had lived back and forth between my grandmother and aunt up until the beginning of second grade. Struggling to keep my mind from going to dark places while sitting in the hospital with my mother, I recalled how I had run away from school to find my family, wanting so desperately to be with my mother, father, and brothers who were in Texas.

I remember how abandoned I felt, questioning why my family had not taken me with them in the first place. I'd decided that if they weren't coming to get me I'd make my way to them, and on one of the hottest days in the state I walked right out the school doors and onto one of the busiest streets in Mississippi. By the time they realized that I was missing, I was already over a mile from the school and drenched in sweat. Returning me to school, they carried me into the nurse's office and removed my dress, leaving only my slip that was plastered against my heated body. In order to accelerate bringing my body temperature down, they pumped me with water and applied cool rags behind my neck.

After running off several more times, the principal called my grandmother to inform her something had to be done to prevent me from constantly leaving the school. Out of concern for me my teacher offered her assistance and promised me a prize if I wouldn't run away again, and for some reason I had the crazy notion that I'd get a watch.

When I had made it several weeks without additional episodes, I asked my teacher for my reward, but when it was a Coke and not a watch like I'd expected, feeling double-crossed I ran away. When my teacher inquired me why, I told her my disappointment about the watch. The next day she brought me a little pink wristwatch that she gave to me after class, and I was so overjoyed that it brought tears to her eyes. I never ran away again, and kept the little watch long after it didn't tell time.

It was a lonely time for me, compounded by the fact that I always felt a burden to my grandmother and aunt, especially when they took me to stay weeks at a time during the summer months to visit my grandmother on my father's side. She lived in Brandon, which was a remote region in Mississippi scarce of homes or anything else for miles. With no one to play with or nothing to entertain myself with while I was there, I came up with the ingenious notion to ride the bike along the nearby country roads. Starting back to the house after a couple of hours, I raised my face to the sun as the warm winds caressed my face, praying to God as if I was the only person he had the time to listen to and the only one that mattered. I missed my family immensely, and as if pushing them out of my mind I began peddling harder and faster.

My ankle suddenly caught inside the chain, causing the bike to fall and land on top of me with my leg pinned underneath. No matter how much I pulled I could not release my ankle from the chain, and no matter how much I yelled there was no response. I lay there for hours before my uncle discovered me, detached my foot, and carried me back to my grandmother's. They bandaged my swollen, black and blue foot while lecturing me on my carelessness, sending me directly to bed for the rest of the day.

I was sitting alone on the front porch the following afternoon as dusk began to descend, crying from my injury and the dejection I was feeling, when I saw my parent's car pulling into the driveway. I was so ecstatic to see them that I forgot about my ankle and eagerly stood to run and greet them, stopping dead in my tracks from the excruciating pain. But it didn't matter, because within seconds of the car coming to a halt my brothers jumped from the car and ran to me, tightly holding onto me as they wrapped their arms around me. I could tell they'd missed me as much as I had them, and dreaded my parents leaving me behind when they all returned home.

But when they left a couple of days later, to my surprise I went with them. While I never understood as a child why they left me to begin with, when I got older the rationale inferred was that they could not afford me at the time. They had chosen to keep the boys together and left me until they could get on their feet. The hurt and insecurity from abandonment was something I never outgrew, in any relationship I had. And as I sat beside my mother in the waiting room at the hospital, I felt that same heartache and loss.

***

June 1977

The first night Billy was in the hospital, they had to perform an emergency operation to remove his spleen. My mother sat alone with me in the waiting room that night, her hands folded, staring at the ground. She absentmindedly shook her head back and forth as if in denial, repeating, "It's not good…it's not good." My grandmother and aunt were called in from Mississippi, and I began to comprehend that if they were coming to Texas, something was terribly wrong.

After his surgery I was briefly allowed in the recovery room to visit my brother, and can vividly recall him lying there against the white sheets, machines pumping and tubes protruding from all parts of his feeble body. I stood observing him for some time, clasping his hand in mine and wishing that he would open his eyes and speak to me. It wasn't too long before a nurse retrieved me from the recovery room and escorted me back into the waiting room. Corey and Colin were not at the hospital with us and I wondered how frightened they were feeling without having either of their two oldest siblings with them. I was torn between wanting to be with them and wanting to be at the hospital, worried for my mother and Billy.

Billy had been in the hospital only a few days when it was decided Corey and Colin should be taken to Mississippi and stay with family while Billy was in the hospital. We sat in the waiting area on Mother's Day, watching as he walked in our direction, grinning as he deliberately walked right passed us as if he didn't know us or didn't notice us. He could barely walk yet was putting forth extra efforts to lighten the mood for everyone, and we all laughed as if there wasn't any reason to be sad, and our visit was all fun and games.

Unable to sit up for an excessive period, we were only able to visit with him for a short while before he had to go back to his room. After we had each hugged him and said our goodbyes I watched as he slowly returned to his room, then turned to find both Corey and Colin crying. No one had to explain that something was wrong with their brother… they knew.

My aunt took Colin's hand and turned for us to follow her to the car where our clothes had already been packed so that we could leave directly from the hospital--and leave our brother. No words were spoken, no one looked at each other. No one dared. My brothers and I drove to

Mississippi with my aunt and grandmother where they remained while we made the trip back to the hospital in Texas.

Before heading back, I called my father to let him know how grave the situation had become, and convey that it was urgent he contacted me. Everyone I spoke with claimed they did not know how to reach him. Years later I learned that he had been with my uncle when I called but refused to speak with me, fearing it was a hoax to locate him in attempts at collecting unpaid child support.

Upon our return to Ft. Worth, we drove straight to John Peter Smith Hospital (JPS) to see Billy and get an update. The news was unequivocally devastating: Billy had non-Hodgkin's lymphoma. From that moment on, time seemed to pass as if I was living someone else's life. His health had been rapidly worsening since first admitted into the hospital, and it became a race to see what we could do to combat his illness.

A publically funded county health network, JPS provided care to men, women and children of Tarrant County regardless of circumstances. Billy could not have received more excellent treatment or care at any other facility. His doctor was indisputably one of the most intelligent, trustworthy and compassionate doctors we could have hoped to attain. He kept Billy under his continuous care and practiced unsurpassed medical treatments in striving for my brother's successful recovery.

Because of his rapid decline, the hospital arranged for Billy to be transferred the following day to MD Anderson Cancer Center where the Oncologists could begin the most unsurpassed, even more aggressive treatments available. In the meantime, the nurse escorted us to the room he would remain in until he was relocated. At the door of his hospital room my aunt grabbed me by the arm and looking into my eyes said in a strange voice, "Whatever you do, do not let him see you crying or upset." and with that she turned and led me inside the drab hospital room.

I could hear him before I saw him, screaming out in torment for the pain to stop. "Don't cry...don't cry..." I repeated to myself as I walked toward his bed. He was sitting up squirming in pain, and I bent forward to kiss his forehead and let him know I was there, wishing I could take his pain away. The scream from merely touching him made me go cold, and I precipitously discerned it wasn't going to be okay.

I turned so that he wouldn't notice my tears, and found myself looking into my mother's face. For all of the differences and heartache I felt she had allowed us, I knew no parent should ever have to endure witnessing their child suffer so horrifically and be helpless to do anything about it. Without caring what my aunt had told me earlier, I grabbed my mother and hugged her, both of us crying together. My brother didn't see our pain or anyone else's; his own pain was far too immense.

My aunt and I returned to Mississippi that night to pick my grandparents up so that they could also go to Houston and be with my mother. With the strenuous trip ahead of her, the doctor had ordered my mother to go home the night before his transfer and get rested. Tommy offered to remain at the hospital with Billy so that she could get a few things she'd need for the trip, take a bath, and attempt to repose. Months afterward we learned that Tommy never stayed with him, but left the hospital to be with another woman.

The nurses did not shy from letting us know that it was Billy's worst night that night, and tortured from his pain had called out for us. After he became even more distraught that no one with a familiar face, a familiar touch or recognizable voice came to him, the doctors and nurses did what they could to keep him tranquilized.

Would he have even known that we were there? It never mattered to me either way when I learned of the details and all he had suffered that night. It only mattered to me that he was my brother, just a little boy afraid and in pain…and that he had been left alone on what was to be the last night of his life.

Billy was transported to MD Anderson in Houston by ambulance, the speeding lights flashing and it's sirens blaring, as our mother and Tommy sat next to him. My aunt, grandmother and grandfather and I were driving from Mississippi to meet them, our own emergency lights flashing as we sped down the highway. Even though we were averaging a hundred miles an hour, I recall feeling like we were not moving fast enough and that time had all but frozen. I'll never forget that evening sunset was one of the most breathtaking that I'd ever seen. Without a cloud in the sky, the sun appeared as if it had exploded with fiery oranges and reds, mixed with the brightest pale yellows that fused with variations of muted purples. The sky was almost silver instead of blue, and filtered rays of light radiated across the sky casting a mystical haze, giving it the look of a painted picture, of an afternoon in heaven.

When the sun could shine no longer or cast its illumination onto the horizon, darkness engulfed the night as if there would never be light again. I kept gazing outside the window searching for the moonlight, but in its place I began to spot little twinkling stars scattered across the sky enhancing the illusion that perhaps the moon had burst, dispersing its light across eternity. I watched for any sign of a falling star to make a wish...just one falling star and a single wish was all I wanted.

But I never saw that falling star, nor did I get the chance to make my wish as the sky gave way to tall, clustered buildings, and the lights of the city diminished any chance of spotting one. We were now in the middle of Houston where you could barely differentiate the sky from the buildings looming massive and ominous, appearing infinite against the sky.

We checked into the hotel room to freshen up from the tireless ride before going to the hospital, and not at all familiar with the area took several wrong turns searching for it. We somehow parked in the furthest garage from the hospital, and to save precious time already lost, we calculated that it would be faster to walk, opposed to parking elsewhere. My grandmother could run circles around any of us, but my grandfather was barely able to walk, so we walked across the road from the parking garage we were at and headed to the hospital. Once we made it in, we then had to establish which wing of the hospital Billy had been admitted and how we could get there.

Riding up in the elevator my stomach began to feel sick, and my heart began to beat faster. I felt as if I had been in a race and couldn't catch my breath. All the while, the elevator kept going up and up...and up. As we stepped off, a young nurse at the receptionist desk politely asked if she could help us. "Yes." my aunt spoke. "We are looking for Billy Carrington who was admitted today. Do you happen to know which room we can find him in?" I noticed that she did not look our way as she excused herself, briefly returning with a man who looked to be one of the doctors on staff. He motioned that we follow him, and expecting that he was taking us to the hospital room where Billy would be, was surprised when he lead us into what looked to be his private office. The office was located on an outside wall, and though I would have normally observed the numerous windows, I did not look anywhere but at the doctor as he motioned for us to take a seat and then sat down directly across from us.

There was nothing to prepare us for what lead to his next words. Without hesitation and matter-of-factly he spoke: "We just lost Billy. I'm so very sorry." I tried to grasp what he had said, insistently questioning where my brother was so that I could run and find him. I jumped from my seat and headed for the exit, but I stood there not knowing where or which direction he was, as my tears gave way to tormented sobs. This could not be happening! Someone took me by the arm and lead me back to my seat inside the room, where they quickly brought my mother to join us.

She began recounting the details of Billy's passing, sharing how she had watched as they attempted to resuscitate him, and then described how she had held his warm body when it was over. Out of nowhere, she mentioned that he didn't have shoes on his feet, and turned to inform the doctor that she wanted him dressed and his shoes on before they took him to the morgue. Her mind somewhat in a state of denial, she didn't want her son to be cold when he left the building.

I knew that she knew it didn't matter about the shoes or clothes, and recognized it was my place to validate that it didn't. "Mother, that's not Billy. He's no longer here. He won't know if he has socks or shoes or warm clothes on..." From deep within the core of my faith, I believed that to be true, but in that heartbreaking moment, I simply didn't care. He was not with us anymore.

The doctor looked at my mother inquiring how old I was, and my grandmother spoke up informing him that I was thirteen. He looked at me as if speaking to himself, and whispered almost inaudibly, "She's a wise young girl and considerably mature beyond her years..."

No, I wasn't wise or mature beyond my years. I was grasping at any plausible approach to handle the moment, grasping for the strength to get through the inconceivable nightmare. Then everyone began to talk as if the tragedy was merely some kind of a routine hospital visit, as if we would be taking Billy home with us in our own car and not in a hearse.

The discussion involving the necessary arrangements for my brother faded into the background, as I quietly advanced toward the windows I'd completely disregarded when first entering the room. Gravely despondent I stared out into the night, longing only to see my brother once more. I stood there, mournfully looking upward into the evening sky no longer searching for falling stars, no longer looking at a sky, but heaven. I blocked everything else out, probing the dark horizon before me as if waiting to behold an angel…an angel finding his way home.

It was almost dawn that June morning when we all returned to the motel. I could not stop crying as my mother held me, just as much for herself as for me. My aunt and grandmother made the necessary phone calls to inform family we had lost Billy, some already arriving from Mississippi believing they were coming to offer support with his stay at the hospital, only to learn their assistance unnecessary. As if the heartache wasn't enough, in the midst of pain came anger, when I heard Tommy and my father shouting at each other outside the hotel room. Their confrontational behavior was because Tommy did not want my father there, vindictively barricading the door and impinging upon his efforts to reach me. My father was overwrought from losing his son and not arriving before he'd died, unsure what his place was at the moment or what to do.

I left my mother's side and ran at them, my arms flailing in every direction, not caring which of them I made contact with or how much my wrath was felt. My words bellowed out with all the passion of unbridled emotion that came with hate, anger, disappointment, and frustration. How could either of them do this right now? Hadn't we all been through enough? My cousin grabbed me and led me to her car, where I fell to my knees at the car door sobbing profusely, wishing it would all fade away. But it was only the beginning of the heartbreak and sorrow to come.

We escorted my brother's body home, each introspective over what had taken place in the two short weeks since Billy had been admitted to the hospital. It was hard to comprehend that only two weeks had passed since he'd been home, and now he was headed home, but not the way we had planned. Brokenhearted and exhausted, no one wanted to put forth the effort to talk.

In a trance, I was drawn back into reality when Tommy randomly began whistling a tune from the backseat that sounded like something you'd whistle while skipping and laughing on a beautiful, sunny spring day. But it was none of those things for us. How could anyone in the car possibly feel up to whistling? My grandfather all but snarled my thoughts out loud, "Who the hell feels like whistling right now?" With that remark, Tommy stopped whistling and never said another word the entire ride home. I never forgot that sound, never forgot that I wanted it to be Tommy's body inside that casket and not that of my twelve-year-old brother. To this day, I can't tolerate the sound of whistling.

Corey and Colin had already been taken back to Richland Hills, and as soon as we arrived my mother quietly led them into the back bedroom and delivered the news that they had lost their brother and he wouldn't be coming home. I can only speculate the sorrow her soul suffered from the burden of having to share such a loss with them. I never heard a sound come from the bedroom, but when they filed out the look on my younger brother's grief-stricken faces made my own heart ache for them. As I went toward them to offer arms of comfort and love, it was even more heart wrenching for me to know there was nothing I could do or say to take away their pain. They too, would have to endure the loss and the suffering only time could dissipate.

To have the death of a child or sibling is a terrible heartache, but not having the finances to bury that child is unfathomable. We didn't have the money to buy a burial plot, nor did we have the money to buy anything decent to bury him in. Because we didn't have insurance or prepaid plot, our only option was to have him buried in a plot that belonged to Tommy's family located in Desoto, Texas. A baby blue suit was donated for his burial, as were the clothes that my brothers and I wore to his funeral. My grandfather and grandmother paid for the funeral service and burial necessities, which included a white hearse and white Town Car for transportation to his resting place.

My mother held both of my brothers against her, one on each knee, and I sat alone until my aunt moved up a pew to sit by me, cradling me against her shoulder. Even with her next to me, the emptiness and heartache was overwhelming and almost unbearable. The doctor he initially had at JPS attended the service, as did the two nurses who had stayed with him on his last night there, sitting directly behind us as part of the family.

The memorial service was short as the story of his life swiftly unfolded, some things known to many, some things only to a few. The sermon included a letter that Billy had written in his class shortly before his death, expressing the things he enjoyed and some of his many aspirations. He loved baseball, horses, and being in the Boy Scouts. He loved animals and fishing with his younger brothers at a nearby pond, often heading that direction whenever they could sneak away. He wanted to own a cattle ranch somewhere in Texas when he grew up, and if he couldn't own a ranch, he wanted to play professional baseball.

The final words accredited to his short life revolved around cherished fragments of who he was and what made him Billy. Like his delightful sense of humor and how he enjoyed making others laugh, his infectious smile reflectively sparkling in his chocolate brown eyes. He had made a lasting mark on all who knew him, and there was no doubt that everyone would miss him, his absence leaving behind a tremendous void. I remember perceiving how short the time describing his life took, and how infinite the amount of time he would be missed every minute, of every hour, of every day. He was laid to rest on a beautiful spring afternoon, and everyone not a part of the funeral procession respectively pulled over to the side of the lanes as we made our way to the cemetery. Men who were working alongside the thoroughfares pulled off their helmets and hats and placed them against their hearts as the white hearse with the tiny white casket drove past them.

When we reached the cemetery, last words were spoken and the final prayer offered in hopes of providing comfort. The brief ceremony was over, and before the last "Amen." was spoken, Tommy turned to leave as if he had somewhere else to be. Never looking back once, he walked across my brother's fresh grave leaving his footprints behind as he did.

Afterward I did what I could to keep things going for the boys and my mother, peering inside her room regularly I'd find her lying across the bed as if she too, had died. I think a massive piece of her did die when she lost Billy, and she progressively became distant and disoriented. Tommy did nothing but bestow his wrath upon us and then leave each night, manifesting even greater depression for her, but giving my brothers and me the relief we needed during our own time of grief. Corey and Colin seemed as lost as I felt. Not only did I feel lost, I felt overwhelmed and needed someone to aid in helping me with the boys.

I reached out to my father by writing him almost every night, imploring his greatly needed comfort and assistance. Not only did he not come, he also never responded with a letter or phone call of any kind. It was my belief that by then his preferential drug wasn't prescribed by a doctor, but one equally as helpful in forgetting. I imagined that he had put us out of his mind as he profusely poured bottles of alcohol into his body and soul.

Our mother disengaged herself not only from us, but also from the outside world, in bed and usually unconscious most days from the medication she was taking for depression. She was completely unaware of what was going on around her and she didn't want to know.

I comforted my brothers as much as I could and ensured they ate, completed their homework, and that they were clean and had clean clothes. There were days when I felt the burden overwhelming, as I avidly begged my father to get in touch with us. But as the weeks and months passed, I recognized that not responding to me was his way of disconnecting, and no matter what I told him I was wasting my time and energy. It would be a considerably long time after my brother's death before we ever heard from him again.

A few months after the tragic loss of her son, our mother announced she was leaving Tommy and that we were moving. The tiny, three-bedroom house we moved into was centralized in the oldest areas in Richland Hills, but the location enabled us to remain enrolled in the same school district and to keep what few friends we had. My mother hired on as a school bus driver, which allowed her with us most of the time when we were home, and therefore when school started that August we all went back, picking up the pieces of our lives as best we could.

Chapter 4

I met Rene soon after mother left Tommy and we moved to our new neighborhood. She lived down the street from us, and attended the same school that I was enrolled in. We fast became friends, and much of the time we were inseparable. Occasionally permitted to visit with friends other than Rene I was invited to watch a football game at the beginning of the season, and that's where Logan found his way into my life.

He was a tall, cool blonde with dazzling green eyes, and there was an immediate chemistry between us that couldn't be denied. Having such a deficit of love for the majority of my life, I grabbed at the opportunity to have someone that I felt cared for me and showed respect toward me. His family pretty much adopted me after I met them, and my relationship with Logan soon became one of the happiest times I'd had in my life. I learned so much about what I wanted from someone, but more importantly I learned what I did *not* want. It didn't take me long to learn that one is just as important to know as the other.

Logan wasn't just older than me in years at the time we dated, he was much more sexually knowledgeable and experienced by comparison, and within months after we met, taught me the skills he'd studiously mastered. I must say that for a young girl never having experienced a loving, physical relationship, I was as ready for us to share the experience of lovemaking as he was. Maybe I thought that if I gave myself to him I'd reclaim something lost, and wipe away my previous experiences at the same time. I simply wanted to be loved and feel safe, and as our relationship evolved, the first time he took me he did everything he possibly could to make me feel both.

He had arranged for us to have an evening at his parent's house while they were gone for the weekend, and I remember him taking my hand as he quietly led me into his bedroom where he had music playing in the background and lit candles flickering against the walls. He seemed to sense my discomfort as I stood at the door feeling shy and awkward, but then gently and lovingly he took me to a world I had never experienced. As "Somewhere in the Night" played softly in the background, I gave him the only thing that was mine to surrender; I gave him the piece of my heart that no one else had ever touched.

When I snuck back into my room in the wee hours of the morning, I took the time to write all of the details in my personal journal, never wanting to forget the experience or the evening. We were together at every feasible opportunity from that point on, and occasionally came unbelievably close to being caught "with our pants down".

There was never a time we didn't want to be together, and generally spent it driving in his '64 Mustang convertible talking, laughing, and excitedly sharing dreams and hopes for our future. He loved that car, and it tickled and surprised me when he offered to let me drive us to Church's Chicken to get dinner for his family. It wasn't a significant distance from his house, and I needed the practice since I didn't have a car and seldom got the opportunity to drive.

I used extra precaution as I drove, and because there wasn't a drive-in I pulled up to the front of the building to park the car so that we could go inside and place the order. I wasn't pleased that the car was not parked in the center of the parking spot, so I put the car in reverse and backed out to re-park. Logan very calmly asked what I was doing, as I explained my goal to perfectly park the car, putting it once more in drive and placing my foot on the gas pedal. I turned just in time to observe his smile disappear and change to absolute chagrin, before I heard him yell, "Stop!" rather than hitting the brake, my foot pressed the gas pedal even harder and the car plunged all the way up to the fryers, both of us sitting there with half the building down around us.

Everyone froze, some with food halfway to their mouths, some standing on the opposite wall acting as if they were holding it up. The employees standing at the fryers looked on as the chicken they had been cooking began to burn. I couldn't tell if it was the chicken, the car, the building, or Logan creating the most smoke! He turned to look at me as if I was an alien from another planet, and at that particular moment I was wishing that I could be on another planet.

The police were called, and as the cop began notating the information on the ticket, grinned a quirky little smile and then looked at Logan and me. "So, what happened? You hit the gas instead of the brake?" For a split second I pondered hitting the officer as well. "You think?" I replied. The officer's smile dissipated and he didn't seem entertained by my response in the least. Logan stood next to me without speaking a single word as if dazed by the entire scene, and oblivious to anything going on.

The most phenomenal thing of all was that Logan's car had only a slight indention. We had just destroyed a building, but that car was miraculously still perfectly capable of driving off the premises, which we did…to a Burger King. Logan drove.

I continued to write in my journal documenting that incident and everything else going on with school, my friends, his family, my family, as well as documenting *everything* pertaining to Logan and me. I was never late for my curfew, which was something that my mother could count on regardless of where I was going or who I was going with. But being on time for my curfew wasn't the concern she had on one of the nights Logan dropped me off after a date. I walked in to find her holding my journal with a look I knew meant nothing short of death, and I considered turning and running away as I had when I was a little girl, trembling with fear for what was about to happen.

There was no doubt she had read my entries, including intimate details of the night I snuck out of my room to be with Logan. She became irate, yelling and throwing things and telling me to tell her that it was not true. I was embarrassed and ashamed, and I was afraid she wouldn't let me be around Logan anymore, so I lied. I told her I'd invented all of it and had merely read about such things, reassuring her that what I had written was nothing but my vivid imagination.

My journal was never returned to me, and I couldn't bring myself to approach her for it. However, I made a mental note to eradicate anything incriminating, or that could possibly disclose other feelings or incidents I didn't want her to know about.

It was a couple of months later when I felt as though I was going to faint. I was in my midmorning class at school when I became so sick I could hardly stand on my own two feet. Remarkably I made it home and into bed, where I began to tremble as if I were standing naked somewhere in the Artic. Earnestly feeling the compulsion to go to the restroom, I barely managed to get out of bed before I lunged over, debilitated from excruciating stomach spasms.

I had difficult menstrual cycles and on average bled for seven to ten days, then would maybe skip a month here and there. All I could assume in that moment was that I was making up for missing the previous month's cycle. I could feel the clumps of blood as they left my body and heard them as they landed and splashed within the toilet. Violently shaking and feeling disorientated, I stood to flush when I observed massive amounts of blood floating in the toilet.

What kind of period was this? I had a vivid flashback of the day Tommy had taken me into the bathroom and made me look into a paper cup at the blood he'd scooped into it, his proud evidence that mother had experienced a miscarriage. At the time, the fetus had resembled nothing more or less than huge chunks of blood to me.

Something inside told me that I needed to get help--and fast. By the time I managed to reach Logan I was almost incoherent and could hardly grip the phone in my hand. He could hear my voice beginning to fade, and all I heard him say was "I'm on my way!" By the time he arrived at the house he found me catatonic on the bed, the phone still clutched in my hand, unmindful to the fact that he picked me up and carried me to his car. As I gradually became somewhat alert I grasped that he was as scared as I was, and that he was speeding to the hospital in a slightly panicked state of mind. Arriving at the hospital's emergency entrance, Logan jumped out of the car and ran to my side, and with one fluid movement promptly swept me into his arms then preceded to carry me inside.

The emergency staff instantly recognized that I required immediate medical attention and whisked me to a private room where the doctors and nurses congregated beside me. Logan wasn't allowed to remain with me as all of this was happening, and laboriously began an attempt to contact someone and convey what was going on. Our neighbor, who we had become close friends with, soon arrived and somehow accomplished reaching my mother. I dreaded my mother being called and was afraid of anything being disclosed to her, especially after the diary incident.

After a thorough exam, the doctor performing my examination questioned if I could be pregnant. My flustered and emphatic response was "No!" He paused for a moment before asking if I was sexually active, and I unswervingly responded with another no. He then turned and left me in the room lying on the table not knowing what was going to happen, and that's when my mother flounced in taking control in her unsympathetic way. As if a young child I had no voice, no thoughts, and no responses to the hospital staff unless she told me to.

I lay there amongst all of them talking as if I wasn't even the patient, wishing my mother would totally remove herself from the room. I shut my eyes to shut her out the only way I could without leaving myself, and heard her say with a heavy sigh of relief, "I just knew something had happened to Colin!" It was said as if my crisis was obviously nothing to be too alarmed over, and I had inconvenienced her for coming. I had nothing to say to her or to the doctors, I just wanted to see Logan and go home.

I was released that same evening, without medications or a follow-up doctor's appointment. Not only did I lose a child that day, but due to the DNC never performed and the lack of proper treatment, the incident ultimately triggered major health risks and jeopardized the hope of having children: all because I was afraid of my mother finding out the truth. Mercifully, no one ever found out that I had a miscarriage, and I never shared with anyone about the fetus I mistook as merely abnormal masses of blood…and flushed down the toilet.

Neither Logan nor I ever spoke of the incident, and I often wondered if he ever put two and two together. We didn't date for very long afterward, and in later years that followed we briefly dated before permanently going our separate ways. He wanted to marry me both times we dated, and while I never doubted his love for me, by then I could no longer conceive him being a part of my future. The future we had outlined and imagined would be so perfect.

Soon after the breakup my mother moved back with Tommy, having apparently grown tired of working and dealing with the challenges of three children. I was older now and much more knowledgeable of things unlike before, which intensified my awareness of his immoral behavior. I knew I would leave sooner than later, no matter what it took. Moving back in with Tommy after the hospital incident and breakup with Logan, took all but the last of my strength and I became less tolerant of everything and everyone, mostly of mother and Tommy.

As I had predicted, there did come a day that the fighting and yelling became too loud and the mood dangerously heated. I could no longer tolerate it and began yelling at Tommy, telling him how much I hated him for all he had done to my family, and cursing the day he had become a part of our lives. My mother started retaliating, antagonistically yelling at me and saying hurtful things in his defense. No longer able to control her anger at me, she slapped me across my cheek with blunt force. My face burned where she'd hit me and I stood there dazed, proclaiming that if she hit me again I'd be gone.

I didn't actually feel the second blow when it struck, but it was a piercing strike that hurt deeper than the last. I turned from her, grabbed my purse, and headed for the door. Her angry threats of me never returning home if I left didn't phase me in the least, as I walked away from that house and the unequivocal misery it held. As much as I wanted to protect my brothers, I walked away from them too. With a determined stride I headed to my best friend's house, unable to see the path before me through the blinding tears. I never looked back.

Not quite sixteen and a year of high school left, I moved in with Rene and her family until I could find an alternate place to live. After graduating high school at seventeen, I was accepted full time at the

University of Texas in Arlington and opted to rent a bedroom close to the college. Attending fulltime during the day while working two jobs on evenings and weekends, I became overloaded after attending only a few semesters. In order to pull myself together and get on my feet, I began searching for full-time employment so that I could alter my schedule and work during the day while attending school part-time in the evenings.

With that decision, I began walking the streets of a rural town called Haltom City, located on the outskirts of Richland Hills. The town was so small that you could literally walk from one side of the street to the other by crossing two lanes of minimal traffic. The buildings were quaint, each connected by a sidewalk that enabled one stop shopping, dining, post office services and banking without ever having to drive your car. The sidewalk ran from the beginning of the town to the end of the town, where the city library sat nestled in a charming park. I began my walk on the first side of the street making stops at every business, and though I wasn't positive what I was looking for, I was unrelenting in my quest to find something.

It became increasingly warmer outside as I went from building to building, my spirits and perseverance growing thin. Finished with the first side of the street, I crossed over to the other side where the local bank was and stood at the entrance, debating on going in or not. I had no experience whatsoever to pursue a financial occupation but figured I had nothing to lose, and at the very least I could perhaps get a sip of water to cool me down.

As my eyes adjusted from walking out of the sunlight and into the bank, I noticed you could easily see across the street from the windows that lined the front of the building. There were people standing and sitting throughout the bank, and I had no indication as to which direction to head or whom I should approach to inquire about an available position. The teller stations were located to the left, each with several people waiting in line for assistance, and rationally concluded that I'd have greater luck if I approached somebody at a desk rather than remain in the teller line. I was in the process of crossing the room to find someone when I glimpsed a tall, handsome man approaching with his hand outstretched to offer his firm, yet gentle handshake, and a calm smile that convinced me he could eliminate my worries.

He didn't introduce himself, but casually escorted me to one of the nearby desks, then politely offered me a chair and something to drink. With my "Yes, please." response, he walked away and promptly returned with a Coke and package of peanut butter crackers, which he handed to me. Smiling in appreciation I accepted the Coke and stuffed the crackers inside my purse, while managing a timid thank you at the same time. I was already guzzling my drink as he made his way to the other side of the desk to take a seat, his penetrating stare almost making me choke on it.

I found that I couldn't even manage another sip, and carefully sat the drink on top of the desk within reach. His eyes never waivered as he crossed his arms on top of his desk and leaned forward; "Well, young lady, what can I assist you with today? You look like you are a little hot and worn out from the heat!" I foolishly felt a different kind of heat penetrating my body as an all-telling flush rose to my face, and my train of thought foolishly pondering, "What *did* I come in here for?"

He sat back in his chair as I took a deep breath and responded to his question, "Well, sir, I was wondering if I could fill out an application and speak with someone about any positions that your bank might have available." It was almost like a game of tennis, as he moved forward in his seat once more and peered directly into my eyes. "What are your qualifications?" The ball apparently again in my court, I rattled them off: experienced in handling cash transactions, good with numbers, worked immensely well with people, eager to learn, and willing to start anywhere.

He stood, and I suspected he was going to shake my hand in farewell and lead me toward the exit, but surprisingly led me to another desk across the room. The desk nameplate read "Mr. James Brenner--President", which gave me confidence that things were satisfactorily advancing since I was going to meet the president of the bank! Thankfully, I had managed to find someone kind enough to get me to the second step of a potential opportunity.

I thanked him as I took a seat, expecting him to walk away after having done his part, then watched him as he walked around the desk to sit across from me. Turning sideways just enough to gaze out the window he crossed his legs and again leaned backwards. I wasn't especially definite what I should say or do, because it seemed he was killing time waiting for Mr. Brenner, as he quietly watched the activity across the street.

Maybe I should have eaten those crackers he had handed me earlier, it seemed this was going to take much longer than I'd anticipated, and I cringed as my stomach let out a hunger growl just as he turned to face me. "Do you know what has impressed me about you?" I contemplated if the answer he was looking for pertained to my aggressive behavior or how unabashedly I had guzzled my Coke without spilling it on my dress.

But before I could speak he answered his own question. "I watched you walk this entire street in the heat, going in and out of each door with a smile and determination on your face. I think that takes spunk, and I'd like you to interview for a bookkeeping position available that needs to be filled immediately." I was elated that I was going to get a chance at an interview, and grateful that he had apparently taken the initiative to schedule an interview and there was no need for me to speak with Mr. Brenner.

He stood to escort me to the Human Resource department and instructed me to have a seat, coming back momentarily to introduce me to the HR supervisor with whom I'd interview. He smiled a reassuring smile and I smiled in return, when it occurred to me he had never introduced himself. I reached out to shake his hand in appreciation, mentioning that I had not caught his name. He glanced briefly at his employee and grinned as she made the introduction: "This is our president, Mr. Brenner!"

I was hired that day and started the following week. It would be years later before I comprehended the degree in which that day irrevocably changed the course of my entire life. I remained there shy a couple of years, working my way up and making a friend who eventfully became my roommate. I purchased my first "new" used car and managed to find an unpretentious lifestyle. Before long I started a new job at a much larger bank closer to home, with an increase in pay and the promise of opportunity and advancement. Having no second guesses that it was a wise decision for my career, I gave my two weeks notice.

Chapter 5

I happened to meet Adam on a girl's night out on the town, after I teasingly implied to my girlfriend that I'd meet someone that night and marry him. Haphazardly joking about that may have altered my destiny a little bit, because once Adam and I met things seemed to accelerate overnight. Scarcely a couple of months into the relationship he wanted me to move in with him, even though he lived with his mom at the time. Live with his mom? I couldn't help but be pensive of the concept after the experience of living with my own mother! And what mother would be ok with her son living with his girlfriend? I knew they had been extremely close, partly because his father had left her when she was pregnant, and Adam never having met him.

One of my motives for living with Adam was the fact I constantly struggled to make ends meet even with my recent increase in income. Though diligent in my efforts to put back money for college, it seemed my money never stretched adequately enough to include that ambition. Moving in together seemed like a prudent solution for both of us to save money and attain some of our goals. So after numerous weeks consisting of several heartrending deliberations, I packed my things and went to live with him--and his mom. As if things hadn't moved swiftly enough by taking that step, he asked me to marry him soon afterward. My analytical assessment was that we already lived together as if we were married, so why not be married? I reservedly said yes to his proposal, ignoring that little voice whispering in my head--or was it in my heart?

Both frequently obscured one from the other more often than not by then, and at the mere age of twenty-one I felt as if I'd already lived a hundred years times two.

With the anticipation of getting married, Adam and I moved into our own apartment with the original objective to get married before the justice of the peace, and thus be done with it. We could not afford the luxury of a big wedding, and it seemed impractical to spend money we did not have. But before we could make it to the courthouse, my mother learned we were getting married and felt we should have a wedding, even though she didn't have the money for a wedding either.

We compromised and planned a cozy, traditional ceremony in a tiny church that she had attended, with me wearing a secondhand wedding gown, sparse decorations and a homemade decorated cake served. Though I hadn't wanted a wedding I now had one, and reassessed the perpetuating dilemma I'd lived with my entire childhood--somehow she had managed to manipulate what I did and how I did it. Hell-bent on mending the relationship with my mother and thinking that if I gave in to her it would do the trick, I prudently forged onward.

Three weeks before the wedding date, I came across a listing posted in the paper for a bank teller located fairly close to where I was working. It was a part-time position that would allow me to attend school as originally planned, and since Adam worked nights, also take up the lonely hours I had during the week when he was at work. We both agreed the change a smart move that would render opportunities to advance my career and with his blessings, I left early from work in the middle of an unexpected afternoon storm to apply. By the time I ran to and from my car in the rain without an umbrella, I was drenched and shaking from the cold.

Once at the interview, I debated on asking for a hot cup of coffee, then decided against it. Through chattering teeth I determinedly explained that my motivation for changing jobs so soon, was because I was getting married and going back to school. The employment manager hired me on the spot, and impatient to begin I provided my current employer with two days notice and not the standard two weeks.

Eager about the changes I was making, it was the first time I'd ever felt excitement for the direction I was headed in my uneventful life.

In the midst of planning the last minute details for the wedding and honeymoon, scheduling classes for the upcoming college semester and training for my new job, I was struggling to maintain some kind of sanity. Though a little on the fatigued side I was still excited and ready for our honeymoon trip to San Antonio over the weekend, convinced the mixed emotions I was experiencing would ultimately pass in time. I was certain all the way up until that Halloween Friday when I looked up to see a virile, handsome man in his mid twenties being escorted in my direction. As my supervisor reached my station, she casually introduced me to Derek as our newest employee. My heart really did stop, and as we were introduced he smiled as if he knew I could barely breathe.

Though no masks were permitted, all of the employees had dressed in costumes for Halloween, myself included. I was dressed as a baseball player with a uniform three times my size, tennis shoes, a ponytail covered by a baseball cap which was turned sideways, and large freckles painted across my face. I became aware that my freckles must have been fading into the flush that I could feel spreading from ear to ear, and mesmerized by him standing in front of me, all I could muster in response to his cordial "Hello!" was a shy smile.

As he moved past me I turned back to my workstation as if he did not faze me in the least, still unable to breathe normally, feeling slightly dizzy. My first whim was that I shouldn't be having that kind of reaction to him, or any other man, since I was getting married the upcoming week...I needed to get a grip for crying out loud! Presuming it was simply because he was so darn good looking and I was about to dive into marriage, I wrote it off as normal pre-wedding jitters. That was all it could possibly be, that's all I'd allow it to be, and I married Adam as intended.

Not a soul detected that the entire time I walked down the aisle I was questioning what the heck I was doing, trying to force any thoughts of Derek out of my head and reassuring myself I was doing the right thing. But no amount of reasoning could stop me from thinking of him or keep my heart from pounding. My thoughts should have been on

Adam, and my heart pounding because of him! It broke my heart and frustrated me that there seemed to be no escaping Derek's power over me: and it certainly didn't make any sense to be walking into the arms of one man while coveting another.

As fate would have it, when I got back from my honeymoon, I was handed the delightful duty of training Derek. My heart filled with excitement and anticipation each day I went to work, for no other reason than I looked forward to being near him. There wasn't a female who worked at the bank that didn't flirt with Derek, including the women that came in to complete their banking transactions, musing over other obtainable services. It was unabashed lust. Outwardly I made a point of disregarding him, determined to be unlike the others just to prove a point. Point was that I was married.

Adam continued working evenings while I worked the day schedule, therefore he'd be gone by the time I got home. Routinely, I'd stand at the window each night watching for his blinking headlights to let me know he'd entered the apartment complex, which was my signal to put dinner on the table. As soon as he came in the door his dinner was served, and in-between chewing his food we'd take that opportunity to briefly visit since he had to leave within the hour. Once he left I'd begin cleaning the dinner dishes and repetitiously preparing for the next day. He typically arrived home a little before I left for work, his day ending and my day beginning--like clockwork. I was sitting at home each night alone and frustrated from being married but not feeling married, inexperienced at dealing with any aspect of a marriage.

A few weeks into Derek's training, I had a vivid and unnerving dream about him. I was in the elevator at work going up another floor, and when it opened Derek was standing there waiting to get in. Nothing was said as he stepped in, but the moment the door closed, it was if we were magnets and came together. An insatiable passion invaded my body, and I woke up drenched in sweat as if I had run a marathon, my body still trembling. I lay there the rest of the night unable to sleep, replaying every detail of the dream over and over in my head. I had never experienced anything even bordering such passion. For the next couple of days afterward, I turned red just being in the same room, and speculative that the other girl's faces turning red when he came near was due to the exact same reason. I hated it, and wanted no part of it.

That theory seemed to elude me as we headed out from work at the end of our shifts, casually discussing the possibility of going to get something to eat as if we had known each other for years. Before I knew it, I found myself seated in his Camaro driving to a restaurant in downtown Ft. Worth as if merely going to dinner with a friend. Seated across the table from him I was determined I'd be the cool, collected woman and keep my distance, not permitting him to make me tremble as he had that night in my dreams.

But by the second drink, I was barely able to contain myself from crawling across the table and sitting in his lap. Instead, I settled for telling him how enormously attracted I was to him and that I was walking out of my short-lived marriage because I could not stay married to someone else while feeling the way I did for him. What I couldn't begin to explain was how I'd wanted this moment all of my life, but never saw it coming quite like this.

I'd planned on attacking him and taking what I could once we were back in his car, but as it happened my body decided the fourth drink I'd consumed was one too many. With the car door opened, I hacked up a lung along with half of the food I had eaten earlier. Nice...couldn't ask for a better impression than that! Derek drove me back to the bank to retrieve my car, and once I became coherent he followed me home.

I made it up the stairs and into the apartment, not caring about anything other than overcoming the night, hoping the following morning I'd find that it had all been nothing but an awful dream. If I could just fall asleep, that would be the trick to put all of this nonsense behind me! I called in to work the next day, using the alibi that I had some kind of virus and could barely get out of bed. In all fairness, it was partially the truth! I needed an extra day to get the "virus" out of my system.

Two days later I stood alone in the elevator as the elevator doors opened, and there he stood. Everything seemed like it was in slow motion, like I was reliving something from the past. The doors closed behind me, and without warning I was swept into his arms kissing him like I had never kissed anyone, or been kissed by anyone before. It felt familiar, and for a split second I remembered my dream.

We pulled apart as the doors opened, and I could feel my heart pulsating wildly, fearful everyone could detect it pounding through my shirt, not to mention the radiant blush spread across my face. I stepped out as if nothing had happened, but in my heart I knew something unconscionable had occurred. In that brief instant, my life changed in ways I'd never begin to distinguish for many years to follow.

I learned a little too late in life how considerably easy it is to discombobulate the dreams we have with the reality we live. We tend to conjure up fantasies that reflect in our minds what we envision we need or want, making something or someone fit into our world of make-believe, frequently creating confusion between reality and fantasy. In my mind this man was everything I had ever dreamt of, all that I could possibly ever want or need. The passion between us intensified with each touch and I couldn't get enough of him. My body would spontaneously melt into his, my appetite for him never satisfied. To this day I have never experienced anything similar to those days and nights, and it's probably best that I haven't. It seemed as if he became my heartbeat and the breath of my lungs. I could not seem to function when I was away from him, or whenever I was with him. I wanted him to be a part of my life every waking moment.

In all fairness it seemed only right to be upfront with my future ex-husband, and I'd voluntarily shared what was going on between Derek and me. An annulment would have been the answer, but unfamiliar with the legalities of ending our short-term relationship, we agreed it logical to file for a divorce. We had already taken steps to separate and file, when Derek asked to visit with Adam at our apartment. Perhaps to tell him his side and apologize? It didn't matter at that point why he wanted to talk with him or even what they had to say to each other, because after their talk my husband of three months left that same day.

The funny thing was, there seemed to be a lack of surprise on both sides. It was almost as if Derek was asking my father if he could court me, and it felt as if my father had lovingly handed me over. The trade was made; freedom for Adam, chains for my heart. A short time afterward we officially filed for a divorce, and I never saw him again. Derek broke up with the girlfriend that he had dated throughout high school and most of college. She had been his first love, and somehow I fooled myself into believing I would be his last.

The more involved we became, the greater I resented the women who did not care if he was dating, married or gay. Derek was aware of how handsome he was, and his charismatic personality created a dangerous combination. He was used to the attention and girls fawning all over him, and unfortunately, he was used to playing the field and giving them attention in return. It was shameless lust demonstrated by most of them, and none of them cared to conceal it.

Some advise that you should never work with someone that you sleep with...you would think I'd have been a bit more privy to that theory. Working together and observing his relentless exhibition of flirtatious mannerisms soon took a toll on me. It was apparent that if our relationship was going to last, one of us had to find alternate employment. Even though I didn't have another job lined up, I gave my two weeks notice, convinced that it was the most favorable decision for us.

As I walked out the bank door my last day I felt displaced and a tad bit stupid, leaving my job and handing Derek over on a silver platter. It dawned on me that the provocations and behaviors I was leaving behind would not be leaving with me! In addition, he still had income, and I didn't even have a concrete plan for employment that would provide me steady income. I was barely making it when I was employed! Would he come to my rescue, or was this relationship on a much different level for him than it was for me? Two weeks after leaving the bank, I still did not have a job, and was quickly running out of time in every viable way.

No matter what level the relationship, there is no level that is comfortable if one person is not working, is crazy jealous, and has too much time to fixate on both! I fell into a slump almost instantly, but persevering I decided the first sensible thing would be to request my position at the bank be reinstated. I couldn't imagine why they wouldn't be thrilled to oblige! I was a dependable, bright employee, and there was no reason on earth why it couldn't be as mutually advantageous for them to rehire me. When I went into the office of my former boss to pitch the idea it was as if she was playing basketball, making a slam-dunk faster than I could grab for the ball. The game was final, and there would be no rematch! I'd have to find work elsewhere.

Feeling dejected and stressed from the predicament at hand, I took a Saturday afternoon drive to the bank to pay Derek and several other friends working a quick visit in-between my errands. I pulled into the teller lane and after a brief moment it became clear to me that he wasn't even aware that I was there. Moreover, was the fact that he was spellbound by the brunette practically sitting in his lap, flirtatiously tossing paper balls at him while laughing as if a seductress in waiting, and she didn't intend to wait much longer!

I calmly pressed the button for service to make my presence known, waiting patiently for the little tart to quit flirting with my boyfriend. But within two seconds of me saying hello and another twenty seconds of waiting for Derek's response, she became enthralled once more with the same beguiling cat-and-mouse game! Of course, Derek was finagling as best he could to play their little game while trying to make sure his girlfriend did not feel the least bit cheated for attention at the same time. But I was feeling cheated, and one paper ball too many tossed at him and I succumbed to jealousy, insisting in a malicious voice that she stop…*OR ELSE*!

The tellers and everyone in the drive-up looked my way as if on the edge of their seat pausing in expectation for the consequences that went with my *"or else!"* His reaction was something similar to a child being caught with his hand in a cookie jar and then acting like he shouldn't be reprimanded! I could have driven right through the wall into both of them. Repeatedly!

Deciding it best to forgo that plan, I brusquely informed him I'd be waiting out by his car for him when he came out. Since that hadn't been a part of his original prospect, that bit of information probably thrilled him to no end. But wait I did. Of course his casual, calm, and indifferent mannerism further infuriated me, which gave him the opportunity to attempt convincing me I was overreacting and should consider going to the eye doctor for an eye exam, because apparently I was seeing things that weren't happening!

Passion is an interesting emotion. It can take you to the greatest heights and it can take you to the lowest lows, and Derek did both of those for me. I was extremely conscious of the fact that women seemed to be drawn to him like the tide to the shore, and the women at the bank were merely a trivial percentage. It seemed as if inherently a part of his life and consequently a part of mine. With the fear of losing him I held on even tighter, while he was doing everything he could to disentangle the noose around his neck and keep me at bay. There were lies I would catch him in and other lies that I wasn't aware of or didn't pinpoint until weeks, months, and even years later.

A day and a dime almost too late, I located a job as a new accounts representative at another bank! In dire need to salvage my finances and thinking it would be a fun alternative to make extra cash, Derek and I both went to work part–time at the baseball stadium that summer. Now, I know what should have crossed my mind; hadn't working together been what started all of this in the first place? But if he was going to be there making spare money and it provided me the extra money I needed too, it seemed like a clever solution. Things seemed to be calming to a degree and I was beginning to feel the choices I had made for the wrong reasons were heading in the right direction. But all good things must come to an end.

I guess I should have been mindful of the old saying "If they'll do it with you, they'll do it to you". Unchangeable by nature or design, it seemed an endless cycle of me wanting a committed relationship with Derek and him being committed to having a relationship with me and everyone else. I don't know why he didn't just let me go. Why the need to hold on and have other women on the side? Was he afraid I'd shoot him if he walked away from our relationship, or perhaps be inclined to shoot the other woman if I found out what was going on between them? It was probably a good thing I didn't own a gun.

The final demise of our relationship took place when I noticed his car parked outside an elementary school one weekend while sitting at a stoplight. I felt a sense of misgiving in the pit of my stomach that something was about to go awry when he wasn't in the car. Where was he? More importantly, who was he with and why leave his car at a parking lot?

The apartments across the street from the school had a sidewalk that led behind the building, so I sat down on the stairwell nearest the street to wait for Derek's return. Fixated on the parking lot, it seemed an eternity I sat there, my heart pounding faster every minute my mind imagined the worst-case scenario: or so I thought! Obscured from their view I observed them pulling into the parking lot, then watched as he got out of the car from the passenger side and walked to her side.

She was young, beautiful and poised, glancing up to him with an exuberant smile as he opened her door. She stepped out of the car, and their body's seemed to instinctively meet in unison to hug. Hopeful the hug between them was nothing more than a platonic hug between two really good friends, I knew differently as they began to kiss. I did not want be the spectator of the scene before me any longer. With unreserved madness I got into to my car and drove across the street, pulling up on the other side of his car. Barely waiting for my car to come to a complete stop, I opened the door and jumped out, startling them.

They both had that same look: guilty. The sad part was that I still wanted to fight for him, wanted him to tell me a lie, tell me something…anything. But to my surprise, he turned his back on me as if I was the perpetrator standing in his spot, with someone that I shouldn't have been caught with. Unable to assault me physically, he mercilessly berated me with his hateful and vindictive words, while she got into her car to drive away. As far as Derek was concerned our little altercation was finished the moment she left, impulsively abandoning me to follow after her.

I irrationally began calculating options inside my head, and came to the dauntless conclusion to trail behind him and prevent him from dismissing me in such a cruel fashion. It didn't take long before he spotted me, and approximately half a mile further down the road he pulled into an old, empty parking lot, and I followed suit. Had he perhaps come to his senses and decided to tell me we were heading home--together? He shot out of his car and in my direction, visibly enraged.

His next move took me by surprise and left me downright flabbergasted! Reaching across me to yank the keys out of the ignition, he threw the keys as if hurling a football into the arms of a wide receiver at the other end of the field. Accomplishing his mission, he promptly got into his own car and then continued following behind the other woman, leaving me sitting alone feeling like a fool.

I'd learned of the girl's name from co-workers at the ballpark so I called directory assistance for her phone number and address, then headed in that direction once I had the information. By the time I arrived it was growing dark, but there was nothing that was going to stop me from accomplishing my objective, too much hurt had been inflicted to turn around. The house was obviously not hers, but her parent's. Derek's car was parked alongside the curb, so I knew it was at the right one. I knocked on the door, and the woman answering introduced herself as the girl's mother after I told her that I was a friend of her daughter's and came by to say hello. She explained that her daughter was not home but should be returning soon and invited me to come in and wait for her. What a *lovely* idea I thought. I accepted her invitation, plopped myself onto the couch, and began to carry on mundane chitchat with both of her parents.

Within a few moments the phone rang in the other room and the woman politely excused herself to answer, and though the conversation started out in a normal tone, it quickly changed to a low, soft whisper. No doubt it was my archenemy calling and my cover was blown. She called out to her husband who excused himself, leaving me alone tapping my fingers against the arm of the sofa. All I could think of was the fact that Derek had met this girl's family, yet he had never met mine. I could feel the knife dig deeper into my heart. Her parents didn't come back into the room, and five minutes later the same girl and Derek walked in together.

Derek had a look of embarrassment and surprise, and the girl dubious and speechless. I blatantly stared him down, and in a cool voice asked if he now wanted to make time for that talk he seemed to be too busy to have earlier. Without another word he turned to walk outside as I silently followed and closed the door behind me, aware that I had irreversibly done the same to our relationship.

We both had antagonistic and demeaning words to say to each other, as blame was dispensed and all pride tossed aside. Everything in our relationship reprehensively stripped of integrity, including any feelings he may have had left for me. Driving off much later, my heartache was magnified visualizing how he would probably go back to her and they would strip each other as well, but not the demeaning way we had performed the act. I was heading off to emptiness and pain, whereas he had turned back to open arms and happiness.

The weeks steadily went by, each feeling to me as if they were endless. I couldn't seem to focus or sleep, imagining what I wished I had said or wanted to verbalize if I saw him again. It was months later when Derek walked into the bank where I worked and acted as if I had seen him a few hours ago, and we were the closest and dearest of friends. To this day, I do not know what kept me standing on my feet or how I feigned being so aloof and unresponsive to his charm.

The casual conversation of "How are you?" and "What have you been doing?" made me want to hit him with something considerably hard, and the thought of him not surviving the hit crossed my mind. With each question I replied indifferently with short and evasive remarks. I was fine…nothing new was going on with me…thanks so much for dropping by. After apologizing profusely for the incident that had ended our relationship, it seemed he was waiting for a reprieve and evidently for my forgiveness.

If he expected me to fall apart or beg him to come back, it was soon apparent I would do neither. On the contrary, my next words surprised even myself. "You were right," I told him, "being apart is the wisest choice for us. Hope you are happy in life." Pleased with my response and the absolution he presumed I was giving him, he smiled and walked away without saying another word.

Lie with Me

Autumn Carpentier

I don't pretend to know I know everything about
anything at all, but a girl knows when things are not
going well and can hear it in a phone call:

The call to say you're running late but you should be home
pretty soon, yet in the background I can hear that you're
not alone in the room, so before you lie with me…

Just remember not too long ago you felt the same for
me as you do for her, is this evening going to be all
it's worth if you should chose to lie with her?

Is it even in your thoughts that I will doubt what you
might say? Do you really think that I don't know
what's going on when you come home so late?

Think twice before you try to deceive me and act as though I
don't have common sense…you best think long and hard about
the ultimate consequence…if you are going lie with me:

Tell me that you miss me and you hate that you're
not here, try to make it all oaky by calling me honey
and dear, as you lie with me…lie to me,

whisper sweet hopes and dreams in my ear like you did when our love was new…go on and on when we make love like our love is true…if you must …lie to me.

Please don't lie with her…

Footnote: I wrote this to show how the word "lie" can mean two different things, depending on which side of a story between three people one is on, and, which one gets the "lie" as in *deception*, or the "lie" as in *lay down beside* someone. I wanted so much to be the one Derek wanted to lie down beside, that I was willing to have him lie (be deceptive) to me.

Chapter 6

Time does have a way of helping you overcome. They contend that loss, i.e. death, has five stages: (1) Denial and Isolation (2) Anger (3) Bargaining (4) Depression and (5) Acceptance. And there are more ways than one to die. I went through each and every one of them after Derek drove off that day. From experience, my personal opinion is that acceptance is the hardest phase to come to terms with. To achieve acceptance, we have to acknowledge the final act of being final by prudently conceding to the termination, followed by eradicating every demented aspect of our thoughts and feelings, thus allowing forward progression.

I've not discovered a blueprint for the recovering process after surviving a loss, or if any step progresses the healing process any faster than the other. But I have learned that laughter soothes the mind and comforts the heart, at any stage you may be enduring at the moment.

Kristy was one of my dearest friends and we had met at the same bank where I met Derek, but had been employed with the airlines for a while by that point. Not too long after Derek walked off into the sunset that day, we sat on her living room floor pessimistically discussing her life, my life, and life in general, when she jumped up exclaiming, "We needed to take a trip to Vegas!" Her strategy began to unfold, with plans that alluded to the fact that she'd instigated similar plans a time or two before. To have fly stand-by free privileges you had to be a family member, so her creative ruse was for me to pose as her sister for the entire trip. We planned to use her upgraded passes and fly out first class, stay for the evening and then return on the Monday morning red-eye, which would put us home in time for work. She became increasingly enthusiastic the more she plotted our spontaneous trip out of town, lifting my spirits with every word formulating our expedition!

It wasn't until we were heading to the airport that I noticed Kristy had a petite traveling bag with her and asked what it was for, since we'd planned to be out of town for only a day. Her brief reply was a little vague, "Just a few things, in case…" The thought "In case what, exactly…?" passed through my mind. Evidently it was to hold all of the money we were planning on winning, or for all of the toiletries we'd take home from the casino!

I don't know how, but we passed through security and made it onto first class. We had both dressed in on our sexiest black dresses, highest heels, and reddest lipstick with our hairstyles piled, teased and sprayed as high as Mount Rushmore! We looked the part, although some may have questioned what the heck part that was as we sipped our initial glass of wine on the plane.

By the second glass I'd simply forgotten anything remotely relevant concerning that little black traveling bag. With alcohol in hand and a warm cloth on my neck, all I cared about was the fact that I was headed to a faraway land of sin and gaiety. I took a deep breath and sat back, counting all the ways to spend my winnings from the casino and concocting how my troubles would end and therefore life become worry-free. The wine had kicked in, I was dreaming.

If you have ever been to Vegas, you know that it really is a world of its own. If Satan lived anywhere on earth, his home address would certainly be there. So many lights make it almost appear as if it could never really be night, even when the sun goes down. Constant movement inside the hotels and along the streets make you imagine time doesn't really matter, and in nothing flat manages to remove you from all that is outside the parameter of that world. That is until you hit your first loss and the drinks don't come fast enough, or worse, you lose count of how many you've actually consumed.

The first nickel slot machine I put my money into ate it faster than a snake devours a little insect for dinner. By the end of the evening I had no money, my feet hurt, my hair was falling, and I couldn't drink anymore because I could not afford to sit at a table to gamble to keep the drinks coming. When Kristy lost her last dollar a few hours after me, she devised yet another scheme.

I came to the astute conclusion that my friend was a professional heister, and that she was exceptionally skilled at it. Before I knew it, we had passed the entrance to the show for Willie Nelson, explaining that our name was on the list, "right there" as Kristy pointed to the list the attendant held in her hand. We were then escorted to the front of the show room and practically seated on stage at a table where we could reach out and touch Willie if we were inclined to do so. The funny thing was I never really cared for Willie Nelson. But hey, it was a free show!

Unfortunately, she didn't entirely think the whole plan through. As we sat comfortably in our chairs, the people we were impersonating materialized before us as if planning to haul us off to jail…and for a little bit I was certain we would be. But being the professional manipulator that she was, Kristy succeeded in convincing them we had made a terrible mistake and didn't know HOW on earth such a mistake could possibly have happened.

By the end of her erroneous story, they were paying for their own new seats located next to their previously purchased seats, that we still occupied. Since we had no money on us, they allowed us to write a check to pay them back for the seats we had confiscated, and then graciously paid for our drinks the rest of the evening! If I questioned her line of work before, at that point I had no misgivings that my dear friend was in the wrong business. She shouldn't have been taking reservations for the airline, but negotiating for our country somewhere. The other side wouldn't have a chance.

At the end of our escapade, we left for the airport to catch a return flight home. I was already feeling and looking a little ragged, and when the last overnight flight departed and we weren't on it, the black dress and heels were suddenly overkill for the airport. We were rolled over to the 5:45 morning fight which meant it was going to be a challenge for me to get to work on time, but all I wanted to do right then was roll over and land in a soft bed. Kristy set off to find the ladies restroom with her little black bag, while I attempted to get comfortably positioned on one of the airport benches in my dress and heels.

I'd about given up on Kristy when I looked up to observe someone who resembled her walk out of the restroom. I thought I might be hallucinating because I was so tired, but at second glance it was unmistakably my friend. She had changed into jeans and a t-shirt, her long hair tied into a knot at the nape of her neck, her face freshly washed, and her toothbrush in hand. She sauntered toward me as if she was heading off to bed in her own apartment, plopping down onto the bench adjacent to mine with a nonchalant sigh.

I wasn't sure what to say or if anything was worth saying as I watched her slapping at the soft bag with her fist to create a place for her pretty little head, then proceeded to lay across the opposite bench and sleep as if she didn't have a care in the world. The following morning I looked a bit different than I did on the trip heading to Vegas. While Kristy looked relatively refreshed, my hosiery had a run, my black dress was crumpled, my hair tousled, and a crease crossed my face where I had been using my bulky purse as a pillow. At that point I could no longer pass for me, let alone as her sister. We never went on another trip together, but to this day whenever I travel I carry a little black bag myself, and I think of her and the valuable lesson I learned: be prepared.

It seemed as if that was to be one of the few lessons learned the first time around for me, unfortunately. I happened to be at lunch and was about to be seated, when I came face to face with Derek as he was leaving the restaurant. It had been a while since we last saw each other and he paused as if uncertain he should approach me or not. His casual "How have you been?" followed hastily by "Are you working close by?" with his last nonchalant statement, "Let's do lunch sometime soon." was the all but one-sided conversation between us. I impertinently replied with an indifferent "Sure." then moved on to be seated at my table.

Two days later he called and asked to meet him for lunch, explaining that he wouldn't have much time but would like to see me. I didn't want him to get the opinion that he intimidated me and lackadaisically agreed, damned and determined to prove that I had moved on. That might have been great...if it had worked out that way. I promptly came to the astute realization that I had mistakenly taken the path that led to unquestionable heartache again. By the end of lunch every passionate emotion had resurfaced, leaving me feeling as if all that we had shared never ended.

The lunches and phone calls impetuously became dinner and hanging out together with friends, the conversations between us inclusive of everything from our jobs, families, daily incidents, and even the people we were dating. Was that better than nothing? Or was it just a different version of nothing? At that particular moment I didn't seem to have a need for anything more, or anything less from him.

It was while we were having lunch that Derek mentioned a position with his company, which offered a pay increase and a marginal amount of travelling. I'm not sure what I said or how fast I may have expressed my interest, but within a month I had already interviewed, given my two weeks notice, and was about to start my new job. I wasn't excited because I would be working with Derek, but because it was the first time since I had left the bank I wouldn't have to work two jobs for a supplemental income or pinch every penny.

Because of our rocky history I didn't want anyone to know Derek and I had dated or had ever been anything but friends. When I told him I'd been hired, I also urged that he not mention we had dated and neither would I. As far as I was concerned it served no purpose for anyone to know. You can picture my surprised reaction as I was heading out of a staff meeting the first day on the job, and the first antagonistic statement hurled at me by a male co-worker was, "So, you and Derek dated?" I soon discovered that while the men had been informed of his claim on me, none of the woman had a clue. It didn't matter to me, although he had driven a stake into my heart once before I would not tolerate him sabotaging any opportunities, and I *certainly* wasn't going to allow him to drive that stake back into my heart, or back!

So on it went. We danced all around the feelings and dated other people as if we were competing and keeping score as to who could conquer every person of the opposite sex that we were acquainted with.

But at the end of the day when we all met for happy hour, everyone stood at a random distance watching us play cat and mouse, while we both seemed to be clueless to any of it.

Working with Derek I had the preeminent advantages of both worlds, or so I presumed. I could talk to him, hang out with him, do everything I enjoyed with him, thus sharing his world without letting him destroy mine. It was a win-win, until I was reminded why the same scenario wasn't a good combination the first time around. It seemed incongruous that as hard as I fought not to repeat history and take that road, somehow that was precisely the road I was venturing.

Derek seemed to feel he had that right to keep other men at a distance, but had no qualms of unashamedly latching onto other women. Because we weren't a couple he didn't have to hide the fact that he was romping around, contrary to his behavior when we'd dated. But as the hours of traveling at work increased, our love/hate relationship began to cast a shadow on our personal relationship and our work relationship. Exceptional attention averting us from the same audit assignments or the people that felt uncomfortable knowing of our roller-coaster relationship became a must at work. We were progressively tearing each other apart all over again. Timing is everything...

The first time I encountered Lance, I was out with several other girls that I had met through Kristy. They were crazy, fun, lighthearted girls and they were all unquestionably beautiful. Although I'd never had much self-esteem, any confidence I had at all seemed completely lost in their shadows when I was around them. But the more a part of the group I became, the more comfortable and self-assured I became with myself. I discovered that I had to exude confidence whether I felt it or not, and came to the realization that there must be something I had to offer, since everyone seemed to enjoy hanging out and spending time with me.

It was on such a night that I felt exceptionally sure of myself and confident of holding my own, I happened to glance behind me in time to witness a couple of the girls sauntering in Lance's direction. He was laughing and talking with a few guys as if undoubtedly assured that the girls would manifest toward them. Of course, one by one they seemed to do exactly that! Unlike the others I acted indifferent, downed the drink I'd ordered moments before, and headed out the door. I'd be seeing the girls at a pool party over the weekend, so didn't bother with courteous goodbyes. Let them have their fun for now, I was tired from the week that I'd had and my mind was not on meeting anyone.

I couldn't pinpoint why, but hanging out by the pool the next day I seemed to be in an unusual frame of mind. I had just started walking from my lounge chair to get a drink from the outside bar, when I saw Lance making his way over to everyone. He had a young boy with him, and the kid looked so much like him that I assumed he must be his son. Standing at the bar I watched him laughing and talking, acting carefree and what appeared to me, a little cocky and aloof.

As quickly as he came into the party he turned with the boy with him and made his exit, but something inside prompted a second look at him that day...and then a third. When I returned to my chair, all of the girls were exploring the idea of going dancing later that night, and I didn't have to be asked twice. Excited about the evening plans ahead of me, I relaxed and enjoyed the afternoon of music, drinks, and volleyball.

Even though drained from being in the sun all afternoon, nothing was going to hinder my night out on the town. I've always enjoyed dancing, nine times out of ten my eyes are closed to everything but the music, using the music to check out from reality. I didn't care if I was dancing with someone or alone as I circled the dance floor that particular night, and danced around it oblivious to the world or anyone around me.

I unintentionally maneuvered my way in-between Lance and a stunning blonde that he was dancing with. She was not a regular in my group, but apparently she was a part of his. I wasn't dancing with anyone in particular when I turned to find myself dancing with Lance, and for a moment it seemed as if I'd acquired a dance partner for the evening. But when I turned to find I was face to face with the blonde, in no time flat I began circulating the floor again without further regard for either of them.

After that night I spoke with Lance perhaps a total of three times in the following weeks with nothing other than a hello or goodbye, and anytime he was around me, the blonde was around him. Her name was Charmaine, and it did not escape my attention that they often arrived together at social gatherings, but managed to leave separately. I also noticed that they were never publically demonstrative with each other, while both were openly flirtatious with other people. I was a bit stumped and a little intrigued, but since there was no evidence to suggest otherwise, I came to the presumption that they were nothing but chummy friends. I was in the process of moving to a new place, and had more pertinent matters on my mind other than their social status or love life.

Even though there was a tremendous amount of work in preparing to move, I was looking forward the changes that it would bring. The last time I moved I didn't have many friends to help with the task, but this time it would be different. I had ample volunteers, and arranged to have them all meet for beverages and pizza after the move, followed by a night of drinking and dancing, to celebrate my new home.

With the assistance of Derek and his best friend Stuart, the first thing I did the day of the move was head to the department store for my new couch. We loaded it onto the truck, and then hauled it all the way up two flights of stairs to my new apartment only to discover that the couch was too big to fit inside the door. I stood there thinking that this could not *possibly* be happening, deliberating on knocking a hole in the wall to make it fit. Standing at the stop of the stairs, Derek and Stuart had a look across their faces that told me they were considering the same.

Unprepared as to what I should do next, I headed to the office building to express the frustration over my predicament, and to request which wall they might be persuaded to destroy in order to accommodate getting my couch inside! Their idea to move me into an alternate unit was a bit more reasonable, but delayed the move into my new place for another week. I'd have to develop a contingency plan for the following weekend, and postpone everyone's help until then. Reluctantly, the couch was hauled back to the bottom of the steps and back onto the truck.

With a new goal in mind I immediately began making calls informing everybody of the change in plans, with the last two calls being to Charmaine and Lance. She had been invited to be a part of the move by someone who knew someone…who knew someone, so I didn't think she would be too terribly disappointed about the change in plans.

As far as Lance was concerned, I wasn't even sure he had really expected to help me move or if he had involuntarily gotten caught in the crossfire of someone volunteering for him. I didn't have his number however, so when I called Charmaine to let her know of the new arrangements, I innocently and casually asked if she had Lance's phone number so that I could call and update him.

It didn't register until much later, but the hesitation on her end was unlikely from granting me time to get a pen to jot the number down, but more likely from biting her tongue while she cogitated a way of getting rid of me before I had time to actually call. I have a feeling it was with great reluctance that she gave me the number, but called him as soon as we hung up anyway.

He didn't answer, so I left a message that if he could make it to the club later that evening I would hook up him then. I never imagined that he would make anything of that brief and generic phone call, having made the exact same phone call to everyone else! But the minute I turned on the dance floor to find Lance in front of me later that night, I instinctively felt he'd construed something more from my message than intended. Unexpected paths in life customarily create detours and take us to crossroads we do not anticipate, which can throw us into an unsettling state of confusion. I did not see it coming, hadn't even a clue, but I hit one of those infamous crossroads that night.

With merely a few weeks before Christmas remaining, Lance coaxed me into Christmas shopping with him the upcoming Saturday afternoon, since I was going out for happy hour that Friday night and wouldn't be available. When everyone got together, "everyone" included Derek. I arrived last at the bar, but eventually Derek meandered over to dance with me, after which the only time we left the dance floor was to rejuvenate with a cold drink. It all seemed fun and carefree until I felt myself being pulled into his gaze, unconscious of anything or anyone. Alcohol and all, I could differentiate between harmless fun and precarious intentions, and sensed it was time for me to leave.

I waved goodbye to the others, trying to leave without Derek noticing, skittish that if he saw me leaving he'd convince me not to. Once outside I placed the keys in the ignition and started the car, preoccupied on going back inside or not, then realize I'd already pulled out of the parking lot and was headed home.

I barely had time to change out of my clothes when I heard a knock on my door. Thinking it might be Lance stopping by, I opened the door with a smile on my face to find Derek standing there instead. He didn't speak, and tongue-tied myself I couldn't manage to utter a single word. Seconds from me opening the door, he walked in closing it behind him and pulled me against him. His kiss enticed me to forget anything to do with sensible or right. I wasn't thinking of the past or the future, and Lance no longer impeded my heart or mind. We spent the night together, making love the entire night. There was truly something deeper between us that night, and we had no way of knowing it would be our last time together for a long time.

Though profusely exhausted, I kept my date with Lance and went Christmas shopping as planned. Years after the fact I'd find out Derek brought pizza and Coke back to my apartment later that same day, along with his appetite and his own intentions. But I was not there when he came by, and I had presumed the night before was the same thing it had been in the prior years for him; sexual release and nothing more.

Within weeks of meeting Lance I became unemployed with my firm, and we began dating exclusively. I recognized fairly quickly that it was Lance who was willing to offer things Derek was not. I needed something I had never had before, someone who wanted to embrace me and be protective of me. I needed someone I could build a life with, someone that was safe and unpretentious. I needed someone that abstained the anxiety and shrouded me in blissful tranquility. What had started out a caring friendship soon became something else between Lance and me, and the relationship moved fast and furious from the beginning.

After Derek and I no longer worked together we infrequently saw each other, subsequently going our separate ways, completely unaware the degree Lance's diversion would influence my life and those associated with me, including people who were not yet a part of my life.

***

As one phase of my life closed another opened, it seemed as if the time I had been with Derek never really occurred. Lance and I moved in together within months of dating, and he eagerly arranged a trip to Houston for me to meet his parents a few weeks later. Both were nothing short of fabulous from the onset, and the first girl apparently to meet them since Lance's breakup with his fiancée a couple of years before, they were thrilled that he was bringing someone home. You could tell we had an immediate connection, and I was overjoyed that they so graciously welcomed me and made me feel a part of their family. It was a relationship that grew as zealously as Lance's and mine, and a bond filled with just as much love.

I did not meet Lance's younger brother Victor on our first trip to Houston, but the first time I walked into the living room and saw him sitting on the couch, I literally turned back to make certain Lance was still behind me. Even with three brothers of my own I had never seen two siblings look so much alike, but as I precipitately began to learn, so characteristically different. Where Lance was responsible and diligent in everything he did, an anchor for those drifting, Victor was the carefree, captivating, and exciting one of the two. I observed those traits because I had seen the same ones in Derek, and it would later prove uncanny how much Lance's brother reminded me of him.

In looking back I should have been committed…to a mental institution of some sort. I had all the signs that pointed me in the direction completely opposite the route I was taking, but I continued on the detour. Positive I knew what I wanted and that I'd find a way to attain it, I had a tendency to perpetually push for a committed arrangement other than living together. Even Lance's mother urged me to be patient, but that did not make me any less stubborn. I had been exposed to a family that showed me what a family was designed to be and eager to start my own, almost as if I was hoping to compensate for lost time. I never doubted Lance's love for me, but I'm not sure if his proposal was because of his love for me or because of my provocation to convince him that was what he wanted.

The proposal wasn't romantic or even a question, but simply a formality of becoming engaged. It took one day at the shopping mall, a couple of days waiting for the credit approval, and a call from the jewelry store to inform him that he could pick the ring up. I even went with him to finalize the purchase, so he simply handed it to me in the middle of the mall parking lot, under the light post where we had parked. We organized the wedding for the forthcoming September, three days before his parent's wedding anniversary, thrilling them with the news of our announcement as well as the date.

His parents were aware of my hardship concerning family and finances and never once hinted for any amount of contribution, but graciously borrowed money from their personal savings to endow us with an exquisite wedding. His mom shopped with me as if shopping for her own daughter, and the dresses, veil, shoes, flowers, church, and invitations were marked off the list before my twenty-fifth birthday.

My first choice for a wedding gown was a sheath dress, and Lance's mom had offered to let me wear her wedding dress since it was the same particular style. It touched my heart that she even considered letting me wear it, and we were both disappointed when it didn't fit. At the end of our quest, we selected an off-white ball gown of silk that was between tea-length and ankle length in the front, grazing just above the ground in the back. It was a simplistic, but elegant dress, designed with a Bateau neckline and fitted bodice, sleeveless arms and an open, plunging back. The veil was fitted like a crown, framing my face with beautiful tiny pearls, which carried into the royal length train cascading behind me in a display of sheer elegance. The low-heeled pumps were died to perfectly match the dress, visible from underneath the dress in all their satin glory.

The only thing missing was a single strand of pearls I wanted to complete the ensemble, which was given to me by Lance's parents on my

25th birthday. I wore them for the first time as I walked down the aisle to marry Lance, on a perfect September fall evening with approximately 200 of our family and closest friends. I had chosen to make the walk unaccompanied, and not a soul would have ever dreamt that my heart was pounding for all of the wrong reasons.

The sun was shining behind me when the church doors opened to let me begin my walk, and for a brief moment all anyone could see was the outline of my dress and veil. For that brief moment I emerged a mere apparition to those watching, moving blindly toward the altar shunning the voice inside my head, inside my heart. It was Derek that kept creeping into my thoughts, making my heart pound sporadically. Why could I not get him out of my mind? But Lance was the man I was about to set off on a new beginning with and build a life. And as I approached the altar he was the one that met me, taking my hand in his to finish the walk together.

Chapter 7

What I distinctly remember about our wedding reception was that there were so many family members from both sides and we had so much fun! Guests and family members had stayed in a local hotel the night before, celebrating our marriage as if it was the event of a lifetime, sharing in the hopes and dreams associated with a wedding day and the union of two people. We were young and had our entire lives ahead with limitless possibilities, ignorant of the challenges that lay before us.

Lance and I had agreed to postpone our honeymoon a few days so that we could visit with family and friends who had come from out of town, therefore we spent the night of our wedding at the Hilton Hotel down the street from where we lived. We did not make love or celebrate that night because we were exhausted, both falling asleep shortly after we made it to our hotel room. The next morning I felt as if I was on top of the world, staring outside the window of the hotel room that overlooked what had been my home for more than twenty years.

I could see the world for miles and it looked to be a perfect September morning, the air crisp from the hint of an autumn chill the night before, the sun radiating its brilliance against the pale, blue morning sky. For a moment I stood alone and watched the world passing by as if remaining there could perhaps keep that moment safe, as if everything I was feeling could be guarded and never tarnished by anything...or anyone. The crossroad chosen, the journey commenced. This was what was best for my life, and I would do whatever was within my power to make it a good life and to do right by Lance and our new family.

Our honeymoon was a week spent in Puerto Vallarta, Mexico. We returned home ready to start our married life together assuming that it wouldn't be any different from living together. At this point I'd like to markedly proclaim that you never really know someone until you are married, and living together is not the same as being married. You tend to romanticize that it is, but that little piece of paper seems to trigger a button that spins your world upside down, and there doesn't appear to be an accessible "off" button. So you spin slowly at first, and soon you are going so fast that all you want to do is get off the whirlwind feeling of being out of control. I'm not sure where or when our spinning started, but I'd be prone to lean toward the moment we began trying to have children and create our own family.

By the time we were married, I was averaging two surgeries a year due to endometriosis and tumors causing havoc to my body. I'd have a surgery, get scar tissue, and have another surgery to remove the scar tissue, thus causing additional scar tissue to develop. Like most health maladies, whatever you do to heal the problem, the treatment generates other syndromes, thus a seemingly endless domino effect. I had so many 'female' impediments that it was hard to know where problems began and others ended. What was even more frustrating was the fact that I could not find a doctor who seemed to be able to stick with one problem or one solution at a time.

Becoming wary of searching for an OB/GYN, another couple fighting fertility complications referred us to their fertility specialist with hopes of determining why I wasn't able to conceive. After I had been cut open, stitched and had accumulated more pictures of my insides than my out, Dr. Gomati's recommendation was that surgery and "deep cleaning" were required, due to the many surgeries I'd previously undergone. However, where other doctors had cut me open as if I was about to deliver by C-section, he practiced the newest techniques and topmost efficient ways to do the same procedures with half the time for healing and scarring. There seemed to be an immediate connection between us, and while people rarely become heroes in our life, Dr. Gomati soon became a hero to me ten times over. He reassured, comforted, and encouraged us the moment we walked into his office.

Dr. Gomati emphasized that I'd require minimal stress and adequate rest after the surgery, so for our one-year anniversary we took a trip to South Padre Island to provide both. We walked the beaches with the intent to do what just what he ordered: rest. We'd also planned to focus on getting pregnant, which included keeping charts of my temperature and other challenging efforts essential to couples encountering conception hindrances. I speculated that the miscarriage in my teens played a huge factor in the difficulties I was experiencing, but didn't want to concede our objective. The alternative would be shots, and I was not looking forward to that. I'd heard stories about those drastic, painful methods and even though I wanted to have children, but becoming ambivalent to the possibility.

If nothing else we returned home feeling rested, and Lance was optimistically reassuring that we had nothing to worry about. I was actually looking forward to my doctor's appointment, up until a friend came over the night before and publicized that she was pregnant. Thrilled as I was for her, I was absolutely flustered that we were trying so hard to have a baby and we weren't making the same announcement. Heartbroken, I began crying the minute she left, no longer interested in keeping my OB/GYN appointment. But the next day came and I forged on, aware I'd have to go sooner or later.

While sitting outside the doctor's office waiting for my visit with Dr. Gomati, I looked overhead to see a poem that a patient had stitched, framed, and hung on the wall in the waiting area. It was the story of a mother and her unborn child soon to be delivered. Before she announces to her husband that it's time to leave for the hospital, she carries on a brief conversation with the child about the journey they've shared for the bygone months of the pregnancy. The mother lovingly shares her sentiments concerning the realization that once the child is born, the relationship between them would forever be changed.

Though the mother was excited to see and embrace her newborn baby, a part of her was saddened by the fact that her baby would soon be physically separated from her. There was something haunting to me about the story, and it touched me in a way I did not understand at the time. I read it at each doctor's visit throughout all of the years he was my doctor, and even after his death I never forgot about the poem... or Dr. Gomati.

I was already feeling a little sad on this particular visit, and when they called my name and escorted me into Dr. Gomati's office to have a seat, I halfheartedly began pulling my temperature chart from my purse. Glancing over it, it was noticeable that I hadn't been diligent in keeping track with logging my temperature as he'd requested. He was going to fuss at me, and I was going to have to redo the entire chart. I was losing my tolerance for the ordeal and was ready to go home, impatiently waiting for him to tell me what the upcoming weeks would entail and how important it was for me to maintain the chart when he caught me off-guard when he glanced up at me and announced, "Looks like we're pregnant!"

I looked up from my downward stare and momentarily wondered what "we" he was referring to, thinking he was much too old to have another child. I had seen many pictures of his grown children, and his grandchildren! I must have missed something. I'd either heard incorrectly, misunderstood what he spoke, or I hadn't been paying attention the past few minutes and had lost track of the conversation regarding another anticipated grandchild he was bragging about. As he smiled into my eyes and repeated the same statement I began to grasp what he was conveying, and started shaking with excitement. I was going to have a baby, and just last night I was convinced I'd never be able to. What a difference a day made, indeed! Dr. Gomati eagerly asked if I wanted to call Lance from his office, as tears from sheer elation rolled down my face. I shook my head no in response, explaining that I wanted to witness my husband's face when I shared the news.

On my way home I bought a 'new mommy journal', and the first thing I wrote was, "I found out about you today. You are already a blessing to both me and your daddy." I then plopped myself onto our couch and impatiently waited for Lance to get home. I could barely contain myself, I wanted to shout it from the rooftops and tell anyone and everyone--but Lance had to be the first.

When he walked in the door and saw me sitting on the couch with a gleam in my eye, he smiled and asked, "What are you doing sitting there looking so cute?" as he walked toward me to kiss me hello. Unable to contain myself any longer, I returned his smile and simply asked, "Do I look like a mommy?" The look on his face must have been the same one I had at the doctor's office, and it took him a moment to digest my question.

Afraid to say what I was feeling, all I could do was sit and anxiously observe his reaction. Inside my head I was having my own conversation: "Tell me that I look like a mommy. Tell me you are as thrilled as I am. Tell me that this is only the beginning of magnificent moments in our life together." My eyes must have contained all the emotions I could not bring myself to voice, as he pulled me from the couch enthusiastically lifting me off the floor, laughing and cheering as he hugged me! It seemed as if the answer to all of the questions in my heart…was yes!

As exciting and thrilled in the moment as we were to find out that we were going to have a baby, my pregnancy with Rylee was problematic from the beginning. I was constantly sick, unable to even tolerate liquids, causing me fatigue and anxiety on a daily basis. I was uncertain what was happening, and therefore became frustrated and apprehensive.

By the second month of my pregnancy, I wasn't improving and Dr. Gomati met me on a Saturday afternoon for a checkup rather than postpone the exam. I never went home, but was admitted to the hospital directly from his office where they pumped me with I.V. fluids for two days straight. Once I was home from the hospital we began the ongoing countdown, and by the ninth month I was overwhelmingly ready to have my baby.

The nurse at the hospital had informed me that walking was an alternative to help accelerate the process, so I walked our apartment complex feeling as if I should be rolled every step of the way. There was no sidewalk, so I walked closely to the cars even though I felt like any car would bounce off of me if it did hit me! Rounding the corner I began walking down the last row when I heard a mechanical voice shout, "You are too close! Jump back ten feet," as an alarm blazed loud enough to wake the dead! I found myself at least ten feet from where I'd originally been walking, all the while the car commanding me to conform to it's boisterous order. For a moment I thought I might possibly deliver in the middle of the parking lot, and once it registered that I hadn't, I knew it was going to be a while before I did.

A couple of weeks prior to my due date I contracted an unknown virus and was put on penicillin to protect the baby and me. Unfortunately, I had an allergic reaction and developed welts that covered me from my neck down to my little toe. Not only was I ten months pregnant, I had welts that itched non-stop and there was nothing that provided me relief. My mother-in-law arrived to take care of me, no less fantastically and dotingly than any mother could have. She stayed with me for over a week and made sure I was as comfortable as possible, hoping I'd deliver while she was there. We both cried the day she had to leave, and after my due date came and went by two weeks, they scheduled me to be induced.

As plans often fall awry, the night before I was to be admitted into the hospital there was every indication I was in labor, and I was instructed to proceed to the hospital to check in and not wait until the morning appointment. Who'd have ever imagined it would be thirty-six hours from the time I was admitted before she was born? It was a grueling experience, and I feared that instead of giving birth to our child, I was going to die. By the time she was born, all of my medications had worn off and I delivered my 10-pound baby girl without an epidural or anything else for the pain, screaming so loudly I could be heard throughout the entire hospital wing--possibly even heaven.

But when they laid her in my arms I could think of nothing else but holding onto her. That and getting something of substance into my body, being that I was outright exhausted from the lengthy labor. Throughout my entire pregnancy I hadn't consumed an ounce of caffeine, concerned it would harm my unborn child. Yet, once I'd delivered I insisted on a Dr. Pepper and managed to down three of them within five minutes, and then promptly proceeded to breastfeed my newborn daughter. We'd barely made it out of the delivery room before Lance got rid of the shirt he'd worn for the last three days, while

I on the other hand finally got rid of my horrific rash, and obtained some much-needed physical relief all around.

At her birth Rylee was basically born almost three months old at 10 pounds, 10 ounces, and 22 inches long, and from the onset she was a hungry little tyke. One midmorning while she was nursing, she made a sound as if she was choking on something! I pushed the button designated for the nurse's assistance, exhibiting panic that I am sure they routinely witnessed in new moms. By the time someone arrived, Rylee appeared to be normal with no signs of choking or any other problems. Maybe I *was* just a new mom who didn't know what she was doing.

But within a few brief moments after the nurse left my room I was buzzing the nurse's station, this time more panicked than before! Since this was my umpteenth time to implore some degree of assistance, I'm convinced she had every intention to sedate me regardless of what I needed. It seemed forever before she entered my room, but as soon as she saw Rylee she yanked her from my arms and inverted her, pounding on her back repeatedly as she ran out of the room. What had happened? She had not relayed any explanation or consolation as she vanished with my newborn daughter.

Lance was called by a staff nurse and informed that he needed to return without delay, and little time was wasted before it was conveyed that Rylee had projectile reflux and severe sleep apnea. The projectile reflux was causing her to choke each time she ate, and the sleep apnea was a potentially serious sleep disorder that was causing her breathing to repeatedly stop and start. She was transferred into the prenatal Intensive Care Unit (ICU) and placed on a monitor and the necessary medications to help her make it through the critical stage.

The hospital provided room accommodations for families with extenuating circumstance, and for the first few nights of her life I'd intermittently leave her side to briefly rest from pure exhaustion. I was taught the precise manner in which to hold her while I fed her, and what to do if she should begin choking. In addition to her feeding schedules, I was available around the clock to comfort her if she began to have attacks and to consult with doctors that had random consultation schedules all their own.

Rigid about her not being fed from a bottle, I was "on call" to nurse her in-between the short times away from the ICU. I was half asleep one night when they called me for a feeding, and looked down to see "Adorable" written on her wristband. I couldn't have beamed more if I was the sun, and couldn't wait to tell Lance how the hospital staff thought our daughter was so adorable that they had written it on her wristband! I bragged to family and friends for days, up until I met one of the new doctors assigned to her: Dr. Adorable.

We took our adorable daughter home after a week of tests, learning how to administer several medications and the proper technique to use the heart monitor they told us she would be on for an unknown amount of time. A wedge was provided that we had to tie her onto each time she slept, with a specialized harness that strapped her upright at an angle to prevent her from sliding downward and laying horizontal. If she did lie flat, she'd either choke on her saliva or stop breathing. Each night we placed the sensors on her chest, and strapped her upright to the crib by her harness. Each night the alarm activated and I'd frantically leap out of bed to untie her, turn her over, check her breathing, pat her back until she stopped choking or started breathing, and then administer her medicine.

After only a few spells of the alarm being triggered I didn't even bother going to bed, but began sitting upright holding her on my shoulder and against my heart day and night. I did that for six months. Lance was using the only car we owned so I had no car, and I was alone day after day with the knowledge that if something happened to our daughter, my only option of saving her would be to call 911.

It was approximately a week after Rylee was home from the hospital that my mother made an unannounced visit. I'd just succeeded in getting Rylee to sleep and thoroughly drained from the episodes she'd had the night before, was planning on getting some rest myself. I apologetically explained the predicament to my mother when she arrived, asking if she would be able to come a different day to visit us. Her rebuttal was filled with frustration and anger as she imperiously ventured into the bedroom to wake her up anyway, stating that the child could simply be put back to sleep once she left. I tried again to explain what I was dealing with concerning her condition, but she demanded I hand Rylee to her and began lecturing me that she was perfectly fine, and that I was overreacting to the medical problems. She further demanded that we should commence to the hospital and visit a doctor so that they could tell me the same thing.

I had no willpower to fight her any longer, and loaded up Rylee so that she could drive us there. I felt bewilderment within the very core of my being, and it was reflective all over my face. I didn't say a word, but sat quietly in the waiting room holding onto my little girl until a nurse or doctor was available to see us. As soon as they called us into the patient's room, my mother began forcefully telling the doctor what *he* needed to tell me. "Tell her that her baby will be okay! Tell her that she cannot constantly hold her and that others can hold her, too! Tell her…"--and on and on she went. She commenced to articulate her personal prescription of what I needed to do or not do, while everyone else stood around unable to get a word in, a dubious expression manifested on each face.

Rylee was checked up one side and down the other and given a clean bill of health, with the exception of her preexisting issues. I was advised to bring her back if for any reason I felt uncomfortable or distressed for her safety, and thought about the insane women taking me home! The entire way back I wished that I were anywhere but with my mother, especially when she invited herself in once we were back home. She was insistent on spending time with her granddaughter, and snatched her from me as we walked inside.

Rylee began crying as soon as she was taken out of my arms, her crying and screaming increasing the more my mother bounced her. As the crying intensified, my mother's voice rose along with it, declaring it was my behavior that was causing Rylee health problems and making her cry endlessly. But telling me that my daughter's misery was my fault wasn't enough, she ranted and raved that I was also inflicting misery upon her, questioning why I'd attempt to keep her from her first grandchild? Didn't I know how much she had already gone through and lost? It wasn't fair that I was going to withhold Rylee from her and not let her be a part of her life! She begrudgingly handed my daughter to me as she was leaving, her immature petulance far from eradicated as she slammed the door behind her. By that time, Rylee was wailing in my arms and I was crying along with her and at my wits end.

An hour later Lance walked through the door and the look on his face told me he was fit to be tied. The attending nurse from earlier that day had called to inform him it was discussed and determined it was in the best interest of his wife and daughter to ban his mother from future visits for the time being. Lance had been confused. He did not know his mother was in town, and why would they request her stay away? Once it was established that indeed it was not his mom they were troubled about but mine, I think Lance was seriously cogitating living closer to his parents and as remote from my mother as possible.

After six rigorous and grueling months of living each day as though we would lose her, we took Rylee off of the monitor. I felt as if I couldn't breathe the first night we put her in her bedroom without the monitor attached. When the morning arrived and she'd slept through the night without any episodes, Lance had to be the courageous one and check on her, because I couldn't bring myself to go into her room from fear of what I might find. We had trusted our hearts in faith and love, and even though there'd be other conflicts and difficulties, we never placed Rylee back on the monitor. She would continue to grow stronger with each passing day.

The passage of time and events can sometimes feel as if lived in another life. At three months after the birth of Rylee, I sat admiring my bundle of joy while on the phone with my mother-in-law unable to contain sharing my thoughts of how fast the months had passed. One minute we were in complete fear of losing her and praying for even a few days, and then we were saying our prayers of thanks that we'd made it a few weeks, and now three months were already behind us. I could hear the smile come across the phone, and in a voice that told me she understood how fleetingly time passed, she said in a melancholy voice, "Just wait! Before you know it, it will be three years that have come and gone. It will all go by in the blink of an eye!" Twenty-two years later I would recall that conversation as if it were yesterday, as time did pass by in the blink of an eye just as she had alluded to, and three years had come and gone.

***

Discord between married couples sporadically comes and goes for the most part. Raising a child can certainly take its toll, especially when you add in the stress of finances and health obstacles. It was almost a year from the time Rylee was born that Lance and I were in the middle of a heated argument on a Friday evening and the phone rang. I let the answering machine answer the call and heard Dr. Gomati leaving a message requesting that I return his call as soon as possible. His instructions informed me to let the answering service know that I was returning his call so they'd put me through to him if I called after hours.

I felt myself shudder, and the deranged remark made to Lance during our quarrel that I hated this life would soon seem ironic. I dreaded making the call, so I finished eating and feeding Rylee, cleaned the kitchen, and put my daughter into her evening bath and left Lance to finish the task while I called the doctor.

I stood with the phone in hand, hesitating long enough to catch my breath before dialing the number, following the instructions I had been given. When I reached the answering service and the "Please wait and we will put you through" at 7:00 in the evening, I speculated the news wasn't good. Looking at my daughter, all I wanted to do was clutch her next to me, protecting us both from whatever it was I was about to be told. As if Rylee could sense something unpleasant was coming she began screaming at the top of her lungs just as Dr. Gomati's voice came across the phone, confirming my worst suspicions...cancer.

My knees buckled and I collapsed onto the floor, asking the first question that crossed my mind: was this going to kill me? I heard him talking but could not hear a word he was saying due to the commotion of Rylee crying in the background, and I yelled to Lance to quiet her, demanding silence so I could hear what Dr. Gomati was saying. His composed voice methodically informed me that the specifics weren't established and therefore extensive tests would be conducted. Cognizant of my anxiety, he was adamant that we refrain from speculating the worst, trying to comfort me before concluding the conversation.

When you have had someone close to you die from cancer, and you've questioned over and over again why it wasn't you--once you absorb that it is now happening to you, the question becomes, "Why me?" We went through the entire weekend not knowing if I was dying or if I had limited time to live. I prayed and then found I could not pray, disheartenment looming behind every thought, the uncertainty for my one-year-old child and what was ahead for her reeling in my mind.

Despite my attempts, I could not elude the despair that shadowed me. After numerous test and surgeries were performed, it was determined chemo treatment was unnecessary at that point. In the meantime Dr. Gomati continuously reassured me that the cancer had been diagnosed in time, and consequently not life threatening. It took two years to get a normal pap from Dr. Gomati, and years of him tolerantly reassuring me that I was going to be okay.

In retrospect, I had to be thankful that the Family Center had denied me an appointment when I'd called their establishment to schedule a visit for discounted birth control pills after Rylee's birth. Due to the fact I had recently delivered a child, they had informed me that it was a requirement to schedule a visit with my own gynecologist before they could provide any medications or prescriptions. If a doctor's appointment hadn't been protocol and the prescription dispensed, the cancer would have been too advanced and therefore untreatable. Feeling backed into a corner I had been extremely angry and discouraged at the time, but was later reminded how wondrously the Lord works in our lives. He can take all encompassing circumstances and use them as tools to benefit, guide and bless us.

Although I never believed that I'd get pregnant with Rylee, I pretty much knew the moment Lucas was conceived. I had stopped taking those birth control pills because sexual relations between Lance and I were non-existent...until I stopped taking the pill. Since we were not having sex, it had seemed like getting off the pill for a while was a logical way to save money. I should have seen that one coming! Trying to save money inexorably cost us immensely, but then proved to be my saving grace in the years that followed.

Though I had already come to the decision to leave Lance, I now had to stay. I headed home to share the news with him, deducing how differently this announcement would be in comparison to the day we learned we were having Rylee. Reflective of my own response his face depicted just as much surprise, with the unspoken question; "How and when did this happen?" I had to be a smarty-pants and remind him of the only date it could be, easily pinpointing the ninth month that our little bundle of joy would arrive.

From the moment I was informed that I was expecting my second child, I was convinced that I was going to have a boy, just as I had been convinced that Rylee was going to be a girl. I experienced mixed emotions about having another baby and the ability to love both, feeling that I was betraying my daughter by even having another child. Rylee had not once been away from me from the time she was born, and I marveled at how I could ever love another child like I loved her.

With a brother or sister on the way I knew it would be beneficial to Rylee if she experienced some independence, and signed her up at a Mother's Day Out program at church. The first day I took her I stood at the window crying as I watched her play, and could feel the snot draining from my nose mingling with my salty tears. My shoulders were shaking with grief as a staff teacher walked in, and promptly inquired if I was okay. How could she even ask? I was abandoning my child to strangers, and I hadn't even had the other baby! My firstborn was going to feel threatened and discarded for the rest of her childhood! I took the Kleenex she extended and turned to go retrieve my daughter, insistent that she'd had enough playtime and no doubt distraught that I had left her!

Getting closer to her I could hear her laughter, and thought to myself how she was such a valiant little girl, but nonetheless prepared for her to come running to me with delight and gratefulness when she saw me. To this day I cannot cogitate on that morning without getting a good laugh. As I stood at the window observing my daughter and crying my eyes out, I can envision someone standing behind me chuckling at the mere idea of me fretting over my child running around outside, playing with new friends her own age. People were undoubtedly getting their fill of laughter as they watched me trailing her around the playground, coaxing her to come to me so we could leave the terrible place, surmising that she would never want to revisit without me at her side.

She began her Mother's Day Out program the next day and never looked back, not even to wave goodbye as I was making promises all the way out the door that I'd come back for her as soon as possible. It only took me a couple of weeks before I stopped crying every time I left Rylee, and no longer needed the Kleenex box they offered.

***

From the time of conception to the time he was born, there was nothing remotely the same about my pregnancy or the birth of my son in comparison to my daughter. Lucas was born in April of 1994, a few months shy of four years to the day Rylee was born. They looked as if they could have been identical twins, but distinctively day and night in personality. To my amazement, the moment they placed him into my arms I discovered with relief and awe that I was capable of loving them both with unlimited capacity. Rylee adored her baby brother, and it seemed they had an extraordinary bond between them from the moment they laid eyes on each other.

We carried him home to the same apartment we had taken Rylee, and perceptively discovered that it was no longer quite large enough for our growing family. With financial assistance from Lance's parents, we purchased our first home when Lucas was three months old. The first week we moved in proved to be challenging. Because neither of us had ever lived in our own house before, we did not have all of the necessities for a new home. We didn't have a refrigerator, so we kept cold items in a cooler, purchasing ice every day to prevent the food from spoiling. I was nursing so I didn't have to worry about keeping formula refrigerated for Lucas, but Rylee had to have milk and juice and there had to be food for us to eat.

Not yet fully recovered from the birth of Lucas when we moved, I wasn't completely ready for all of the unpacking and cleaning that was necessary to establish our new home. It wasn't funny at the time, but I can recall standing in the middle of the kitchen amongst unpacked boxes as my milk seeped through my nightgown, crying away! Crying because--well, I had just had a baby, and the houseful of boxes that needed unpacking weren't going to unpack themselves!

As if being without a refrigerator wasn't an ordeal in itself, we couldn't afford blinds on the windows when we moved, either. We'd temporarily hung inexpensive curtains, with the exception of the arched window above the master bedroom window. It so happened on a weekend while nursing Lucas, Lance came into the bedroom and glanced up to see every roofer working on the rooftop of the house behind us gawking through the window, tongues wagging as if they had never seen breasts before.

They could probably see us as closely as we could see them, and noting our surprised awareness hastily turned back to their project in hopes that the man of the house wouldn't shoot them. Lance determined that they had viewed the spectacle long enough, and after throwing a sheet across the entire wall, purchased temporary paper blinds for every room in the house to obstruct the incident from reoccurring. With blinds on the windows, it gave us the privacy and peace of mind we needed. I would raise the blinds in the living room during the day to let light in, and I'd close them when it started getting dark outside. I made sure the bedroom window shades were closed whenever I was nursing Lucas, day or night.

Even though we had been in the house a short time I'd gotten a tremendous amount accomplished, but had more to do. At the time of the move I had requested the movers place the packed boxes in the garage, so that we could move them one at a time into the room they belonged to be unpacked. Having a bout of energy after feeding the kids breakfast one morning, I felt the urge to make some progress and unpack the last of them. I placed Lucas in his bassinet for a nap and sat Rylee in front of the TV to watch one of her favorite shows, then headed to the master bedroom and into the closet to unpack as much as I could while I had time.

I had just reached the end of the hallway when a foreboding sensation overcame me so intense that I turned and headed back into the living room. As I rounded the corner into the den I first noticed the empty bassinet, then my eyes went toward the direction of the couch where Rylee was sitting, with her brother on top of her lap. Facedown on the pillow she had lovingly placed there for his comfort!

I raced over to lift him in front of me, holding him at arms length trying to determine if his little neck was broken. If you have ever had children, you know that newborns cannot lift or avoid bobbing their heads back and forth if their head is not supported. So there I was, watching his little head bobble back and forth, imagining Rylee had broken her brother's neck! I frantically called the doctor, and as I described the scenario I could have sworn there was a hint of a smile, if not a whimsical giggle in the nurse's voice, when she assured me all would be fine.

I placed Lucas back into his swing and grabbed my daughter's hand, pulling her across the house as I psychotically scolded her all the way to her room. Lucas began crying harder, Rylee was crying, and I was crying. Months later I was cleaning underneath the sofa cushion and ran across something that for the life of me, I couldn't figure out what in the world it was. It took me a few minutes before a light bulb went off in my head and I identified it as Lucas's umbilical cord, which must have fallen off when Rylee had pulled him onto the couch.

That was one account of numerous stories that entertained us and filled our home and our hearts with memories, courtesy of our children. I walked in countless times to find them immersed in playful destruction, unaware of my stunned presence until they heard my reaction. I once walked in to find talcum powder sprinkled throughout the bedroom so thick it looked like it had snowed, Rylee finishing it off by pouring the remainder on top of her brother's head.

Not too long afterward, I found them both in the master bathroom where Rylee was avidly painting red lipstick onto her brother's face from ear to ear, in attempts to make his lips match hers. Much to my chagrin

I discovered red lipstick could not be removed from beige carpet, but left remnants of a lovely bright pink stain after endlessly scrubbing on it. Nevertheless, the look on their faces was priceless after I walked in on them and screeched at the discovery. I've wished time and again that I had taken pictures instead of worrying so much about cleaning the kids and the carpet. Eventually we replaced the carpet, but the memory could never be replaced.

I thought I was beginning to acclimate to the new routine of having two children, a husband that I catered to and a new home, when Lance started traveling more extensively than he did before we moved. It's hard to be the one home doing the monotonous chores, losing your individualism while your spouse is building a career and pursuing a separate life and identity other than father and husband. While we had moved into our new home, my old feelings seemed to have tagged along for the ride. I felt trapped. However, if I hadn't been so lost at the time I might have considered many of the incidents amusing to some degree...after the fact.

Like the night Lance traveled to Las Vegas on a business trip and was hours late checking in, and called me from the hotel casino. By the time he called, I was on the couch frantic some harrowing mishap had prevented him from reaching his destination, tossing around my strategies to locate him and uncover what had gone awry. Answering the phone in a flustered rush, I heard Lance's voice on the other end and anxiously vented my apprehensions with him, ultimately asking him if he was okay. Before he could say anything, I heard the "Cha-Ch'ing" sound of slot machines in the background, followed by the sound of at least three girls laughing. Needless to say I did not find it humorous in the least, and he never made that mistake thereafter. When either of us ever told that story, all he could proclaim was, "You'd think I would have had enough sense not to call her from the hotel lobby of a Las Vegas casino, given that I was already four hours late calling home." One would have thought.

Lance and I continued to struggle within our marriage, but remained devoted to making a solid, stable home for our family, joint in the efforts to acquire the American dream. Enduring all of the trials and tribulations over Rylee participating in a Mother's Day Out program, she was enrolled three days a week and loved it. When Lucas was nine months, I became extremely sick and could no longer nurse him… and I think it was just as painful for me as for him. We cried together each night until we had both dried up and both completely exhausted. By that point I did not have to be at his disposal any longer, the days coming and going as I grew restless and a little resentful.

Due to Rylee's medical problems when she was first born, I did not work outside the home. Even though sacrifices had been required, we soon calculated the numbers and decided that we could survive without my paycheck, so I never went back to work. I remained home with the kids, washing, cooking, and cleaning--and then doing more cleaning and more cooking. When Lance was in town he would arrive home late, and I'd listen to his day of events and problems nodding as if I really did find it interesting, trying to reassure and comfort him, and portray the supportive and appreciative wife. Without question, staying home with my children was a blessing, but the disheartening feelings continued surfacing.

Perhaps I had been speculative that once I had kids and a family I would come to terms with my life and it would free me from those unresolved disparities. Throughout my lifespan I had nothing of relative substance, and now I had so much. Many presumed that I had it all! But what do you do when everything isn't enough, and you don't know what else to do to make it enough? What was it that I kept an eye open for? Did I anticipate that it might fall into my lap? Was it something I could acquire? Was it something I once had and no longer possessed? Was it something resonating from a much deeper place inside? I had no answers. I was appreciative of my life, it was a much greater life than I had ever known. Nevertheless, something was missing in my life that I was unable to identity.

I was home day in and day out without a car and not a single person to talk with, and no one to listen to the events of my day. I felt repressed, as if I had no desires or needs that were my own, and growing bitter toward Lance for making me feel that way. He was traveling, coming and going every week, and when he wasn't away on business he would come home to his children and a dinner prepared and served to him.

There are limited things to share and ways to share the day when you don't do anything or go anywhere, and the trivial conversation you do have is with two young children. Lance didn't care or need to know the details of my tedious routine, including the challenges with Rylee and Lucas. Regardless of my day, the conversation would turn to his within moments of him walking through the door from work. He didn't seem a bit interested in talking beyond his workday by listening to me talk about mine, and I had no reprieve from the monotony I lived day after day.

Whether boredom set in, or desperation to ascend over the walls of confinement in my life, I started looking through my old phone list, desperately reaching out to friends I had not spoken with or seen in awhile. I should have stopped at the letter "Q", or at least skipped the letter "R", because under "R", there was Derek Roberts. What harm would there be in calling someone primarily to touch base? What could it possibly hurt? We had seen each other in passing a time or two while out for lunch, and since he had no reason to doubt I wasn't anything less than happy, he wouldn't speculate about my call. It seemed like an innocent enough idea...

When we last spoke, he had mentioned he was employed with the same company that he had been with for a while, so I called the number that I had listed. My call was rolled directly to voicemail where I left a brief message for him to call me during the day if he wanted, along with my number. He returned my call the next day, and to imply that the call was brisk between the two of us would be stretching it.

He apprised me of his life in a few vague sentences that took less time than the original message I'd left when I called him. He was living with someone, was currently under temporary contract for work, and he'd kept the same friends he had when we were dating. Not too much had changed for him, but things had changed for me. I now had two children, a house, met several new friends and had lived through various surgeries and survived cancer. I was on the other side of the road, waving a farewell as I journeyed ahead full speed. We ended the call as though we were strangers simply making polite conversation but both anxiously counting down seconds to get off the phone. This time it was a mutual goodbye, and I made sure to hang up first. Click! It was as simple as that.

Chapter 8

I believe that as we live our lives, we truly do not comprehend the concept or the value of time. It can be so consequential and yet so irrelevant. In our unrequited battle to negate its essence, we seem never to be in control of it, need a surplus when we have none, or less when we have too much of it. Either way time will come and go, and somewhere in the middle of it coming and going, our lives happen.

Returning from a day at the park with the kids, I could hear the phone ringing as I frantically turned my key in the front door. I could not tell if it had rung once or twenty times, and because I had not turned on the answering machine, I debated whether I should toss the bags and my children and run for it. It was probably Lance telling me he would not be home for supper, or telling me that he would be bringing dinner home. Out of breath, I answered the phone with a windblown, "Hi!" Silence met me on the other end, and deduced from the lack of response that I had missed the call. I was about to hang up to get a dial tone so that I could call Lance's number when I heard a voice say my name. Placing the phone back against my ear, I heard Derek's voice.

Of all the sentiments that could have crossed my mind at that moment, the first that entered my thoughts was the day the phone company asked if I wanted to change the existing phone number or keep the same number once we moved from the apartment into the house. It seemed silly to change a perfectly good number, so why on earth would I do such a thing? New phone number, new baby, and new life. If only time could warn us beforehand of the consequences we bear when making such minuscule decisions. If I haven't mentioned it before, God definitely has a sense of humor--as does Satan.

Our chat was brief, abruptly ending after I heard the garage door opening, which let me know Lance was home. "I have to go!" was all I had time to say, and as I was hanging up his last words to me was a hasty "Call me." I didn't even say goodbye before I placed the phone back onto the base and turned to put my things away, just in time to greet Lance as he walked into the kitchen. I began dinner while we began our routine conversation that we had every evening after he came home. I stood at the sink nodding as if I were attentively listening, but if anyone had asked me the last words he had spoken to me I would have been unable to repeat a single one. I was focused on the last two from Derek, and the way he had sounded.

Perhaps thinking time in between the calls would make it less meaningful, I didn't bother calling him for a couple of weeks. I debated whether I should call at all, riveted with guilt for even contemplating reaching out to him, but convincing myself I was doing it so that he wouldn't feel bad for calling me in the first place. We would visit for a few minutes and that would be that. This time when I called he answered, and after briefly speaking we hung up after Lucas began crying, and I moved on with my day trying to eliminate the entire farce from memory.

But that wasn't the last phone call he made, and after several additional calls and a few months passed, we arranged to meet for lunch so that we could "catch up". Compelled to depict nothing but sheer happiness and bliss, I walked into the restaurant poised and self-assured. I wanted Derek to realize how much he had missed out on, while at the same time recognizing my personal accomplishments since we had last parted. As lunch concluded I could sense my spirits falling and the emptiness I had been experiencing difficult to hide, even greater when he walked me to my car afterward. Unfortunately, it seemed as though I was the one who felt had missed out on something.

My hand on the car door and half turned in his direction, he leaned forward as if to kiss me, and I pulled away rattled and a little shocked that he would be so bold. I guess the fact that I pulled away embarrassed him and made him feel it necessary to justify his actions, as he apologetically explained that he felt led to kiss me because I seamed so unhappy. My initial reaction was thinking to myself, "Well of *course* you kiss everyone when they look sad." I surmised that if he had any clue of my desolation, he would have gladly volunteered to make love to me in the middle of the parking lot. I was diehard not to let anything develop further between us, and placed myself in the car, waving as I drove off, feeling as if the lunch had not gone totally as I had imagined; and afraid nothing else would.

As much as I promised myself I would have nothing further to do with Derek, by November we were talking a few times a week. Lance continued to travel and I continued to be the wife and mother I was expected to be. Tommy had been diagnosed with Cancer a few months prior and was now in the final stages as the cancer was rapidly ravaging his entire body. They had placed him in hospice care and administrating the necessary dosage of morphine to minimize his pain. As much as I wanted nothing to do with Tommy, I helped my mother take care of him and take care of herself, doing whatever I could. Since I lived nearby I was able to assist with their needs and managed to deliver food, fill prescriptions, clean the house and provide diversion from the misery she was in each day by keeping her company.

I generally spoke with my mother on a daily basis for that specific reason, but had left one morning with the kids to run a few of my own errands before calling. I returned midday to find that our caller ID indicated I had missed several calls from her, and I didn't have to call to know what that meant. Instead of calling and making her explain the details over the phone, I loaded the kids back into the car and drove to her house. She met me outside on the porch, grabbing onto me without saying a word as I held her while she cried and released her suppressed emotions. I was never positive if the emotions she released were those of sadness and loss...or relief and freedom.

She later shared the eerie details of his death with me, and the chills shook me as she conveyed the image as Tommy was dying. It seemed he had been afraid of something or someone, and kept asking who the man in the dark cloak was at the end of the bed, proclaiming he did not want to go with him. A dark cloak did not sound like someone waiting to escort you into the direction that you wanted at the end of your passing. I'd assumed that when the time came his destination would not be that of bright lights and angels, but just imagining anyone going through that horror made me cringe.

The entire drive home I wanted to call Derek and hear his voice, to tell him I wanted to see him, and as soon as I walked into the house I dialed his number without hesitation. The upcoming week was his birthday, and we arranged to meet for lunch the day afterward to celebrate. I organized where and when we would meet, strategizing ahead by reserving a booth in the back of the restaurant where we would have adequate privacy. While we had spoken on the phone a few times, I hadn't seen him since the last time we had met for lunch and he had feigned his concern for me to get a kiss.

Now finding that moment bittersweet, I was first at the restaurant and waited on him before being seated, and when he walked through the door my heart practically leapt out of my skin. The waiter promptly escorted us to our table, smiling at both of us as he took our drink order. I had purposely sat across from him so that I could inspect his face and look directly into his eyes, while at the same time keep my distance in hopes that I wouldn't make any illogical moves. But by the end of our lunch and after several glasses of wine consumed, I no longer had any uncertainties about what I wanted.

With all of the pent-up passion I'd harbored for so long ready to be unleashed, I told him everything I was feeling in my heart! That I'd called him to lunch because I needed to be with someone, and someone that could breathe life into me again. With Tommy's death, I was struggling to come to terms with the end of a lifespan of heartache and sorrow, unable to comprehend why something that should have brought me such a positive closure could bring me such mixed emotions and a deeper sense of emptiness. At that facet of my life I needed to feel like a woman, to feel alive again.

Regardless of whoever moved across the table first, within seconds after sharing my feelings we were embraced in each other's arms, kissing as deeply and closely as we could without stripping away our clothes in the middle of the restaurant. If I had been sober I am sure I might have been embarrassed by our indiscretion, but at that particular moment, I didn't care about anything or anyone else. Irrational move or not I had gone to a place where the cold no longer encompassed me, as all my sorrows and anxieties melted, filling me instead with rampant passion. It was the beginning of a significantly tumultuous and heartbreaking affair that was filled with nothing less than torment, disappointment, guilt and regret.

After we had lunch that day, Derek and I managed to see each other as schedules and time permitted. The fact that I stayed home and he worked a few miles from the house helped facilitate the relationship a great deal. February came, and we had already started planning the time that we could spend together on Valentine's Day. It was right at a week prior Valentine's Day that I could not manage to sleep and got out of bed with an unsettled feeling, as if I was waiting for something to happen and needed to be on guard.

I began roaming throughout the hushed, dark house and eventually made my way into the kid's bedrooms. Seeing them safe and sleeping peacefully greatly comforted me, despite the impalpable anxiety haunting me. I left them and strolled back to the living room and stood at the window, staring into the dark night. There was no movement outside or inside the house, and it was as if I could almost hear the silence encompassing me. A slight fog had emerged, and the streetlights cast a hazy glow into the darkness giving an eerie appearance to the night. An unexplained quiver rippled throughout my body and I wrapped my robe tighter against me and folded my arms across my chest, seeing nothing but the vast darkness before me.

Strangely, I didn't manage to sleep much that entire weekend, and by the time Monday came it was as if depression had set in and I was in some sort of funk. I called a friend to arrange taking her kids to the park with Rylee and Lucas, hoping I could shake it off. Dropping me off at the house afterward, she asked me if I was ok, mentioning that I didn't really seem like myself. I simply shrugged in response, knowing I had no inkling how to explain it to her should I have even attempted.

Later, she would tell me that it was almost as if I had experienced some type of premonition of what was to occur. What I couldn't forecast as we visited and watched our children playing throughout that afternoon, was how drastic my life would soon spiral catastrophically out of control in a way I never imagined possible.

We hadn't been home from the park but a brief span of time, when my sister-in-law Jessica called to ask if I had seen or heard from my brother, Corey. She explained that they had gotten into a fight, and he had not come home in two days. Aware they struggled financially and often had controversy, it did not surprise me that they had argued, but it surprised me that he had not been home in two days.

He had moved to Mississippi years earlier to attempt at mending his relationship with our father, the same father who had not been a part of his life throughout his childhood. Though the answer had eluded me, I have repeatedly questioned why so many things we seek to have in our lives are ultimately the very things that chronically become our demise. There are no signs directing us on which way to go or which way not to go, or what to seize or what to let go of. Whatever the reasoning for our choices, we possess an innate thought process that breeds our perception of what's right and what's best for us is ultimately that which *we* desire or feel necessary. Unfortunately, in the midst of planning our lives, we oftentimes get in the way of God's plans for us.

Those thoughts flooded my mind while reminiscent of why Corey had felt the need to move in the first place, as I echoed Jessica's statement; "Two days?"…I was startled that she had waited two days to call anyone and wondered why. After hearing further details from my sister-in-law of how he had left her and the boys during an argument, I ordered Jessica to contact the police since it had already been a couple of days since she had heard from him.

I then called my grandmother in Mississippi to inquire if she had heard from him recently, or if by chance anyone else had. No one had spoken with him or seen him in a few days. I instructed her to contact as many family and friends as possible and have them attempt to trace his whereabouts. About to hang up at the end of our conversation, I half-jokingly made a twisted comment that would haunt me for a long time to come; "She probably had someone kill him for her." I said it in such jest that my grandmother and I laughed together as if the statement had been a punch line to the end of a joke.

We hung up agreeing to keep each other informed, and taking a deep breath I called Jessica back with hopes that she had determined his whereabouts by then or he was now home. Other than the fact she had spoken with the police and informed she would need to complete a missing persons report, there was nothing new to share. It had been over 48 hours since anyone had seen or heard from Corey. The search for my brother began.

***

Lance arrived home shortly before 5:30 that evening and I was in the process of updating him on what had occurred since we last spoke, when the phone rang. I looked toward Rylee and Lucas sitting on the floor in front of me as Lance moved to stand beside me, and heard my cousin Renda's voice on the other end inquiring if I was alone. My response was a simple "No." I don't recall wondering why she asked, but do remember feeling a nervous reluctance when I questioned if anyone had located or heard from Corey.

My question was met with silence, so I timidly repeated the question to her. I then heard myself pose the rhetorical question that in my mind I had already feared: "Is he dead?" Her blunt "Yes" caused me to drop the phone and run outside to the empty field across the street where I dropped to my knees, beating my fists against my legs, screaming in denial. It was a moment forever burned within my memory, as would be in the memory of both of my children, looking on as their father lifted my limp body from the ground to lead me back into the house.

People commonly allege that it is easier to lose someone when it is unexpected, that it is easier not to watch someone you love have to suffer before they die. From my perspective, death is death. There is no easy way to lose someone you love...there is nothing that can prepare you and nothing that can ease the pain. It becomes a void in your mind, heart and soul that cannot be filled; not by time, or by anything or anyone, no matter how much you might try.

Once I managed to become less hysterical, I called Colin to tell him that our brother's body had been discovered. A local man had made a bathroom stop for his dog along a secluded rural road, and the dog had wandered into the forest and discovered Corey's body. If the dog hadn't made the discovery, the probability of finding him would have been minimal at best, and the truth ultimately revealed would never have been discovered otherwise.

I had requested that everyone refrain from contacting my mother and informing her until I could get to her, I did not want her alone when she heard the news. Lance took the kids to our neighbor's house while he left to fill the car with gas and get it ready for the trip, since we would be leaving later that night. While he was gone, I called Derek to explain what had happened and to inform him that I would be leaving for Mississippi later that night, assuring him I'd call back once I heard anything further.

I was inundated with grief and guilt. Lance was trying to do everything feasible to take care of things with unfailing love and support, and my self-centered thoughts were of Derek. I ached for him to be the one beside me, holding me and shielding me from the ensuing travesty. At that moment I was in the house alone, and felt as if I would never experience being so lonely again in my life. Feeling suddenly drained in every aspect both physically and emotionally, I slowly sank back to the ground in a daze.

That's where Lance found me when he got home, and gently lifting me to my feet all but carried me to our bedroom, where he laid me onto our bed and covered me with a blanket. He said nothing, and I knew there was nothing to be said. I lay in the dark, thinking back on the last day that I had seen Corey. He and Jessica had come for a visit with the boys right after we had moved into our new house. As little as they possessed in this world, he seemed genuinely happy for all that we had. I recalled that as he had walked toward his car, I had a strange sensation that I would remember that moment for the rest of my life.

He had turned back to look at me, smiling and laughing at something I'd said to him, waving and saying goodbye. Goodbye....

Once again the tears began to fall at the memory, and I turned and sobbed into my pillow, wishing I had been able to spend more time with him over the passing few years. I thought I had cried all that I could cry by the time Colin arrived at our house close to midnight. For the first few minutes he was there we didn't say a word, clutching each other in comfort as we both cried together. The moment I'd called to tell him the news, he had asked without any hesitation, "What do you need me to do?" My blunt response had been, "Just get here." We were solemnly aware that it would require both of us to break the news to our mother, to help her endure the disastrous news. It was an appalling undertaking that no mother should ever have to incur: she would bury yet another child.

The drive to my mother's house was slow and peculiarly quiet. I sat in the front seat between Lance and Colin, numb and disconnected after taking the medicine that our neighbor had given me earlier to calm my nerves, wishing I could remain that way. When we arrived at her house, it was pitch black outside. She lived alongside an access road that a major highway ran nearby, so she would think nothing of hearing a car, if she heard it at all.

With every step I took in the direction of the house, I wanted to turn and flee. Walking onto the front porch, Colin knocked several times on the door and then took a deliberate step aside, silently expressing my queue to proceed. I stepped forward and waited for her to answer, opening the door after she had confirmed who we were. I walked in, followed by Colin and then Lance.

She had been sleeping, and a small pistol in her hand conveyed to me that she had been ready for impending malice or danger. "What's wrong?" she asked as soon as she saw us all file in, quiet and foreboding. All I could do was look at her, thinking that as estranged as our relationship was I wanted to shield her from what we had to tell her, knowing she was not prepared for such news.

But I didn't have to say it. She looked at me and stated the question more as a fact, just as mine had been hours earlier. "They found him?"

All I could do was nod. "Is he dead?" I could not vocalize a response, but nodded confirmation as the tears came to my eyes. Yes, they had found him. No, I did not know all of the details. Yes, we would be leaving for Mississippi immediately. We then packed a few things for her, and loaded it into the trunk of the car along with the weapon she had held earlier.

Observing the night from a car as you travel into darkness takes you to all kinds of thoughts and places when you are looking for answers. Your imagination grows with every mile you drive and the further you drive, you increasingly feel as if in a dream you pray soon to awaken from. You cling to the surefire process of time, assured that the light of day will theoretically chase away the surrounding darkness and the unknown as if it never existed.

But as the sun rose on Valentine's Day morning and we pulled into the morgue, I despairingly surmised that it was not a dream and no amount of daylight would dissipate the darkness into which we were heading. Though I had no insight to the sorrow and tragedy that loomed ahead, I led the way as if I had no misgivings.

My father met us at the entrance of the city morgue that morning to escort us to the homicide offices of the U.S General Attorney, where three federal prosecutors relayed the gory details of my brother's death. It was conveyed to us that the specifics weren't entirely known, but that the police would unquestionably be conducting his death as a homicide investigation. The Chief Officer corroborated their conclusion with the gruesome details of Corey's death, exposing how he had been strangled, severely beaten, shot twice in the back, and once in the head at close range. From the amount of disfiguring, it was evident there had been several involved in the malicious torturing. Their evidence also supported that my brother had died fighting for his life.

As they were describing the suffering tolerated and the palpable signs of his fight and willpower to survive, I could no longer maintain my resilience or composure as the sobs escaped me. My brother had died alone with no one there to help him or defend him. There had been no one there to share his trepidation or his pain. What did it feel like in those last moments, when he must have known his life was about to end? What were his thoughts as he took his last breath? Did his life flash before his eyes, did he know that he was loved and cared for? It was heart wrenching that he conceivably felt as alone, unloved and uncared for throughout his life, as he had while battling for his life.

Once they relayed what had been unveiled concerning his case, we were informed we could view him, but my father protectively rose to stand beside me expressing that he didn't want us to see him yet. He had already done the disheartening task of identifying his son, the scar on his chin from hitting the bunk bed as a child while playing helped to identify him. His fingerprints confirmed the fact.

On Valentine's Day 1996, we were making the necessary arrangements to bury my brother. As I ironed the shirt that he would be buried in, an indescribable feeling inundated me that made me halt in my tracks. My brain began to register that the local TV station had Corey's picture exhibited and they were sharing the story of his homicide. The more I listened, the more anger took over my hurt and sadness. It was all being uncovered, every element concerning Jessica and her lover and how they had conspired to kill him. How they had dumped his body, obviously counting on the fact that the body would never be located. But the truth has a way of being exposed. It's like God in heaven and fire in hell; you can count on it.

The information continued to evolve, and with it the awareness that we had to address what would happen to his three sons if their mother went to jail, in addition to losing their father. Would the boys be placed in a foster home? Could any of us assume the responsibility of taking care of them? There were so many things to consider and take care of. I felt my mouth become dry and sudden panic rise inside. Lance emphatically made the attempts comfort me, but I turned away from him and leaned on Colin for support.

Looking back I can't imagine the hurt and dismay Lance must have stomached, attempting to be there for me emotionally while I purposely put a wall between us. From the first time I had been with Derek, in my heart I was no longer married to Lance and there had been no further relations between us. Our disengaged relationship was both physically and emotionally. As preposterous as it might have seemed to anyone on the outside, turning to Lance for consolation was a betrayal to Derek, and I was attempting to be loyal to the man that I loved.

Lance faithfully remained my protector, indomitably deterring me from seeing Corey in his casket. He had not wanted me to view the condition his body was in at the morgue, nor did he want me to see him even after the mortician diligently worked to make his appearance resemble what he looked like before he was murdered. No prepping or makeup would be able to hide the violence he'd undergone. In addition to his demise, it seemed we had travelled the same road before with Billy, and soon discovered there were no resources to bury him. Without the slightest hesitation, Lance pulled the money together for Corey's funeral, including his burial plot.

My husband was the one willing to accommodate my every need and want, his arms graciously extended to me without any reservations or expectations attached. How could I not want to be wrapped within that love and protection when I was in need of it most? How could I deny a love that was so freely given? To a love that emphatically wanted to lift me each time I fell to my knees, wipe away every tear that crossed my cheek, provide a shoulder to rest my weariness? In that moment, I felt as if my brother wasn't the only who had perished.

I am a steadfast believer in closure. I don't care what you are leaving behind or how you are leaving it behind: for the soul to move forward and heal there must be closure. By the afternoon of the funeral service I'd yet to physically see Corey, and it didn't feel real or like he was actually gone. Over and over my thoughts recalled the day he was leaving to return to Mississippi after his visit, and almost to his car had turned to look back at me. His smile had been as bright as the sun, his laughter carried by the wind as he joked with me and waved goodbye one last time.

My mind remained frozen in that moment, thinking how he seemed so young and carefree, that he, Jessica, and the boys appeared happy that day. What on earth had happened? What had gone so wrong that I was now standing in front of his casket, and we were saying goodbye for the last time? Did I tell him that I loved him that day? Did he know that I loved him? And as he was dying, did he know that his death would create a hole in our hearts that we did not even realize would be so deep and so painful?

Throughout the entire ceremony everyone had continuously stared at Jessica with disbelief at how ludicrous it was for her to be there, and for the boys to be sitting alongside one of their father's murderers. But as Lance led me from the graveside and gently placed me into the car, my mind was no longer wrapped around any of that. As he was about to close the door, I glanced back at the casket waiting to be lowered, and wanted to run back and make them open it to confirm it really was my brother. I wanted to say goodbye. I wanted...no I *needed* that closure. But the last thing I saw as we drove away from his gravesite was that of his three sons being taken from Jessica, and the police cuffing her hands behind her to escort her to jail.

Chapter 9

*...I will not abandon you or leave you as orphans in the
storm – I will come to you.*

(John 14:18 TLB)

Lance had been awesome in the midst of the tragedy but promptly
resumed his busy work schedule, leaving me alone from early in the
morning until late at night. He would be gone overnight much of
the time, and I was left with everything that had happened. He was
not there to share my heartache or offer comfort, to help me heal the
heartache and overcome the endless nightmares. Even Derek had felt it
necessary for us to spend some time apart, allowing me space and time
to grieve. Time? No, what I needed was someone to give me hope. I
needed someone to be there for me.

I began feeling desperate, so I called the church we'd been attending
and requested to speak with priest, but he wasn't available. There wasn't
anyone available to take my call. By the time I received a return call,
I had catapulted into the abyss of my own hell and no longer cared to
discuss my despondency. How could I begin to explain or share with
anyone that my hurt wasn't solely from the heartbreak of my brother's
death, but also from a relationship outside my marriage that I coveted
but in every aspect shouldn't pursue? I was becoming unresponsive to
anything or anyone, and as each night passed I was having an extremely

difficult time sleeping. I couldn't close my eyes without seeing Corey lying on the slab at the coroner's office, or his face as they beat him to death, eminently envisioning how he must have tenaciously fought for his life. It was becoming a vicious cycle, so I attempted to use a non-prescription sleep aid mild enough that I wouldn't get addicted, but at the same time would offer me the relief that I desperately needed.

A week turned into two weeks, two weeks turned into three, and I gradually found myself sleeping all day, and when I wasn't sleeping I was groggy and crying. I could not muster the vigor to stop myself from spiraling downwards, yet it seemed as though I was never going to hit rock bottom. How was I going to pull it together? When I wasn't sleeping, my thoughts often felt as if they would overwhelm me, creating restlessness in what little sleep I did manage to get.

It was during one of those restless nights that I began writing and expressing my thoughts and feelings to try and pass the time. Reading what I had written provided insight into my subconscious and became a therapeutic outlet for me. It was a refuge where I had none before, a soft place to fall throughout my battles of confusion and solitude. It practically killed me, but I stopped taking the sleeping pills and opted to write when I couldn't sleep, eventually gathering the strength to crawl out of the vast abyss and focus on my children. I was slowly beginning to feel some degree of normalcy and more hopeful in vanquishing the nightmares that tortured me, when I answered the phone to hear Derek's voice.

An equitable amount of time had elapsed since we last communicated, and his justification in calling was that he simply wanted to check on me. His timing was characteristically infallible, and I found myself numb as I sat there with nothing to say. What did he want from me? Sensing my lack of response we said goodbye after a few meaningless topics of conversation, and shortly afterward I received another call from the county courthouse informing me the date of my brother's murder trial. It seemed it would get worse before it got better, but in some tangible way it would be a step toward finding closure to the nightmare. That was something I'd yet to grasp, but knew I had to muster through this particular passage of my life if for no other reason, than for my children.

Lance arranged to postpone any travel during the interim of the trial, and I made necessary arrangements for Rylee and Lucas during the day while he was working. Having no specific timespan prearranged to be absent from home, I packed my bags and drove my mother and myself to Mississippi to attend the trial.

***

Supreme Court of Mississippi.
David CALLAHAN, a/k/a David P. Callahan v. STATE of Mississippi.
No. 98-KB-00693-SCT.
Decided: November 12, 1998

STATEMENT OF THE CASE

¶1. David Callahan was convicted of murder by a Rankin County jury and sentenced to life imprisonment in the custody of the Mississippi Department of Corrections. Aggrieved, Callahan brings this appeal, assigning as error the following:

I. WHETHER THE TRIAL COURT ERRED IN ALLOWING THE IDENTIFICATION OF A CAR BY TAMARA BROWN AND ADMISSION OF PICTURES OF THE AUTOMOBILE OVER CALLAHAN'S OBJECTION.

II. WHETHER THE TRIAL COURT ERRED IN ALLOWING RONNIE PENNINGTON TO TESTIFY AS TO THE STATEMENTS OF JESSICA CARRINGTON OVER CALLAHAN'S OBJECTION.

III. WHETHER THE TRIAL COURT ERRED IN OVERRULING CALLAHAN'S MOTION IN LIMINE REGARDING ALICE BRINKS'S TESTIMONY.

IV. WHETHER THE JURY VERDICT WAS AGAINST THE OVERWHELMING WEIGHT OF THE EVIDENCE.

STATEMENT OF THE FACTS

¶2. Corey and Jessica Carrington had been married for eight years in 1996 and had three children. They were experiencing marital problems and Jessica had been away from home in the weeks preceding Corey Carrington's murder. They lived in Rankin County, Mississippi, within 150 yards of David Callahan's trailer. David Callahan borrowed a .25 caliber automatic gun from Mark Brinks during the first week of February 1996, ostensibly to shoot a dog which had been harassing children in the neighborhood. There were three rounds in the gun when Brinks loaned it to Callahan.

¶3. Corey Carrington was murdered February 8, 1996. He was shot three times with Brinks's .25 caliber automatic gun. He was also strangled with a nylon rope which was recovered with the body. There were two shots to his head and one shot to his back. His blood, a belt loop similar to one missing from his jeans, and his watch were found around 50 feet behind Callahan's trailer.

¶4. Lora Roberts, a neighbor who lived a "stone's throw" away, heard two shots around 10:00 a.m. or 11:00 a.m. on the morning of the murder followed by a third shot a few minutes later. She testified the shots came from the direction of David Callahan's property.

¶5. Tamara Owens, a student on her way home from Pisgah High School, saw a maroon late model car which she later identified as Callahan's car backed up to a dirt bank on Highway 43 in Rankin County around 2:00 p.m. There were two people standing outside the car, including a white man fitting Callahan's description.

¶6. A day later, Daniel Stephens found Corey Carrington's body behind the dirt bank near the side of Highway 43 in Rankin County. A rope used to strangle Carrington was found along with a blanket covering a large portion of Carrington's body. The Rankin County Sheriff's Department could not identify the body. Around lunch that day or the next day, David Callahan returned the cleaned gun he had borrowed from Mark Brinks. The three rounds left in the gun by Brinks had been used.

¶7. On February 13, five days after the murder, Jessica Carrington reported her husband missing and his body was identified later that day by Lisa Canton, Jessica's friend and co-worker. William Carrington, Corey Carrington's father, saw Callahan's car in Jessica and Chris Carrington's driveway on Sunday, two days before Jessica Carrington reported her husband missing.

¶8. The school bus driver for the Carrington children took them to Callahan's residence instead of their home on the day after the murder occurred and again on the day before Jessica Carrington reported her husband missing. The bus driver testified that parental consent was given, as required, before leaving the children at a location other than their own residence.

¶9. Lisa Canton, a friend and co-worker of Jessica Carrington, testified that Callahan and Jessica Carrington were "going together" in the weeks prior to the murder. Canton and her boyfriend, Robert Britton, recounted Callahan's oral accounts and Jessica's approval of ways he could kill Corey Carrington. Callahan described how he could kill Corey Carrington during a card game at Canton's home where Callahan, Jessica Carrington, Canton, and Britton were present. Britton testified Callahan and Jessica had been at Canton's house together at least twice while he was present. Additionally, Canton testified she did not know a gun was used in the murder until Callahan asked her whether or not prints were lifted from the gun.

10. Timothy Vance, a cell mate of Callahan, testified that Callahan confessed to the murders while awaiting trial. Callahan contends Vance's statements were made only in an attempt to receive special treatment or a plea bargain. However, Vance testified that he had received no "favors" because of his testimony.

¶11. At trial, Callahan disputed his location on the day of the murder. Debra McLeigh, a neighbor, testified he was at her house working on her frozen pipes the day of the murder and two other days that week from 7:30 a.m. until lunch. The appellant's brother, Tina Callahan, also testified that the appellant visited him at work from around 12:30 p.m. until just before 2:00 p.m. on February 8, 1996.

I. WHETHER THE TRIAL COURT ERRED IN ALLOWING THE IDENTIFICATION OF CALLAHAN'S CAR BY TAMARA BROWN AND ADMISSION OF PICTURES OF THE AUTOMOBILE OVER CALLAHAN'S OBJECTION.

¶12. Callahan contends there was a violation of his Sixth Amendment right to a fair trial when Tamara Owens was allowed to identify his car. He objects to her identification at the police station where she was shown a picture of the car, and he objects to her identification of the car at the impound lot. Callahan asserts the car was the only auto on the lot when

Owens identified it while Owens testified there were several cars but the car she identified was the only maroon one.

¶ 13. The state contends the appellant failed to raise this error in his motion for a new trial and is thus procedurally barred from raising it now. Alternately, the state contends the defendant cites no authority for his position that identification of cars should be afforded the same procedural safeguards as identification of suspects. Finally, the state contends the identification of Callahan's car did not deny his right to a fair trial. Tamara Owens had an adequate opportunity to view the car on the day it was parked near the dirt pile. She testified that she noticed the car because it was similar to one driven by her boyfriend and no doubt she spent time trying to distinguish the car from her boyfriend's car. She described it to police before being shown a photo of the car or identifying it at the impound lot.

¶ 14. In prescribing which errors must be included in a motion for a new trial to be preserved on appeal, this Court has held, "[a]ll new matters, no[t] shown of record and not merely cumulative irregularities, mistakes, surprises, misconduct and newly discovered evidence" must be brought to the attention of the trial judge before the Court is allowed to review them. Jackson v. State, 423 So.2d 129 (Miss.1982)(quoting Colson v. Sims, 220 So.2d 345, 346 n. 1 (Miss.1969)). Counsel for Callahan objected during the trial to this evidence; therefore it was a matter of record and it was not necessary that he list it in his motion for a new trial. "[I]t is not necessary to make a motion for a new trial grounded upon errors shown in the official transcript of the record" Colson, 220 So.2d at 346 n. 1.

¶ 15. We have held an appellant's failure to cite any authority in support of assignments of error precludes this Court from considering these issues on appeal. Grey v. Grey, 638 So.2d 488, 491 (Miss.1994) (citing Matter of Estate of Mason, 616

So.2d 322, 327 (Miss.1993)). While failure to cite authority should not be considered a procedural bar, this Court is not bound to consider an unsupported argument.

¶16. In Ohio v. Roberts, which Callahan cites, the United States Supreme Court allowed the testimony of a witness who did not appear at defendant's trial when the witness had testified at the preliminary hearing. Ohio v. Roberts, 448 U.S. 56, 100 S.Ct. 2531, 65 L.Ed.2d 597 (1980). She had been subject to questioning that was the equivalent of crossexamination and was unavailable to appear at trial. Id. Ohio does not address identification, the very issue for which Callahan cites it as support. The United States Supreme Court has dealt with identification and the attachment of Sixth Amendment rights in several cases. See United States v. Wade, 388 U.S. 218, 87 S.Ct. 1926, 18 L.Ed.2d 1149 (1967); Kirby v. Illinois, 406 U.S. 682, 92 S.Ct. 1877, 32 L.Ed.2d 411 (1972). However, this line of cases addresses the identification of human beings not automobiles. There is no rational basis for Callahan's argument and we find it without merit.

II. WHETHER THE TRIAL COURT ERRED IN ALLOWING RONNIE PENNINGTON TO TESTIFY AS TO THE STATEMENTS OF JESSICA CARRINGTON OVER CALLAHAN'S OBJECTION.

¶17. Callahan asserts Officer Ronnie Pennington's testimony should have been limited to what he personally observed or did. He asserts that Pennington's testimony as to what Jessica Carrington said was hearsay and should not have been allowed by the trial court. Callahan objects to testimony by Pennington which relates to Jessica Carrington's inconsistent statements regarding her relationship with Callahan. Pennington testified Jessica Carrington first stated she knew Callahan only vaguely then later admitted they had a sexual relationship.

¶ 18. The state contends this matter has not been preserved for appeal since the judge's reasoning for overruling the appellant's objection is not part of the record. In the alternative, the state submits any harm was cured by rephrasing the question to limit the testimony only to the inconsistent statements of Jessica Carrington.

¶ 19. This Court has addressed a similar situation in which the appellant specified all "in chamber conferences" were to be included on appeal and nevertheless a bench conference on a hearsay ruling was not included in the record. We held:

Under the circumstances, we perceive no grounds for charging [the appellant] and his attorney with responsibility for the fact that the court reporter did not take down what transpired. On the other hand, we do not think it appropriate that we invent matters not fairly within the record. We approach the critical portion of the trial with a common sense awareness of how at the trial level court and counsel proceed regarding objections of the sort here made.

Lambert v. State, 574 So.2d 573, 577-578 (Miss.1990) (citation omitted).

¶ 20. In this case, Callahan noted that all "objections, arguments, responses and rulings by the Court" should be included in the record for appeal. At the first possible moment, counsel for Callahan objected to "hearsay" and was sustained. However, upon renewing his motion later in the testimony, counsel for the appellant was overruled after a bench discussion which had been designated "Off The Record."

¶ 21. The distinction between the two rulings appears to be premised on the fact that Pennington was exposing inconsistent statements of Jessica Carrington. This sort of testimony might have been allowed under Miss. Rule of Evid. 613(b) as impeachment evidence if Jessica Carrington had been a witness and was afforded an opportunity to explain the inconsistency. However, Jessica Carrington was not a witness in this trial. Therefore, Pennington's statements fall into the category of hearsay under Miss. Rule of Evid. 802. His testimony does not come within an exception to the hearsay rule enumerated in Rule 803 and allowing this testimony was error.

¶22. Callahan asserts that admitting hearsay constitutes reversible error. He cites Balfour v. State, 598 So.2d 731 (Miss.1992). However, the defendant's case in Balfour was reversed for violations of the Fifth, Sixth and Fourteenth amendments. Id. at 756. Our inquiry is whether the error merits reversal. Did the admission of this evidence abridge Callahan's right to a fair trial? Lambert, 574 So.2d at 578. Pennington's testimony served to impeach Jessica Carrington's character for truthfulness. It may have also lent credence to the state's theory that Jessica Carrington and Callahan were having an affair, showing Callahan's motive for murdering Corey Carrington. The testimony of Jessica Carrington's friend Lisa Canton and her boyfriend Robert Britton brought out similar facts. They stated that Callahan and Jessica were "going together." Additionally, William Carrington's testimony that his son and Jessica had been having trouble and that he saw Callahan's car in the couple's driveway reinforced evidence of a relationship. The bus driver's testimony that she was instructed to drop the Carrington children at Callahan's house in the days before Jessica reported Corey missing did the same.

¶23. In addition to the similar testimony, there was sufficient evidence to convict Callahan without Pennington's account of Jessica Carrington's statements. Garry Simon, a forensic scientist with the Mississippi Crime Laboratory, testified that the bullets recovered from Corey Carrington's body were fired from the gun Callahan borrowed from Mr. Brinks. Blood evidence fifty feet behind Callahan's trailer pinpointed the site of Carrington's death, and Tamara Owens identified Callahan's car as the one she saw later the day of the murder backed up to the bank where the body was found. She also testified a man fitting Callahan's description was standing near the car. Finally, Timothy Vance, a cell mate of Callahan, testified Callahan confessed to the murder while awaiting trial. The jury would not have returned a different verdict had it not heard the hearsay testimony in issue; therefore, the error in admitting this testimony is insufficient to require reversal.

III. WHETHER THE TRIAL COURT ERRED IN OVERRULING THE DEFENDANT'S MOTION IN LIMINE REGARDING ALICE BRINKS'S TESTIMONY.

¶24. Callahan contends the trial court should have sustained his motion in Limine regarding the testimony of Alice Brinks since he contends all Ms. Brinks's knowledge about the events in question came from her husband, Mark Brinks. The state argues this motion is not preserved on appeal and is therefore barred. The state also asserts that no hearsay testimony was allowed from Alice Brinks except one sentence which was remedied by an instruction from the judge. The state contends there was no error by the trial judge.

¶25. A trial judge enjoys wide discretion with regard to the relevancy and admissibility of evidence. Fisher v. State, 690 So.2d 268, 274 (Miss.1996). We will not reverse a trial judge's evidentary ruling unless the judge commits an abuse of discretion prejudicial to the party bringing the motion. Fisher, 690 So.2d at 274.

[Motions in Limine] should be granted only when the trial court finds two factors present: the evidence in question will be inadmissible at trial under the rules of evidence and that mere offer, reference, or statements made during trial concerning the evidence will tend to prejudice the jury.

Hopkins v. State, 639 So.2d 1247, 1254 (Miss.1993).

¶ 26. A contemporaneous record of the motion in Limine by the appellants was not preserved in this case. However, it was later made a part of the record. While any testimony by Ms. Brinks which simply reiterated her husband's testimony should be excluded as prejudicial, it is clear that she did have first-hand knowledge of some of the events around the time her husband loaned the gun in question to Callahan.

¶ 27. She described where the gun was kept. She testified it was last fired six months prior to the week of February 5, 1996. She personally knew there were three rounds left in the gun prior to the week of February 5, 1996, and she personally discovered the gun was missing that week. She also saw her husband walking down the hall with the gun. All objections by appellants to Ms. Brinks's testimony were sustained and in one instance an instruction was given to the jury to disregard what she said. The trial judge instructed the parties that the hearsay objection would be sustained unless Ms. Brinks could testify based on her own knowledge. Callahan suffered no prejudice since the trial judge carefully protected the testimony to avoid entry of inadmissible hearsay. The judge did not abuse his discretion in denying the appellant's motion in Limine and allowing Ms. Brinks to testify. This assignment of error is without merit.

IV.   WHETHER THE JURY VERDICT WAS AGAINST THE OVERWHELMING WEIGHT OF THE EVIDENCE.

¶ 28. Callahan contends the jury's verdict was against the overwhelming weight of the evidence and therefore the court erred in failing to grant any of the following: a directed verdict motion, a preemptory instruction for acquittal, a motion for judgment notwithstanding the verdict, or a motion for a new trial. In opposition, the state retorts that there was ample support for the jury's verdict and it should not be overturned.

¶29. It is well settled that our authority to interfere with a jury's verdict is very limited. Benson v. State, 551 So.2d 188, 192-93 (Miss.1989). This Court has held, "To determine whether a jury verdict is against the overwhelming weight of the evidence, [this Court] view[s] all of the evidence in the light consistent with the verdict and we give the State all favorable inferences which may be drawn from the evidence." Strong v. State, 600 So.2d 199, 204 (Miss.1992) (citing Corley v. State, 584 So.2d 769, 773 (Miss.1991)). We will reverse only when the trial court has abused its discretion in refusing to grant a new trial. Strong, 600 So.2d at 204. We will only grant a new trial when allowing the verdict to stand would "sanction an unconscionable injustice." Harris v. State, 527 So.2d 647, 649 (Miss.1988)(quoting Groseclose v. State, 440 So.2d 297, 300 (Miss.1983)).

¶30. The primary basis for the appellant's contention here rests on the alibi evidence provided by Wendy Nance and Tina Callahan. Additionally, the appellant cites the circumstantial nature of the physical evidence. Finally, the appellant refers to Mark Brinks's uncertainty about the date the gun was returned. It is clear that the jury is the only arbiter of the credibility of witnesses. Collier v. State, 711 So.2d 458, 462 (Miss.1998). When asked to reverse on the ground of inconsistencies or contradictions in testimony, we have held this is clearly in the jury's province and flatly refused. Id. "Jurors are permitted, indeed have the duty, to resolve the conflicts in the testimony they hear. It is enough that the conflicting evidence presented a factual dispute for jury resolution." Groseclose v. State, 440 So.2d 297, 300 (Miss.1983)(quoting Gandy v. State, 373 So.2d 1042, 1045 (Miss.1979)). Since the credibility of the testimony of

Mark Brinks, Debra McLeigh, and Tina Callahan was a decision for the jury, the Court will not reverse the jury's verdict. Finally, the appellant claims the physical evidence is not strong enough to warrant the jury's finding of guilt beyond a reasonable doubt. In reviewing the record in the light most favorable to the state, it is clear there was an evidentiary basis for the guilty verdict. Therefore, the verdict was not against the overwhelming weight of the evidence.

CONCLUSION

¶31. Callahan presented no basis for error in the identification of his automobile. While the testimony of Ronnie Pennington recounting Jessica Carrington's statements was hearsay, it is clear the jury would have reached the same verdict without this testimony. No motion in Limine was required for the testimony of Alice Brinks since she was able to testify to facts based on her own knowledge. Finally, the verdict of the jury was not against the overwhelming weight of the evidence presented. There was no reversible error in the trial court's proceedings and so we hereby affirm the jury's verdict.

¶32. CONVICTION OF MURDER AND SENTENCE OF LIFE IMPRISONMENT IN THE CUSTODY OF THE MISSISSIPPI DEPARTMENT OF CORRECTIONS AFFIRMED.

***

The details throughout the trial were horrendous and heart wrenching. The public defender consistently implied that Corey's death was due to a drug deal gone wrong or a robbery gone amiss, and not that of my sister-in-law, her lover and her lover's sister taking his life. The prosecutor provided substantiating evidence of a plot discussed on various occasions to murder Corey, bringing witness after witness to the stand corroborating the facts. The prosecutor presented how they'd placed his lifeless body in the trunk of their car after murdering him, picked up his oldest son from school, then drove to an isolated countryside road to dump his body with his son still in the back seat of the car. The day before Jessica reported my brother missing, the school bus driver had taken the children to David Callahan's residence rather than taking them home, and then again the day after the murder. He testified while under oath, that the mandatory parental consent to leave them at a location other than their own residence was officially documented.

It was determined by the authorities that the man sitting in the courtroom was the individual who pulled the trigger of the gun that had ultimately taken Corey's life. Apparently, he was unwilling to renounce his lover or his sister. As each horrid detail was divulged, it wasn't until the prosecutor displayed my brother's jeans drenched in his blood that I thought I might lose control. I could think of nothing but attacking the man that sat on the other side of the guardrail, the man with no degree of remorse for why he was there, and confident that he would never be convicted of his crime. I was thankful a break was ordered and the court temporarily adjourned, needful of a breath of fresh air before I literally threw up.

As I walked past him, he turned to look at me and gave me a ruthless sneer as if to suggest he was enjoying the memory of what he had done to my brother. I didn't even blink when I lunged forward, reaching for the bailiff's gun with the intent to blow his brains out. In that split second I had no thoughts of my beliefs or morals, as every conviction in my heart and soul seemed to die with thoughts of revenge, casting all else aside. Someone reached out to restrain me, and as the disturbance swept through the courtroom, the man kept sitting calmly in his chair...still smirking.

I was inconsolable as they sat me on the stairs outside the courtroom, my shoulders shaking with the pain that resonated within. It wasn't just the death of my brother or the shocking revelation that my sister-in-law took the life of her husband and the father of their children. It was also about my own death, my own future, and that of my children and my husband, which seemed to run parallel to the nightmare I was living in. Deaf to everything and everyone around me, I could only hear my mother reassuring me that there would not be a pardon for the man on trial, and not to give into his repugnant performance. I become so distraught that the judge approached me out of concern for my wellbeing, and said in a stern but gentle voice, "Have faith." I didn't appreciate at the time that it was voluntarily more than he probably should have said to me, and a comfort that he should not have publically extended. I lifted my head from my knees, rose to stand, and followed the judge back into the courtroom as if I would be the one sitting behind his desk and wearing the black robe.

But all I was doing was making my way back into hell, praying that this man who awaited his destiny would find damnation himself. The experience of feeling that you are living in hell makes you thirst for a cool drink of water to quench your thirst, only to find that the water you thirst for is limited and never enough. During the trial, there came a point that I could no longer recall anything but the sadness or the pain of what was in front of me, and by the time the jury returned with a guilty verdict and a life imprisonment sentence, I knew my thirst from living in that hell would not to be quenched despite the outcome adjudged.

Several weeks after the trial was finalized we received a call from the Mississippi police headquarters to speak with someone from the district attorney's office. They wanted to discuss what options lay before us concerning Jessica and the boys. Did we want to charge Jessica with the evidence already collected, chancing an innocent verdict? Or prefer to release her and wait with hopes that the State might possibly compile additional evidence against her, with a greater possibility of a conviction and sentenced to prison for her crime? They explained the double jeopardy term, which prohibited a defendant from being prosecuted twice on the same (or similar) charges subsequent a legitimate acquittal or conviction. Basically, it meant that if arrested at a later time we could not prosecute via a second trial, if she wasn't convicted during the first trial.

Weighing our options, something inside told me that if we opted to let her walk, chances were slim of a second arrest or returning to jail once they released her, let alone a trial by jury. I wanted to proceed with a conviction, but my vote was not the one that counted. The decision was made to detain her for as long as possible while probing to collect crucial evidence condemning enough that a jury would convict her. But as the postponed court day drew nearer nothing admissible had been uncovered, and went before the judge dreading the fact it was highly probable she would soon be walking out a free woman.

Regardless of the outcome of her case, I had made the decision to go before the court requesting the judge grant my brother's family guardianship of his three sons, imploring the court take them away from her under the circumstances. Jessica was not present in the courtroom throughout the trial, and I had not seen her since Corey's funeral when she had been taken into custody and separated from my nephews. Now I stood alongside her wanting to permanently take them from her. I could feel the anger and distaste projecting from her as if she was verbalizing it aloud, as if she wanted to perform the same malevolence upon me that she had been accused of doing to my brother. But the county's orange overalls she donned while in prison and the fact that she was about to be on parole after having served time did not seem to sway the judge. As our testimony concluded, the harsh pounding of his gavel sounded in the room, and Jessica was granted full custody of the boys, our request denied.

We had lost my brother, and now my nephews. It seemed to be one loss shadowing another, and I would have to confront another heartbreaking loss when I returned home. I wasn't convinced that the road I was on was ever going to get back on track, but I no longer felt

121

obligated to pretend or to settle, and the day after I returned from Mississippi I asked Lance for a divorce. Right or wrong, I wanted out of our marriage. The passage of change was at hand, and I had come to the decision to move on with my own life.

Consecutive weeks of hurtful and wearisome discussions wore us both down, but Lance obstinately conceded to the fact that I was going to leave. As we sat together outside on our back porch drinking coffee in the cool morning air on a Saturday morning beforehand, an undeniable sadness gripped us. Yet that morning I still believed Lance was my best friend, and as he stared across the yard beyond the kids jungle gym that we had put together the previous Christmas, the glazed look in his eyes told me he didn't really see anything. Not sure what to say or do, I sat next to him tentatively awaiting him to pull his thoughts together, when he abruptly turned and looked at me. "You are trying so hard to not be like your mother, you are going to become just like her. You'll lose either way, whether you stay or whether you leave."

I looked at him speechless, letting his words sink into my thoughts and wishing with all of my heart he was wrong. But he was not wrong. I could stay for our kid's sake and blame them for staying in a loveless marriage, or I could leave, ending my marriage and taking my children away from their father. However you looked at it I was going to be repeating the cycle, the cycle I swore I'd break. I had calculated that my life and the lives of my children were going to be different, because I was never going to make the same mistakes as my mother. The thought was mind-boggling, and I suddenly felt bewildered and scared. Not only was I continuing the vicious cycle, but it also seemed as if I was adhering to the blueprint. He'd arbitrarily struck a chord, and there was nothing else to say. He stood and turned to go back into the house, leaving me on the porch in the cold air, with my cold coffee and my chilling thoughts.

Lance and I both discussed how and when I would move, with the joint understanding that he did not want to watch me pack, or watch me walk out the door with his children. Therefore, it was agreed that the separation should occur while he was on a business trip. I would learn years later that he lied to his parents, telling them and everyone else that he'd no warning that I was leaving, and that he came home to an empty house and his wife and children gone.

Before I could do any packing or leaving, there were several things necessary to organize in order for me to leave. By then Lucas was almost a year old, so I placed him in daycare and acquired a part-time job. Getting back into the workforce was going to be the expedient way for me to wean Lucas from being with me twenty-four seven. But as I was leaving in the mornings he would cling to me crying his heart out, and when I picked him up in the afternoons I could tell he had been crying before I arrived. My heart was torn. How could I walk away from my child and place him somewhere that he was so plainly miserable? How could I walk away from the opportunity to stay home with my son and be the parent that he needed?

By the second week, it was an irrefutable fact that a change was imperative. My son was not improving in the least, and I could no longer stand the heartbreak of his ongoing unhappiness. Rylee was in school, so it never really registered to her that I was working. I would drop her off at school on my way to work, and then pick her up once I'd picked her brother up from day care. Lucas could not tell me what was happening, and Rylee was not there, so she could not tell me anything, either. I withdrew them from that daycare and transferred both to an alternate daycare down the street. It was a newer facility, and the caretakers seemed so much friendlier and attentive. By the second day there was no comparison to his disposition, and he'd already bonded with one of the young girls whose class he predominantly stayed in. With the matter satisfactorily resolved and content with my decision, I moved forward with the other arrangements to separate from Lance.

About six months later there was an available slot for Lucas to attend daycare full time, and I went from part-time to full-time employment where I currently worked. Lance and I agreed he'd remain at the house, so I rented a modest, two-bedroom duplex around the corner. I requested he reside in the house so he wouldn't be tempted to move out of state for a job opportunity, and hopefully remain close to the kids both personally and in proximity. I traded in the used car his parents had given us and bought a new and dependable car. Now I was employed, had a daycare for my children, and a new place to live. Everything seemed in order…but the hardest part was yet to come.

It puzzles me as to what determines family members or friends to remain by your side without hesitancy or deliberation, while others tend to ridicule and judge at every opportunity. Oftentimes sacrificing a relationship in a matter of moments, that may have taken years to build. The weekend I began moving I sought the help of my friends, but only one of them made themselves available. Even when I requested help from my lifelong friend Misty, her husband David, vented that "they" didn't support me leaving Lance. He "forbid" her to help me move, but offered they would be happy to help me move back in once I came to my senses. The irony of that statement would be in my mind not even two years later when Misty left David: for cheating on her. Within ten years from her leaving David would die from alcohol poisoning, literally drinking himself to death. They would find him sitting in a chair by the window, alcohol bottles surrounding him, his house in shambles. He died alone.

At that precise moment however, I felt as if I was in a fight for my life and fighting for it on my own as well. Lance was on a business trip as agreed, and without the help from anyone other than Kelly, I made the move from our home to the new duplex in one grueling, nonstop day. I left with so little that it required nothing but a paltry trailer and two carloads to complete the move. I took nothing but the living room furniture purchased when we first moved into the house, the guest bed, one TV, and half of the dishes and pans. Before I left, I cleaned and moved some of the furniture from the living room into the den so not look empty when Lance came home. The whopping $585.00 income tax refund was part of my "settlement" since the equity in the house wasn't divided. I used it to purchase twin beds for the kids and other miscellaneous items needed, including food. I worked nonstop striving to make the new place a home they'd feel comfortable in. I didn't want them walking into complete disarray and that be the first image of our new residence.

Though physically and emotionally drained from the move, I was originally scheduled to begin my fulltime job the Monday after I moved. My phone wasn't yet connected, so I went back to the house to call and make them aware of the extenuating conditions, and let them know I would not make it in. I'd barely made it into the workplace the next day, when my manager brusquely called me into her office, informing me that they were releasing me because I had been negligent in corresponding about my absence.

Feeling the severity of the issue I forced myself to remain calm, but could feel myself beginning to unravel as I deliberated on the fact that I had two young children relying on me. I apologetically began explaining the calamities incurred over the weekend, attesting that in fact I had called. I further alluded to my practice of exceptional work ethics, and that I would never be careless concerning my responsibilities. They permitted me to remain, and within six months I was promoted to a vice president position, which thankfully added a pleasant and much needed bolster to my salary.

I picked the kids up from daycare that same Tuesday and carried them back to their new home, explaining the new living arrangements as simply as I could in terms they could comprehend. In my mind I'd envisioned Lance a part of our children's lives, sharing the burdens and the joys of raising them as if we were married. He'd remain my friend, and the people we remarried warmly welcomed into the family. We'd all live harmoniously, our lives ordinary and uneventful as though a divorce never occurred, none of us skipping a beat. It wasn't long before I realized I was apparently living in a fantasy world, and seemed to be the odd man out with such auspicious aspirations.

In the meantime the poignant roller coaster of a separation, moving, working again as a single mom, all shadowing the aftermath of losing my brother and witnessing his murder trial, took its toll on me. Keeping my children unaffected by my dysfunctional feelings and helping them adjust to our new life was a challenge I thought I was prepared for, but soon discerned...not so much! Where I'd considered myself to have many friends before my divorce, virtually all of them appeared to have fallen off the face of the earth during my divorce. I had no family I could turn to, and where writing was formerly my emotional outlet, I merely stared at a blank piece of paper now. Within a few weeks after the move I began questioning myself for the reasons behind my choices, theorizing all of it was brought on by temporary insanity.

I find it most incongruous that people put so much preparation, money, time and invested emotions into getting married, and it can all end ninety days from filing a piece of paper signed by someone saying irreconcilable differences simply can't be reconciled. Lance tried several times to talk sense into me before our separation became a divorce, but to no avail. The day the divorce became finalized I decided to walk across the street to the park before picking the kids up from daycare. There was no one else in the park, and I sat looking down at the ground, barely pushing the swing I was sitting in.

An afflicting sensation that I had elected a deviant path from the road I was ordained to travel, became inordinately troubling. The sun warm on my skin, I didn't feel the cool spring wind as it blew my hair across my cheek, mingling with the tears that fell. I'm not sure how long I sat there, when I sensed someone was standing near me and looked up from the ground expecting someone there, but discovered I was clearly alone. A subtle chill caused me to shiver even in the warmth of the sun, and I stood to go home.

I started walking across the parking lot to make my way home when I passed a parked police car, and glanced into the bluest eyes I'd ever seen in my entire life. They were almost mesmerizing, and I found myself unable to look away. He smiled sympathetically and spoke in a reassuring voice…"Don't worry, everything is going to be ok." All I could do was acknowledge his words with a meager smile of my own, and continued to walk past him to the exit of the parking lot. I waited for the oncoming traffic to clear so that I could cross the street, turning to look back at the police officer that had been so kind moments before…to discover there was no car.

I slowly turned full circle scoping the parking lot behind me, aware that there was only one way in – and one way out. He had not passed me to exit. This time, the chill traveled up and down my spine and caused the hair on my skin to rise, until warmth filled my entire being and a peace encompassed me. While I may have appeared unaccompanied in that moment, I knew that I'd just been given a miraculous reminder that I did not walk alone.

Chapter 10

The experience at the park that day carried me through some of the darkest days and darkest nights that followed. Somewhere in-between, I came to the realization it was imperative that I discover forgiveness. I had to be willing to extend *sincere* forgiveness to others, and render *myself* the grace of forgiveness as well. I wasn't perfect by any means, and I was aware of my faults and the unlimited mistakes that had created my life and generated the challenges I faced. But I faithfully believed that somewhere along the way, God would be forgiving as well as understanding of my shortcomings, and somehow take my worst and turn it into my best.

I was preparing to climb into bed after a demanding day at work and hours of cooking, cleaning and preparing for the following day, when I looked to see my bible on my nightstand and opened it to a verse that seemed to reach to me.

Romans 8:28

And we know that God causes all things to work together for good to those who love God, to those who are called according to His purpose.

As I read the scripture I could all but feel God's arms wrap around me, reassuring me that I just had to persevere and he would direct my path. I closed my bible and closed my eyes to find restful sleep that I greatly needed.

The day afterward made the night before feel as if nothing but a dream, however. The peace I'd felt dissipated into a vapor and I could no longer feel God's arms. Instead I felt delimited by Satan, as if he had virtually kidnapped me in the middle of the night and taken me straight to hell. It began first thing in the morning on my way to work, by being pulled over for speeding. Upon writing up the speeding ticket, the policeman directed my attention to the expired inspection sticker on the windshield, and was kind enough to write a citation for both. Luckily, he let me off for the insurance card I did not have on hand with a mere warning!

Saying my "Thank you" like we typically do for some reason, I hurried to work even later than before, triggering the security alarm upon my arrival, and for the second time that day, I had to deal with the police. I then discovered two scheduled employees had called in sick and I had to work late to cover their shifts, thus picking up the kids late from daycare. There is nothing worse than dropping your kids off at daycare in the dark and picking them up in the dark, unless they are also the last ones to be picked up and you have to pay a late fee because it's after hours.

The day had not ended any better than it had been throughout the entire day, and unlike the night before, I tossed and turned until falling into a deep and troubled sleep. I was grateful when Friday arrived, and for the first time I was even appreciative that Rylee and Lucas were spending the weekend with Lance. I had arranged to meet some friends at a nearby venue in Dallas that evening for cocktails and some live music, looking forward to the diversion I hoped the night would bring. I'd made the decision to take my own car to meet up with everyone that evening, in case I wanted to leave. Arriving early, I ordered a drink and sat down next to the front windowpane so that I could spot them whenever they arrived.

The uptown hangout included several bars and restaurants, while some were inclusive of both. With food, live music and all the alcohol you could consume as you partied from venue to venue. It was my first time in uptown, and I sat alone humorously "people watching" when there was nothing funny about what--no *who* I saw, walking down the sidewalk not five feet from where I sat. Derek was walking with his cousin whom I'd met the first time we dated, and they seemed immersed in conversation that was evidently funny to both.

I remained motionless as I watched them make their way through the entrance of the club, scheming a discreet way to make my exit once they were seated. I hadn't quite come up with a strategy, when my name was called from behind. I instantly distinguished that it wasn't one of the friends I'd been waiting for, and intuitively knew that it was the man I'd remained resolute to avoid for years, and yet perpetually ended up in front of.

My friends and I never succeeded in connecting that night as prearranged, and I hung out with Derek, his cousin and his friends for the evening. Before the time the night had concluded, I'd showed pictures of my children, unreservedly informed them of my divorce, and divulged irrelevant details the foregoing years had encompassed. Everything seemed to flow as if time had never separated any of us, and as the night progressed it seemed me and Derek progressed along with it. He drove me home that night, and didn't go back to his own apartment where he was currently living with another woman. I never questioned how he managed not going home to her, but then I already knew he was an expert at deception. Regardless of his intent, one night did not make amends for the past, either previously or currently. Had he now come to the conclusion that enough time had elapsed and all of my heartaches and troubles were vanished and he could just waltz back into my life?

I didn't see or speak with him the remainder of the weekend. Once I completed the usual morning routine and settled into work that following Monday morning, I sat at my desk drinking a cup of coffee, trying to recover from my lack of sleep over the last couple of days. Going over reports and on my third cup of coffee, my assistant transferred a call, and picking up the main line I heard a familiar voice, and I all but spewed the last bit of coffee I'd sipped onto my desk: it was Derek. We exchanged the customary conversational niceties between us before he finally asked me if I'd like to get together for a drink, or maybe for dinner the upcoming weekend? I thoroughly enjoyed telling him I'd already made plans, and abruptly reminded him I was at work and needed to get off the phone.

Hanging up before hearing the disconnect click of his phone felt appropriate, and the fact that I was assured he'd call back gave me a power that I had not felt with him before. I liked it. I avoided taking any further calls from him for days following his date request, not sure how I felt or what I wanted to say or do, after all I had been through with him…and because of him. I had betrayed my family and my beliefs to be with him, and he'd disdainfully tossed me aside.

Several weeks afterward I arrived home from work loaded down with Lucas held in one arm, groceries and purse on the other, and Rylee trailing on my heels with her homework in hand expressing how hungry she was. I managed to make it to the front door from the parking lot despite the chaotic hassle, to discover a piece of paper inserted into the front door. Preoccupied with getting the kids inside, I grabbed it and threw it into my purse as I walked in, making my way into the kitchen to fix dinner. Hours later, after homework, baths and bedtime stories had been read, I tucked the kids into their beds and fell exhausted into my own bed.

As my head it the pillow, I suddenly recollected that I hadn't unfolded the paper left on the door and went into the living room to find out what it was. I stood in disbelief as I opened it to find a handwritten note from Derek briefly stating that he wanted to meet up, then provided his phone number at the end of it requesting that I call. I refolded the note and placed it on the kitchen table as I walked to my bedroom.

I lay in bed for some time musing over precisely what I should do with his request. He seemed uncharacteristically tenacious in his mission to be with me after so easily walking away time and again, while I had been willing to leave everything behind and give up all that was dear to me to be with him. Willing to do so even after his unfaithfulness to me years earlier, and still here I was alone and just as betrayed by him recently as I had been then. Once again, sleep was evasive until the early morning hours, and when I finally succumbed to it's mercy, it was a restless and troublesome slumber.

Giving into his woes and temptations, we went out a few weeks after he wrote the note. He'd called me at work again to have lunch, and then we met for drinks that very same evening since the kids were with Lance. After a short period of casual dating, Derek broke up with his girlfriend and requested we become exclusive after he had arrived unannounced one evening, to find me on a date. I teasingly contested with him for about a month, but soon gave in knowing that I was fighting a losing battle.

Rylee and Lucas had not yet met him, because I did not want them subjected to men coming and going and confusing them anymore than need be. And until I was assured the relationship was going to work, I wasn't going to create further disorder or undue anxiety for my children. On the weekends the kids were with their father, he would stay at my place in order for me to be nearby the kids and because I didn't feel comfortable at his place.

With the relationship between Derek and me rapidly developing, it was imperative that the kids met Derek sooner than later, because whatever happened between the two of us was contingent upon what happened between the three of them. The protectiveness for my kids was compounded by the fact that it would be revealed to Lance I was dating Derek, and I'd be lucky if he merely became enraged and made horrible threats over choosing to kill me, claiming the act a justifiable homicide. But I knew ultimately he would have to find out, so I took the first step by explaining to Rylee and Lucas that although I cared for their father in a very special way, I had met someone I loved in a different way, and wanted them to meet. I think it was love at first sight! Derek had never been married and didn't have children, and I was astonished at how well he did with them and how well the kids responded to him.

Inside a few short months from Derek meeting the kids it was as though we were practically a family, yet try as I may, I remained incapable of relinquishing the past. I felt no consolation that Lance had come across blasé when I'd told him who I was dating, knowing inside he was torn apart by the fact that Derek was a part of my life once more…and now his children's.

Chapter 11

The first Christmas we were separated I elected to let Rylee and Lucas spend their holiday with Lance in Houston, feeling it critical they be with family under the current circumstances. That meant I either spent the day with Derek and his family, or spend the holiday alone. I remembered how much his mom didn't like me the first time we dated, and I wasn't looking forward to spending Christmas with her or with people I didn't really know and that didn't know me. What would they say about us dating when they learned that I wasn't divorced yet but in the process of a divorce, and had two small children? All I could hope for was to get through lunch before they kicked me out with a good riddance and their thanks, but no thanks arrogance.

Being alone is one thing, being lonely is another, and sitting there that Christmas morning without my children while waiting for Derek's arrival, I felt overwhelming loneliness. By midmorning I'd given up waiting for the kids to call and called them, frustrated that I hadn't already heard from them. I wasn't certain who would answer the phone, or exactly who I wanted to, but it was bittersweet when I heard the familiar voice of my mother-in-law. We used to talk at least a few times a week, but I had not spoken with her in several months due to the separation. Not thinking twice and purely from habit, my usual; "Hi, Mom! Merry Christmas!" burst from my lips, as tears filled my eyes and a smile sprang to my lips just hearing her voice.

Her response stung me like a direct slap to the face. *"Excuse* me?" It wasn't so much what she said, as the tone I could hear in her voice. My mother-in-law, the woman who had been like my own mother, was relaying to me that she had severed our relationship. I was speechless, but it seemed she didn't expect a response, when those words were swiftly followed by her abruptly asking if I wished to speak with the kids. Unable to reply, I think I must have nodded into the phone, but she had clearly walked away because I could hear her calling out to the kids informing them I was on the phone.

Within moments, I heard my daughter speak into the phone telling me she missed me, curious as to why I wasn't there. I notably deduced two things when I heard her voice: I could not let my daughter know I was disturbed, and I had to make sure she knew that I wanted to be with her as much as she wanted to be with me. And that's exactly what I did, even though I felt an overpowering hopelessness engulf me. I was convinced it was only the beginning of my punishment for selfishly causing the unraveling of my family, and after speaking with Lucas and then Rylee a second time I hung up the phone and began to cry.

I'd already spent the majority of the morning alone and dealt with assorted turbulent emotions by the time Derek arrived. It didn't help that I was feeling resentful that he'd not given up anything for this relationship and was getting to spend the day with his family, and bitter that I was sacrificing my world for someone who hadn't made the appropriate choices the first time he had the opportunity. If he had, Rylee and Lucas would be his children and this wouldn't be the scenario I was living. How could he have screwed up so much, and then end up with what he had been so careless to let go? In that moment I should have known I was in trouble…but I didn't, and Derek seemed insensible of my quandary or feelings. As if a soldier going into battle I pulled myself together, my imperious will to prevent additional grief giving me strength. Gathering up the packages and grabbing my coat, I optimistically reminded myself that these feelings were temporary and Christmas was merely one day of the year.

Pulling into the driveway of his sister's house, I couldn't help but gasp with surprise. The man walking up to the car was someone from long ago, someone I had formerly dated. The relationship had never really evolved because of the ten-year age difference between us. At the time it felt as if twenty years, and I had no aspiration for the relationship to become anything other than a friendship. He had once told me that ten years was nothing, and if I'd overlook the age difference and risk chancing it, we could be outstandingly happy! While I sought nothing more between us he'd continued to extend a comforting shoulder for me throughout our friendship, and he remained a superb friend for many years. That same man was now standing in front of me, and was evidently Derek's brother-in-law. Fate is funny that way.

Recovering from my shock, I was indubitably thankful that any innocent handholding and hugs between us never developed into anything substantial. At the same time I was grateful that I had someone presumptively on my side, pulling for me and cheering me on as I headed into the slaughterhouse. He greeted me as if he was as surprised to see me, then walked us into the house and reacquainted me his wife and mother-in-law. Before I could speak, with genuine astonishment he announced that we had previously met years before during an external Financial Audit performed at his bank. That was the truth, and since nothing major ever occurred between us, no harm could possibly come of leaving it at that.

Once the broadcast was over and everyone had said hello, he politely offered me something to drink and escorted me into the kitchen, where we discreetly agreed that no further rationalization of our "relationship" was necessary. I certainly wasn't going to further clarify if he was good with that.

I helped clean up in the kitchen after we ate, and helped clean up the paper, ribbons, and bows once we finished opening presents afterward. When it came time to say goodnight, I sincerely thanked them for a lovely day and for inviting me to spend Christmas with them. What had begun as a dark and heartbreaking day ended on a ray of sunshine and hope! Derek stayed the night that night, and we savored a closeness that abated the day's hurt, sadness, and emptiness. With the formalities and concerns at being welcomed by his family behind us, I was confidently optimistic that I knew precisely how to remain on course.

Reoccurring health ailments wasn't a part of that strategy, but as the holiday season came to a close I began experiencing some of the same hurdles that had plagued me before Rylee was born. Even with the passing of time my phobia of cancer returning seemed never to dissipate, and I was even more assiduous at knowing my body and being aware of any changes I detected. When the symptoms started reoccurring, I wasn't devastated like I was initially. Dr. Gomati counseled me on my options contingent on the prognosis once I was in surgery, and prepared me for the worst while hoping for the best.

This would be the first surgery since being married to Lance that he wouldn't be at my side, and I was mentally torn between the desire to have him there and permitting Derek the opportunity to step up to the plate. What seemed intrinsically different between the two and the way I responded to one over the other baffled me. What was I afraid of? Was I testing Derek, subconsciously afraid he might fail by comparison to Lance and what I had come to expect? Why on earth would I doubt that he couldn't or wouldn't be all that I needed him to be, any less than Lance had been for me?

Unfortunately it was the afternoon I came home from having my surgery that the obvious seemed to knock me between the eyes. I was lying in bed, still groggy from the anesthesia I'd been given, when I opened my eyes to see that Lance was in the bedroom. I felt discombobulated, as if in a dream where time had eluded reality and I was back home still married to him. Kneeling beside me, flowers in one hand and stroking my forehead with the other, he tenderly reassured me everything would be okay, and not to worry about the kids. His touch and his voice seemed to be the soothing antidote from all that I suffered, and I looked into his eyes and saw a tenderness I'd not allowed myself to appreciate for some time. It was the moment Derek walked through the door after picking up my medicine that I knew I wasn't dreaming.

The look in Lance's eyes changed to something I had never seen before, and it seemed as if it was now perfectly clear to him how this storyline would transpire...not just our marriage, but also our friendship. In a flash, I comprehended the hurt, anger and embarrassment he was experiencing as he knelt beside me in front of the man I'd betrayed him and the life we had together, to be with. He stood up, and though still incoherent, it was unambiguously understood that things would never be the same between us. The damage was irrevocable. He did not speak, but simply walked past Derek and out the door, shutting it behind him as he left.

Derek hadn't uttered a single word, but as Lance closed the door he walked over to place the prescriptions he'd picked up for me onto the bed, before turning off the light and leaving the room. Lance had wanted to comfort me with his words, his actions and with his touch. Derek apparently felt picking up my medicine was ample effort, and had no intention of providing the same comfort. It dawned on me that up until Lance had knelt beside me, I'd not been cognizant of the fact that Derek had offered me no more or no less even before he saw Lance next to me. Unable to reach the light switch to turn it on, I couldn't read the instructions or differentiate between the medications placed on the bed beside me. I closed my eyes as the pain intensified, aware that there was nothing I could take that would eliminate the pain I was experiencing.

Chapter 12

Although I had met Derek's family, we remained a clandestine relationship to his friends, and didn't socialize with any of them as a couple or go out much over-all. On the weekends the kids were with me he'd party with his friends, but on the weekends the kids were with Lance, he stayed with me throughout the weekend. Whenever he visited during the week he'd sit on the couch while I fixed dinner for him and the kids, then afterward watch TV while I completed my nightly routine of housework and mommy duties, exhausted by the time I finally joined him. He seemed to have the optimum benefits of both worlds, while I was the one continually making tremendous sacrifices for the sake of our relationship.

I was offered another promotion shortly into our new routine, and excitedly called Derek at home to share the news with him. It was early evening and to my surprise, a girl answered his phone. Thinking I dialed the wrong number, I simply hung up and redialed the number. I took the time to confirm the number, carefully dialing so not to make the same mistake, but heard the identical voice the second time. She freely informed me her name was Tiffany when I questioned who she was, and when I explained that I was looking for Derek, told me that he wasn't there and asked if she could take a message. I could think of a few messages to give them *both*!

Tiffany was the ex-girlfriend who had lived with him for the previous two years, and she was supposed to be completely out of the picture. Why was she at his apartment, and why was she answering the phone? I felt that same familiar sickness in the pit of my stomach, and without another word hung up. When he eventually answered his apartment phone and I rampantly shared what had happened, his impassive defense was that I must have inaccurately dialed a wrong number. He shrugged it off as a mere coincidence that the girl on the other end also had the name Tiffany. I didn't want to determine otherwise, and conveyed the news I'd originally called about regarding my promotion.

We made dinner plans for later that evening to celebrate, and I'd managed to completely erase the incident from my mind by the end of the day, only to be reminded of it when he called a few hours later as I was leaving work. I noticed that he seemed slightly breathless and peculiarly preoccupied, as he informed me that his friends had requested they get together, so he would be spending the evening with them. When I reminded him of the plans already made to celebrate my promotion he all but screamed at me, implying that I expected him to shirk his friends, and there was no reason whey we couldn't go to dinner on another night.

His impertinence caused me to physically flinch, and I no longer cared to have dinner with him, or anything else for that matter. I simply told him to enjoy himself and said goodbye, hanging the phone up before he could say anything further. I wasn't going to go through all of his bullshit and become emotionally detached and just as drained as before. I didn't want or need all of the lies, betrayal, disrespect, or hurt that he had inflicted upon me the first time around. Nothing was worth that.

He called every single day the following week at all hours of the day and night trying to reach me, and I refused to answer his call. When I finally did, I candidly informed him of my exact position concerning our cancelled plans, recapping that our relationship wasn't just about us any longer. I had two children to consider now, and it was my obligation to prevent them any hurt due to his selfishness and immaturity. I ended with telling him it was over and that I never wanted to see him again. A few days later when he showed up knocking on my front door, I didn't find it necessary to open it. I had never denied him anything in any way, so I assumed he knew I was serious, and that he'd made a grave mistake. He had allowed himself to become complacent and overconfident thinking I'd never contemplate walking away after everything we'd gone through. He was wrong.

***

After being unresponsive to his innumerable attempts to reach me, I came home from work to find him waiting outside my door with a small bag in his hand. It was filled with a toy car for Lucas, and a Barbie doll for Rylee. He apologized profusely, asking if he could visit with the kids for a little bit and deliver the toys, working every angle. But I was unremitting to his wish, and took the bag promising they would receive the toys, then turned to walk inside and closed the door behind me. Slamming the door against him felt as though I was slamming the door against the hurt he had caused. Surprisingly, it felt liberating.

Several weeks went by, and I continued to stay busy trying to maintain some kind of balance between the kids and work while keeping my sanity. It was remarkably satisfying to do whatever I fancied for a change, with no worries of having to care for anyone other than myself, when I didn't have the kids. I couldn't remember a time when it had been that way, and for Valentine's Day a couple of weeks later, scheduled the preponderance of my day out of the office to pamper myself as a reminder that I didn't require someone to enjoy the day.

Even when I wasn't at the office, I periodically checked in with my assistant to get messages and check the status of work related matters, but on this particular day she was the first to call. Before I could even get a "Hello!" spoken, she eagerly informed me there was an exceptionally handsome man in the office waiting for me. I was used to that tone from women around Derek, so I automatically knew who it was. I debated on going back to the office or not, but decided that it was time to resolve the issue one way or another.

As I walked into the building and headed toward my office, he stood up from the chair he was seated in. Unfortunately, he did look exceptionally handsome with his jeans, boots, and long black coat on, and holding a gift-wrapped box which he held out to me. He told me that he had lunch reservations for the two of us and asked if I would please accompany him. Enough time had passed that it felt a little awkward standing across from him, and I hurriedly calculated the pros and cons in my mind before agreeing that we could have a quick lunch.

His idea of a quick lunch and my idea of a quick lunch did not coincide, and before the receipt for lunch was in hand we were back together and had plans for him to have dinner with me and kids that evening. They both seemed thrilled to see him, and as the evening came to a close it was evident that Derek had missed us all, assisting with dinner and the evening routine with the kids before he left. He never stayed overnight when they were with me, regardless of how much we wished that he could, period.

I'm not certain how or when I expected it would happen, but in the end it seemed Derek and I were always fated to be together. But when he called to tell me to pack a bag, all I could think about was how incredibly romantic and charming it sounded, until my female co-workers heard I was requested to pack a bag for the weekend. The initial response to my broadcast was an excited, "He's going to propose to you!" I know I must have looked like I felt: skeptical. The possibility never crossed my mind, but it did now. It seemed a little too soon, and frankly doubted that he was ready for our relationship to proceed further after some of the things that had originated between us in recent months. Long overdue for a night on the town, the incentive for going out or where we were going was irrelevant to me. I blew off their absurd comments and finished my work, anxiously waiting for the day to end so that we could be together and begin our weekend.

He had specified I dress up for the evening and added that we would only be gone overnight, so there was no need to pack but for one night. When he picked me up, he mentioned that I looked nice and took my bag, offering no details of his plans for me. Realizing that we weren't heading in the direction of the airport, I became additionally curious as to what the rendezvous entailed. What was the purpose of an overnight bag if we were staying in town? My question was revealed when we pulled into the four star hotel *La Mansion* on Turtle Dove in Dallas, where he'd made dinner and hotel reservations at the for the night.

Once we enjoyed a delightful dinner, we moved to the smoking lounge and enjoyed more drinks and cozy conversation while the pianist played sensual music in the background. There seemed to be something he wanted to say but was doubtful, abruptly leading me onto the dance floor for another dance. We slow danced to a favorite song and then went back to our seats for another drink, quietly relishing the music and each other.

As the drinks we'd consumed kicked in we could barely keep our hands off of each other until we were in our room. There was champagne chilling in the ice bucket and champagne glasses waiting to be filled. Uninterested in filling the glasses, we fell into bed and drank of each other's love and desires. As we looked into each other's eyes, it felt as if there could never be another moment as perfect between us. He reached toward the lamp, and for a brief moment the impending wedding proposal that had been placed in my thoughts made me smile.

I'd already closed my eyes to the light when I heard his voice saying my name. I reopened my eyes, rolling onto my stomach as I placed a pillow underneath my head, crossing my arms below my chin so that I could look directly at him. He now held a black velvet box in the palm of his hand, and without further delay extended it to me as he tenderly asked, "Autumn, will you marry me and make me the happiest man in the world?"

I'm not sure what I felt or what I was thinking when he asked me, but it seemed utterly surreal to hear him utter the words. Had the man I'd loved forever just asked me to marry him and spend the rest of my life with him? My heart throbbing, I breathlessly whispered he repeat the question, tears of happiness filling my eyes as he granted my request, the "Yes!" coming from my lips before he had barely finished repeating the question. As he placed the ring on my finger, my repeated "Yes!" fell silent against his kiss. It was much later that he reached for the light, turning it off this time and giving me a final kiss before we fell asleep without a care in the world…as if we were the only two people in the world.

Chapter 13

For the amount of excitement that I felt over our engagement, I had no idea the anguish that it would bring to so many. It's entertaining how life can work that way, feeling that you have everything under control and your plans are rolling along accordingly, only to find that's not necessarily the case. The kids were with Lance for that weekend, and we had already scheduled to have dinner with friends later that evening, so we headed to his parent's house to share the news with them before anyone else. They weren't home when we arrived, and try as we could to connect we were unable to reach them throughout the entire day.

Our dinner was being hosted at Mark and Jennifer's house, along with his lifelong friends Jason and wife Misty, both whom I knew from the first time we dated, along with a few other friends he'd met since we dated. One reason I had been inquisitorial about Derek keeping in touch with recent girlfriends was from my intuitive, faint-hearted suspicions that something more once existed between he and Jennifer. The female that answered his phone claiming to be Tiffany had prompted my inquisitive investigation to ascertain the number of his intimate involvements, and if he kept in touch with any of them. I'd freely and openly shared where I'd been and what I'd been doing for the last ten years, but while I kept no secrets from him, I was suspicious Derek had not afforded me the same.

When I'd questioned him with my concerns, he had dismissively told me he wasn't keeping in touch with *any* of them, so what purpose would it serve for me to know their names? I wasn't sure what that meant, but the fact that he said he was not keeping in touch with any of them was enough for me, reasoning there was no motive for him to lie to me about such a lame thing. And Jennifer seemed happily married, so when we'd made the decision to publicize the engagement at their house, I hadn't hesitated to agree. I had no way of knowing that I'd later have cause to reflect on his rhetorical response, and feel even greater resentment and anger toward him than ever before.

Upon arriving at Jennifer and Mark's, I made a point of keeping my left hand obscured until dinner, busy assisting with things that could help me to do that. As soon as everyone had taken a seat at the dinner table, Derek stood to make a toast, raising his glass in proclamation of his love for me followed by the announcement. Barely a few seconds had passed before Jennifer jumped up from her chair, complaining of a sudden migraine attack and "unable to function because of it". One of the other girls got up to follow her out, and I immediately felt the awkwardness from everyone else left in the room. Unsure at the time what to think, I dismissed their responses as nothing more than shock from the news we had just publicized.

The dinner was cut short because Jennifer didn't feel well, and the evening ended with us making plans to try and visit Derek's parents again the following day. We arranged for his sister and brother-in-law to meet at his parent's house to kill two birds with one stone, leery that they might possibly hear about it from friends. We'd have to share the news with Rylee and Lucas once they came back from their weekend with Lance.

Arriving at the house, I sensed something in Derek change as we headed inside. I was unsure if the change in his disposition was because he was on edge, or from the anticipation of sharing our news with his family, but passed it off as nothing to be uptight over. We made our way into the living room where Liz and Joel were seated on the couch, and his mom and dad seated in their recliners. Once I got close enough to examine the look on Doris's face, I realized that they knew what was coming--and that they were not pleased in the least! Derek seemed to sense the same thing and wasted no time in telling everyone. The predictable "Congratulations!" and "We are so happy and excited for you!" was followed by hugs and inquisitive demands to hear all about the details.

The only person who had not spoken was Doris. As an uncomfortable silence fell I became a bit apprehensive, speculating what she intended to say and then perceptibly presumed "proposed" wasn't the word befitting of the occasion...or apparently for her in general. Her initial question was curt and matter-of-fact, that of a subjectively pretentious statement. "So you told your friends before you told us?" Followed by the bombshell Doris specifically directed at Derek. "Why didn't you discuss this with us before you asked her? Do you think anyone at the church will marry you given that she has already been married before?" Then she scathingly articulated what she wanted to protest from the moment we revealed the engagement; "I can't believe you didn't discuss this with me before you proposed to her!"

Hello...! Did she not see me sitting there? Did she not realize I could hear every word she was speaking to her son? Red lights! Red flags! She seemed to be digging a dagger into my heart, and I could feel it twisting and turning as she ripped it apart. Although my children were not there, her antipathy instigated an overwhelming urge to run to them and protect them. I sat observing as inconspicuously as possible, while Derek obligingly answered his mother's piercing questions as if they were deserving of a response. What he did not say or indicate to his mother during any part of their conversations was, "I love her, and if you cannot be happy for us and accept her and the kids, then you will be missing out! We want this to be a family, and you a part of that family. Furthermore, we hope that you will want that too!" He said nothing vaguely close to that. She had control over the moment, just as she had control over him.

Pride aside, in an optimistic gesture to make amends and smooth the ruffled feathers, I took coffee cakes and scones to them for breakfast the next morning. Knocking on the door, I nervously waited for someone to answer, unprepared for the condescension on the other side. Still in her bathrobe, Doris barely cracked the door open, peeking from behind. I could tell that she had been crying by the puffiness of her eyes, but the abhorrence toward me was till detectable. "I brought you some breakfast." was all I could muster in an almost apologetic voice before she closed the door in my face without further response.

I stared at the closed door, shaking my head in bafflement, tears filling my own eyes. This wasn't good, and I didn't have a clue what I could do to improve matters. Feeling slighted, I turned away and walked back to my car, leaving the breakfast behind on the front porch. Maybe the bugs would eat well, if nothing else.

Later that day at work I received a beautiful floral arrangement from Derek's sister. The card read, *"I have always wanted a sister. Glad it's going to be you."* There was the backing and the approval that I needed. I would have to hold onto that encouragement if I expected this union to be minutely successful, otherwise I might as well turn and run from the crazy snags threatening our relationship. I stood at a fork in the road, and either direction was going to be nonetheless challenging along the way.

Rylee and Lucas were ecstatic at the news of us getting married, they loved Derek and yearned to have a traditional family, and I wanted nothing more than to provide one. I kept them from Doris, anticipating that she'd say something spitefully derogatory and create unwarranted confusion. As an adult I was perplexed by her repugnance, how could I expect them to understand when I didn't? Nevertheless I held onto the faith that with time things would gradually pan out, seizing the moments we enjoyed with the kids and with each other, enjoying the anticipation of our future together. By then I had learned that we should appreciate the good in life as it happens, to help you through the times not so good.

Time flew as we began preparing for our wedding. I had never known a man so capaciously involved in the details of a wedding, engaged or not. What threw me most, was the fact that Derek's mom managed to become a part of the planning and decision making for the wedding also. She wasn't financially subsidizing anything concerning the wedding, yet she requested to participate in the floral visits, the cake tasting and everything else in between. I became a little exasperated, but wasn't comfortable with confronting the already delicate situation.

Before there was an opportunity to mention my concerns, he began commenting on suggestions his mother had contributed, vocalizing that it would be practical to go with some of her recommendations so that she'd feel involved in the wedding. Before long, it was almost as if she and Derek were planning for *their* wedding and I was the third party.

Nothing she suggested ever went with my suggestions, and it didn't take much time before it was hard to identify and differentiate between the suggestions he offered and those of his mother's. It became discouraging, and I felt as if my hands were tied and unable to fight back. If anything was said against her, he had a tendency to instantaneously become overly protective of her. I felt as though he was abnormally attentive concerning her thoughts and feelings over mine. Yet another "red flag" was raised in warning. Surely once we got married that would change, I reasoned to myself. He was new at this, and even though she knew what she was doing, eventually he'd comprehend what was going on for himself and set it all straight.

Those times were the beginning of the hurdles and havoc we encountered that habitually tested our patience, love and tolerance of each other, even prior to our marriage. I periodically make an effort to remember that there were numerous, worthwhile times in between those not so great times in our relationship. I cherish those times, and focus on those that remain affectionately ingrained within my heart. One memory dearest to me is the Christmas Eve prior to or marriage, when the kids witnessed "Santa" setting up their presents around the tree. The two-story townhome I lived in made it easy to look into the living room below and was perfect for watching Santa as he moved around the room. The fire was burning brightly, and a faint jingling of bells sounded across the room, identical to the Polar Express story we had read earlier that evening. The story was about outgrowing the magic of Christmas and holding on to what you believe in, even when it might not seem possible.

I woke Rylee up and pointed down in the direction of the living room, putting my fingers to my lips for her to be quiet, then did the same with Lucas. With awe and amazement written across their faces, both knelt alongside me on top of the bed and watched the activity below. Suddenly, in a voice that solely comes from the innocence of a child, Lucas leaned into me whispering his concern that Santa might forget to eat the cake we left beside the tree for him. I assured him every bite would be eaten, and smiled to myself knowing what a remarkable memory the night would make for them in the years to come.

Noting their expressions fill with wonder while Santa meticulously worked to finish the task at hand, I too was captivated by the moment and unaware that Lucas had already gone back to bed and fast asleep, as if he knew Santa would not disappoint him. Shortly afterward I motioned for Rylee to lie down beside her brother, but before her head could hit the pillow she turned to me with a look of distress on her face. In a hushed voice she asked, "Mommy, is it okay to love Daddy and Derek, too?"

I saw the worry in her beautiful blue eyes, and gathered she'd been fretting over this concern for some time. "Yes Rylee, it is ok…you can never love too many people, and you can never have too many people love you!" With a content smile she sighed, and without another word rolled toward her brother and placed an arm around him, succumbing to slumber herself. I looked down into the living room to watch Derek closing shop and leaving discreetly as possible, knowing that we had accomplished our goal.

Turning back to my children lying in bed it appeared as though nothing in the world could have disturbed them, but in the hopeful chance Rylee could subconsciously hear me I wanted to tell her anyway: "Yes, Rylee, there is a Santa Clause, just believe and be open to the magic, and the magic of love is that it doesn't discriminate, doesn't have a title, name, gender or boundaries. There are no limits imposed, regardless of whomever you share that love with. Love simply implores you to embrace and accept."…What greater gift could there possibly be?

My daughter witnessed what may have been nothing short of a childhood miracle for her that Christmas Eve. But as her mom, that night I witnessed the love of a child who wanted to take nothing from no one, who wanted only to give unconditionally and without restraint. She already understood that love could sometimes be about making choices and of the sacrifices preeminently required. I sat for a while observing them peacefully sleeping and my heart filled with something that went beyond comprehension or explanation. To this day I'm not sure what I felt, but I know with certainty that my children were not alone in witnessing a prodigious occurrence.

Chapter 14

We opted to buy a house prior to getting married so that we could move into it as soon as we returned from our honeymoon. Even though the house needed some improvements it afforded comfort for the kids by allowing them to remain within walking distance from Lance, and stay in their current school district. The momentous amount of preparation for our move was hard work and time consuming, but nose to the ground I worked at making the house our home. I was mindful of expenses, so as we began receiving gift cards from wedding guests I thought it wise to use them for necessary household purchases and save the cash. With that philosophy in mind, I made the impulsive decision to use a gift card and purchase a comforter for Rylee's room that was on sale. In my mind the incentive was to buy it on sale and not have to pay full price at a later time. I'd be making the purchases with someone else's money, and as an additional bonus saving our money.

Derek was sitting on the couch when I returned home from shopping, and I smiled at him in anticipation of sharing my bargains. Putting the comforter in the storage closet, I heard him ask what I had bought before I saw his face. I enthusiastically turned to tell him about my sensational bargains when his remark stopped me in my tracks. "Why are you spending that money on the kids? That is my money, too! You don't get to be the only person to spend it!"

I thought for a moment that he might be kidding, until I realized that he wasn't. As I stood there appalled at what he was insinuating, I felt one of those chills not brought on from the cold. I did not want to have to justify expenditures and I didn't want to feel as though it was necessary. Most of all, I didn't want him to feel that way simply because of a meager purchase I'd made for our new home, anymore than I cared to be patronized by his display of disparagement.

Without saying a word, I closed the closet door and turned to walk into the kitchen for a glass of tea, gulping it down along with the tears I felt surfacing. I never took another gift card from that day forward to spend on anything. I'd later learn that the gift cards he was so obdurately insistent that I not spend on the kids were never redeemed, and suspiciously managed to get lost.

There were so many warning signs that I should have detected but closed my eyes to, simply choosing to ignore them. I think that when you have it in your mind something will be one way, it's difficult to imagine it any other. As with the gift card, yet another foreshadow occurred that ought to have solidified my misgivings, and prompted me to bolt when I had the chance.

We happened to be visiting his parent's lake house during a weekend and hanging out on the dock, when a young woman from next door came strolling leisurely across the yard. She had legs up to her perky breasts she proudly flaunted, enhanced by the tight tank top she donned. I could tell by the look in her eyes that she wasn't merely a friend, the connection between them transparent. He walked away from me to meet her at the opposite end of the deck, leaving me behind with the assurance that he would be right back. They both laughed and visited while I stood tolerantly waiting where he'd left me, trusting that any moment he'd beckon me to come stand beside him so that he could introduce me to her.

Growing aggravated at the scene and offended that he had already left me there for a lengthy amount of time, I started toward them with a determined stride. Midway to where they stood I saw her turn to watch me as I approached, Derek turning from their conversation to do the same. Before I could get much closer to them they exchanged a brief, but close hug, and then she abruptly turned to leave. As I reached his side he said nothing in the way of an apology for his manners--or lack of. He then headed back to his parent's house, while I helplessly stood watching him walk away. That was the second time he had left me standing alone, and I followed behind his footsteps wishing they led me back to my own home and away from the neighbor that was too near for comfort.

A couple of weeks later, we were invited to Mark and Jennifer's house for a barbecue party. Not too long into the afternoon, Lucas started feeling ill and I was debating on leaving. I had him in my lap trying to soothe him, when I looked up to see Derek standing extremely close to Jennifer near the stove, discussing personal details about the possibility of her requiring a partial hysterectomy. Stove or not, that was a hot topic to be discussing with someone other than your husband. I thought it weird that the two of them were immersed in such a conversation, but was distracted from the scene when Lucas needed my attention.

It wasn't until Derek came and sat down next to me, that I noticed a strange exchange between the two of them: Jennifer came over behind Derek and placed her arm around him, rubbing his arm, asking him if he wanted her to get Lucas an aspirin. Derek jumped back up and followed her into the kitchen, where she climbed up onto a stool, intentionally stretching her long legs underneath his nose to reach for them. The moment I saw the look he gave her, I knew my suspicions about them were accurate. I was seething inside.

When we arrived back at my place, I put Lucas to bed and sat down beside Derek. With my eyes on the TV, I nonchalantly asked how he had met Mark and Jennifer. He couldn't remember. My next question was to inquire which one he'd met first, Mark or Jennifer? He wasn't sure. I prodded a bit more…"You don't remember?" At which he finally admitted it was Jennifer he first met. My final twist of the knife was to straight up ask him if he had ever dated Jennifer, with a look in my eyes that told him I already knew and he best come clean! His flat "Yes." Made me jump up from the couch! "I KNEW IT!! I *knew* you two had dated! You lied to me!!" I exploded!

When I asked him why he'd lied about keeping in touch with her or dating her, he angrily retaliated by telling me he knew that what just happened would have only happened earlier. I quickly communicated to him that if it hadn't been a big deal or if she no longer meant anything to him, he would have been open with me about the relationship. Not being upfront about it meant that her relationship was worth jeopardizing our relationship, and betraying me. Worse, I felt humiliated that all of his friends and family knew that I didn't know about them. Including Doris.

Conspiracy. Duplicity unmasked in its highest form.

But for every deceptive and hurtful act he chose to inflict, it seemed my love for him frequently diminished his behavior in my eyes, and even caused me to recklessly discount what was flagrantly conspicuous to others. And to my own astonishment, on the day I married him I felt nothing but a quiet calm and happiness that I had always presumed he alone could provide. Rylee stood beside me, and Lucas beside Derek, with Misty and Jason as our matron of honor and best man.

Who would have ever guessed moments before I'd almost poked my eye out trying to find a contact lens that I had just inserted? Don't ever make the mistake of getting contacts two days before your wedding if you don't know what the heck you are doing. I had everyone poking and prodding, sticking flashlights and fingers in my eyes as they persistently searched to locate the lost contact.

My makeup, which I had applied ever so carefully, began sliding into oblivion! It was at that particular moment someone came into the room disclosing that the two roses I'd designated placed at the alter in remembrance of Billy and Corey, had been mistakenly placed at the entrance in the reception area. I frantically headed down the hallway to pinpoint anyone who could resolve the issue, with at least three of my bridesmaids trailing behind me. I probably looked something akin to a runaway bride!

With mere seconds to repair my makeup I returned to the dressing room without sufficient time remaining to dig for the contact which I speculated was now lingering somewhere in the back of my eye. As I began my walk down the aisle unaccompanied I could not see my children, my friends, or my family. I could not see Lucas being fed gummy bears by Jason in order to encourage my four year old to stay focused for longer than a minute. I could not see Rylee's sweet face and glowing smile, tears in her own eyes. I could not have seen Derek any less if he had been lost somewhere in a thick London fog, therefore unable to see his face or read his expression.

What I would be thankful for not seeing that day, was what the video camera caught as the preacher began to pray for our new family. At the moment the prayer ended with, "And watch over Derek, Autumn, Rylee, and Lucas as they begin their new life together." the cameraman happened to scan the crowd in time to catch Doris as she raised her head, chin set as if in defiance of the blessing, pure coldness radiating from her eyes. The minute I saw it, I had this ludicrous image of her discreetly whacking me across the skull and running away with her son if she thought there was a chance she might not get caught.

Fortunately, I wouldn't discover the nefarious scene until we watched the video of the ceremony several months later. Once the prayer was concluded and all eyes opened and all heads lifted, Derek and I kissed the kiss that sealed our wedding vows, turning as the preacher presented us as husband and wife to our and family and friends. As the clapping and celebrating continued, we all but ran down the aisle like we were teenagers who knew nothing of love but the joys, hopes, and benevolence love promises.

The kids stayed with Jason and Misty while we were on our honeymoon, and when we came back, we all moved into the new house to begin our life together. As with any marriage, fundamental adjustments are necessary and develop with trial and error. It would be presumptuous of me to believe our marriage would have been less or more successful, if we'd not dealt with so many of those trials and errors. But I would maintain that what makes any relationship successful takes so much other than love, and expand even further by saying that love is at the bottom of the totem pole, with respect, grace and laughter topping by far. We had been married almost a year when Derek's dad was diagnosed with Amyotrophic Lateral Sclerosis, also known as Lou Gehrig's disease.

ALS is an incurable, fatal neuromuscular disease characterized by progressive muscle weakness resulting in paralysis. The disease attacks nerve cells in the brain and spinal cord. Motor neurons, which control the movement of voluntary muscles, deteriorate and die. When the motor neurons die, the brain can no longer initiate and control muscle movement. Because muscles no longer receive the messages they need to support function, they progressively weaken and deteriorate. It is a horrible way to die and a horrible way to live while watching someone die from the disease. As much as I wanted Derek to be there for his dad, and as much as I wanted us to be there for Doris, I predicted what she'd do well in advance.

From day one she constantly requested Derek at the house with her. Therefore, during the week he'd ordinarily leave directly from the office to have dinner and spend the night with them. On the weekends he all but lived there, and when he wasn't there, she'd call for him at all hours of the day and night with absolutely no desire for Derek's sister or me to be there. As the illness gradually debilitated his father more, and his mother required more of his time, it seemed senseless for him to constantly be commuting back and forth between our home, their home and work. I did the only thing I could to make it less stressful for him, and offered him the alternative to temporarily live with his mom and dad. He mulled over the proposition for a moment, and then responded with a mere "No." So I didn't pursue the matter.

I felt as though we were already in a relationship that comes after several years of marriage, not the first year. Time came and went, and I did what I could when I could, trying to allow him to do whatever he felt he needed to do for his parents. I didn't question the amount of time he spent away or complain how his absence created inconvenience in our home during the time he was absent. I hardly saw my husband, but as the month of July approached and with my birthday fast around the corner, I'd hoped we might have a little bit of time together and a much needed break from our unsettling schedule.

I was optimistic that Derek would take the initiative to plan some kind of celebration...up until he called from his mom's and apprised me of the news that Doris had scheduled his father a hospital appointment for some extended tests that day. I was afraid to ask, but as if suspecting my thoughts, Derek was quick to promise that we would spend my birthday together that evening as planned.

When the day arrived and he left early in the morning to be with his parents, I maintained the comfort that the evening would bring us together, attempting to abate the uneasy feeling I felt, even though instinctively something was telling me to be prepared. I picked up a cake and told the kids that once their dad got home we'd eat out for dinner, and then return home for cake and games. By 6:30 p.m. I still hadn't heard from Derek to update me on the prognosis or any changes to our plans. At nearly 7:00 p.m. I received a call informing me that it wouldn't be much longer before his was home. By 8:00 p.m., the kids and I were famished and I was becoming frustrated from the "I told you so!" that kept raging amongst my exasperated thoughts. Pretty certain we were no longer going out for dinner I cooked spaghetti, and by 8:30 the kids and I were eating, trying to delay cutting my birthday cake until Derek was home. By 9:00 that evening he still wasn't home, and as far as I was concerned, he had missed my birthday.

It was straight up ten o'clock when he came through the door with an unwrapped gift box, acting as if he was running late by merely a couple of hours or even minutes. "That had better be some terrific gift!" I was thinking to myself, when to my surprise he handed it to me and told me it was from his mother, and that she also sent her apologies for making him miss my birthday.

I didn't know how to react or if it even mattered, he had not gotten me a gift of his own or even a card, but came in bearing a gift from his mom as if that should suffice. It was apparent he felt that I should be understanding that he'd remained there throughout the entire day, even though his sister could have stayed at the hospital and provided support for their mom, too. It didn't seem to matter or register what time of evening he'd come home on my birthday, that the kids were already in bed, or that we never cut my birthday cake.

While he was absorbed with his father's illness, my endometriosis and cancer invariably kept rearing its ugly head, and it was no longer advantageous to delay the inevitable. A few months after my birthday I began having health complications once again, and after several exams and tests it was determined that I could no longer delay a complete hysterectomy. It was a bittersweet realization that I no longer had an option, regardless of the numerous surgeries and treatments to postpone having one. Dr. Gomati had told me on many occasions that it would not be feasible for me to have children anymore, and that it was more important to be around for the two I already had, often reminding me how miraculous it was that I'd given birth to them.

Regardless, I also felt remorseful over my reproductive organs being taken from me. It felt a little bit like my womanhood was being taken, and made me question just how significant reproductive organs contributed to me being a woman? Would my husband look at me differently? Though I'd voiced wanting another child many times, he radically opposed the thought and did not covet having children of his own. Would he change his mind and want to leave me if I couldn't afford him that fulfillment? All I'd wanted was to give him the ultimate gift that a woman could ever bestow the man she loves; a child of his own flesh and blood. But he had rejected that gift, and now it would be too late.

The procedure was prearranged well in advance so as not to create too much inconvenience or disruption for work and school. We kept the family abreast of the schedules ahead of time, to prevent interferences with upcoming appointments for Derek's dad should he need to assist. Even still, I was a little thrown off when Derek answered the phone a couple of weeks later, and it was Doris calling him about her own health condition and not his dad's. He was noticeably uncomfortable with the evolving discussion with me sitting nearby, so I left the room to give him privacy.

Though he had been uncomfortable with me sitting nearby during the actual conversation between him and his mother, he felt the need to share their entire conversation with me afterward, elaborating on the graphic information about the severe rectal bleeding she was experiencing when she went to the bathroom. I asked him if she had called the doctor, and he said that she'd already scheduled her colonoscopy a few weeks out, but hadn't mentioned the exact date to him. I questioned the fact that if she were having such severe symptoms, why wouldn't they rush her hospital admittance? I deduced that it wasn't really that bad and dismissed it from my mind, until a few days later when Doris came by.

Bemused over her rare visit, I paced myself with inconsequential talk and concerns for her health, before inquiring if there was a date scheduled for her procedure. Derek had taken a seat beside me, and the moment my question about a date was brought up, I could literally feel him stop breathing. With a look of skepticism, she shifted her gaze from mine to his, questioning why he hadn't told me the date? I watched my husband's response as I stepped in before he had a chance, and contended that he wasn't aware of the date. At my interjection she turned from her son directly toward me, with a bogus look of astonishment. I could almost hear the depraved wickedness in her voice as she spoke. "Oh no...when I told Derek the date he informed me that it was the same date as your procedure. I told him then that I remembered thinking there was something else happening on that date, but I couldn't remember what it was for the life of me! When he reminded me of your surgery, I just didn't consider it necessary to change it."

I sat in shock as a spiteful look crossed her face, both of us conscious of the fact that everything she'd said from the time she walked through the door was nothing but a barefaced lie. There was no doubt in my mind that she'd intentionally scheduled her procedure for the exact same date as mine, and that my husband had known about it prior to her showing up at our front door. At the time I questioned Derek about the scheduling of her appointment, he had talked as though she was dying...and I fleetingly entertained the notion that her demise might perhaps agree best with my schedule.

Acting puzzled, I posed her the same question about what kind of doctor permitted someone to bleed for weeks without an expedited office visit? Was there nothing available for her to get in any sooner? She seemed blasé to my concern, and after a few moments she got up to leave, the gleam in her eyes conveying that she was satisfied that she'd accomplished her mission. Her sinister look clearly validated that she had unmistakably used her superficial visit as a camouflage to achieve her ulterior motive.

No sooner was she out the door than I turned to Derek demanding to know why he hadn't relayed the information when I'd first questioned him? He had not only lied to me, he had deliberately lied to me for the exact reason she'd wanted me cognizant of the fact that he'd been aware of the specifics beforehand. He had hoped Doris might resolve the matter by changing her appointment, therefore eliminating issues she had created that he hadn't deemed worth inflicting on me. While he may have envisioned such, she and I both knew that was never her intent. Her intention all along was to cause the strife that she had deliberately created within our home.

She relentlessly toiled at manipulating her son into choosing between the two of us, whatever that took. Incidents kept occurring one right after another, but I was committed to the concept that Derek would inevitably identify that his mom was the instigator producing the gargantuan, dark hole we were perpetually descending into. Unfortunately, his dismissive responses were the same each time: "She is just that way! She didn't mean to!" And my favorite; "You should attempt to handle it differently and accept that's the way she is. I have lived with it all my life. Why can't *you*?" Every time he asked me that, my fierce comeback was that she'd obviously been allowed to get away with that method of behavioral exhibition and therefore habitually continued.

I proceeded with my operation, and Derek stayed with me throughout the procedure leaving to help his mother once I was settled back at home. He never said another word about it, nor did I. Though unspoken, we mutually conceded there would be no purpose served in rehashing the predicament.

Subsequent to my surgery, we received the upsetting news that my Aunt Doreen had died after battling cancer for over a year. Aunt Doreen held a special place in my kids' hearts, and especially in mine. She was my mother's sister in Mississippi, who I'd temporarily lived with in between living with my grandmother. She was the same aunt who came to pick me up when I ran away from school. I was extremely close with her and her daughters, just as Rylee and Lucas had become extremely close to them as they were growing up.

Even though they were both young at the time they understood what cancer indicated, and both were shaken upon learning she was terminally ill with cancer. Therefore, at the time of her death I didn't feel the need to inform them straightaway since the funeral arrangements were for the successive Saturday, and both had exams that upcoming week. Derek and I had both agreed it best we wait until closer to the time we left to attend the funeral.

The Sunday after we'd received the news of her passing, Derek and I headed to his mom's in the early afternoon to allow us time to get home before the kids arrived back from their dad's. As it habitually happened, Doris hinted to Derek there were several things that needed to be taken care of outside, and as usual, he graciously responded with "I'll take care of that!" I was uncomfortable with Doris even if a mediator was there to be the buffer between us, but was particularly edgy anytime I was alone with her. I had the distinct impression she was aware that I felt that way, and thoroughly enjoyed having the upper hand.

Wishing he would stay and not leave me alone with her didn't deter him from heading out the door, and as the sliding glass door closed behind him the conversation instantly turned to my aunt and the details of the funeral arrangements. Doris openly weighed her question momentarily before asking if the kids had been informed of her passing. I briefly rationalized our approach and the viewpoint supporting our decision to wait and inform them of her passing, and then we moved onto the next topic of conversation.

As timing would have it, two days later I was in bed with a fever when Rylee came tearing in from soccer practice crying, and inconsolable. She was fretful over the death of her Aunt Doreen, and just as rattled by the fact that I'd not told her. I held her against me, explaining that I hadn't wanted her upset during the middle of taking school exams. I turned to Derek standing at the foot of our bed, and my eyebrows rose as if questioning, "What the heck happened?" He could tell me nothing but the truth while Rylee lay beside me, cradled in my arms, sobbing uncontrollably.

He glibly described how his mom had brought Rylee a cake, and when she'd prodded what the cake was for, Doris had bluntly conveyed that it was for her Aunt Doreen dying. Before he could expound further, I imagined making my way over to her house and wringing her neck, claiming temporary insanity induced by high fever. As if a lion with her cub, I was innately protective of my child and began questioning about the incident, challenging her fatuous logic. Why on earth would she make a cake and deliver it at Rylee's soccer practice, when less than two days ago I'd specifically shared that we hadn't told the kids yet?

Derek unrelentingly defended his mother, exclaiming that she'd claimed to be unaware of the fact that we had not told the kids. I condescendingly reminded him of the conversation between his mother and me over the past weekend, as he curtly reminded me that the conversation must have taken place while he was outside, because he never heard us discussing the matter. He had gone outside and was not present during our conversation, and apparently it was now her word against mine.

He continued to stick up for her, and I continued to argue, bewildered that he could not admit that she had created discontent between us once again. Getting tired of going in circles with him, I brashly posed the question that boggled my mind most: Why did he so readily believe her and look for her best, but so readily didn't believe me and looked for my worst? His bitter response was that he was not going to assume the worst in her, as she was his family too. He'd always grant her the benefit of the doubt, and hoped that I'd do the same.

The rollercoaster ride of our relationship wasn't just merely derailing, but plummeting off track going full speed with no way to dodge the catastrophe. I insisted on acquiring a counselor, and scheduled what would end up being the first of six counselors. I methodically selected a male counselor each time so that he couldn't use the defense that a woman would philosophically perceive things differently, or naturally take my side during our counseling sessions. Every time we would get to the phase where Derek would have to address disagreements or the counselor would begin telling him things he did not want to hear, he'd question their viewpoint and demand to go to someone different.

The negative emotions and growing controversies soon played into the sexual aspect of our relationship, and by then it had been a year and a half since he had touched me. My romantic, unprompted and teasing advances with enticing negligées, or planning spontaneous dates for dinner or drinks seemed to have little affect on his desires. The more I attempted to achieve closeness in our relationship, the more he pulled away and the more we became isolated from each other, both physically and emotionally.

Chapter 15

Derek's dad died about a year after his diagnosis, and with his death we were bombarded with maintaining two homes and doing piddling things like putting gas in his mom's car, because she never had to before her husband's death. Thinking we had surely hit our limit with adversities, Derek lost his job and the only income was from my employment and the child support from Lance.

In the midst of trying harder than ever to save my marriage, I received a call while at work one morning from Lucas's elementary school informing me that his heart was racing and pounding, asking if I want them to call an ambulance? I was at the school before the ambulance arrived, but by the time I reached him his heartbeat was in a normal rhythm mode. Maybe something had frazzled him or he was troubled about something that had triggered the erratic heart rhythm.

Not taking any chances and as a precautionary measure, I took him home so that he could lie on the couch with me for the afternoon. He made it through the remainder of the day without any abnormal or inconsistent heartbeats happening until later that night, when I heard him calling from his bedroom. "Mom! It's doing it again!" I raced to him, placing my hand against his chest, feeling his heart pounding as if it was going to explode. My own heart began to pound.

I thought back to a Sunday afternoon when we had invited family over for barbeque and to swim in the pool. Lucas had jumped out of the pool and plopped himself onto Doris' lap, when a strange look crossed her face. I assumed it was due to him getting water all over her clothes, but she looked at me, placing her hand over Lucas's heart. "Feel his heart beating!" she exclaimed. "I've never felt a heart beating like this." I had lightly placed my hand over my son's heart to feel the same rapid and pounding beat of his heart. At the time I had smiled at her and dismissed it, attributing it to the fact that he had been running, swimming, and playing hard. Yet as I was sitting there on the edge of my son's bed feeling that same heartbeat, I knew this time it was not from any physical strain on his heart.

His next words caused me to gasp and my own heartbeat to increase. "Mom, it hurts right here." as he pointed to his chest. I was prepared to drive him to the emergency room, but Derek reassured me he was fine and that we should wait a bit to see what happened. Lucas began to calm, his heartbeat normalizing, so I sat with him until he went to sleep checking on him throughout the night.

The next morning I took him to be examined by our general practitioner, who arranged to have us admitted into Dallas Medical City in order for a cardiologist to perform an array of comprehensive tests. Fearing the unknown possibilities I called Lance to inform him that his son would be admitted into the hospital, and the specifics of what I'd been told. Frustrated because he didn't answer, I left a message with the basic information, pleading he call me as soon as possible.

Once admitted, they X-rayed Lucas from head to toe, drew several vials of blood and then shaved his head to attach sensors that would enable his brain activity to be monitored. He was so little, and though he seemed to be fine on the outside, I wondered how he felt on the inside, because I knew how worried I had become. Every time I watched them take his stats, draw blood, and run him through scanners, it took me back to another time and place. Surely, God would not allow anything to happen to my son…but my job was to reassure him everything was going to be okay, and as I comforted him I was silently trying to comfort myself.

I still hadn't heard from Lance by the second day Lucas was in the hospital, and called him from the hospital room to find out when he was coming. It was quickly apparent the conversation wasn't going to be a positive one between us, and even more disturbing that Lance didn't feel the need to be there and had no qualms informing me he wasn't coming. Aghast and unable to conceive how he'd come to make that decision, I determined it was in my son's chief interest to finish the conversation outside of his room. *Surely* Lance was able to conceive the urgency of what was happening and just how pressing it was for him to be at the hospital. Exasperated, I realized that it was useless to try and convince him to come because no matter what I said or how much I pressed, he'd stubbornly resolved not to.

When I questioned his rationality behind the lack of alarm for his son, he had no response other than to imply that he didn't deem it necessary to deal with an unsubstantiated and unwarranted situation. Before hanging up, I told him once more how Lucas kept asking for him and wanted him to be there. Not even that swayed him, nor did he seem the least bit contrite for his attitude. I didn't say anther word, but disconnected the call feeling like I'd just disconnected from someone I didn't know.

When I walked back into the hospital room, Lucas asked me when his daddy was going to come. I fought the tears that welled up in my eyes as I explained that his daddy had to work and could not come up immediately, but planned on coming as soon as he could. Lucas didn't respond, but went back to the toys he had been playing with before the call, in silence. As much as I wanted to, there was nothing I could say to assuage his disappointment and hurt.

At the end of the week we were sent home with a cardiac event recorder, which was a portable device that tape-recorded his heart's electrical activity (ECG) for approximately five minutes before and during occurring events. We would send the recording by phone, which transmitted the information to a receiving center. If the tracking indicated an emergency we'd be instructed to proceed to the hospital. Each time the alarm was triggered, we expeditiously called the number provided us and communicated any symptoms he appeared to be experiencing. Afterward we'd reset the monitor, and it was simply a matter of time before it recorded the ensuing episode. We were hopeful each episode would render insight into what was happening and why, at the same time fearful the episode might happen to be detrimental.

He wore it for the duration of a month, and the stress of not knowing when or why the alarm would activate terrified me, unsure what any of it signified for my son. By the end of the month, the monitor hadn't provided us any additional information other than what we started with. Forthright, I questioned the results consequent to the occurrences, and the lack of an established diagnosis or anything remotely concrete identified. Lance was sure I was crazy and outraged that I had caused our son to go through such traumatic stress for nothing, additionally adding a financial burden from the substantial doctor and hospital bills incurred. "Money would be his concern!" I remember thinking. I did not care what anyone said, I had been with him during his episodes and something was not right.

We were referred to a pediatric electro-physiologist, a doctor categorized with specialized training in the electrical conduction system of the heart in children. Normal function of the electrical conducting system (ECS) is required to maintain coordinated contraction of the heart chambers at an appropriate rate. Subsequent to our first visit, the doctors labeled his reoccurring disorder as Mitral Valve Prolapse (MVP). MVP occurs whenever the valve between the heart's left upper chamber (left atrium) and left lower chamber (left ventricle) doesn't close properly causing inadequate blood oxygen delivery to the working muscles, and causes a "clicking" sound that can be heard with a stethoscope by a doctor who's specialized in that particular medical field. Once I knew what we were dealing with, I took the diagnosis as "good and could have been much worse."

We didn't know it at the time, but Lucas's condition would progressively degenerate. Years later he'd shatter his jaw while attending a friend's graduation, and within a year afterward roll his vehicle approximately six times over a major interstate bridge. Both due to a cardiac syncope: both due to passing out.

An insertable cardiac monitor (ICM), also referred to as an insertable loop recorder (ILR), would be implanted under his skin for monitoring his heart. The small insertable device would continuously monitor his heart rhythms and record them either automatically or while using a hand-held patient assistant. Two years following the implant, we'd be informed that eventually he'd be required to have a pacemaker, which had to be replaced every ten years. But that would be years afterward, and all that mattered to me was that Lucas was with us and we believed he was at minimal risk. I never took that for granted for one moment of one day.

Unfortunately, the costly prognosis contributed to the outstanding bills that had accumulated, and money rapidly became tighter. I was thankful I was employed, but the money was nowhere what we needed to pay all of our bills since Derek wasn't working during that time. Lance's child support helped, but it simply was not enough. After another year of financial dissension, we risked the prospect of losing the house and concluded that our most advantageous option was to file bankruptcy. The bankruptcy included Lucas's medical bills, our time-share in Florida that we purchased at the beginning of our marriage, and the credit cards we had borrowed against to help us pay our monthly expenditures. It had all become a vicious cycle. My greatest consolation was that my children did not experience any type of deprivation. In the midst of our predicament, nothing in their world was ever disrupted or disharmonious in their lives.

We made it past the various health impairments and past the bankruptcy, thankfully able to keep possession of the house and both cars. After a year had come and gone from the time Derek lost his job, he was finally hired. The kids began to get older, and we were busy with daily living that came and went. Heartbreakingly, the singular thing that remained constant was the lack of affection between us. Derek and I spent ample time behind the door of our bedroom in hostility, but when it came to the kids we took tremendous measures in keeping up the appearance that our relationship was genuine and not the farce it had become.

Unfortunately, it became harder and harder to conceal our portentous disputes from them as he became increasingly impudent with his words and actions, showing his anger and frustration in ways that alarmed me. While I was aware of his passive aggressive behavior,

I had never perceived him as someone who would use physical force. He did not like confrontation, so the first time he punched a hole in our bedroom wall sent shockwaves throughout my entire body, and the kids were witness to the episode. Eventually, throwing plates of food and dumping trash onto the floor became a habitual behavior.

Disillusioned with our marriage we tackled our conflicts with a counselor. I was hopeful we would rebound, up until our sixth session when the counselor had the bright idea to provide Derek "homework". I know my look of disbelief was transparent, as he coached my husband how to respond to my needs in a way that would promote emotional and physical intimacy. The more the counselor referred to Derek's project as homework, the more it became apparent that I was the homework. I had gone from the woman he had once ardently pursued, to a compulsory assignment.

I was doubtful that it could get any worse, until the following session when the counselor asked if he had completed his assignment for the week...and Derek had to tell him no. I never totally heard the word "homework" the same way, and both of my children were in school for many, many years afterward--with homework.

As the sessions progressed I became reflective of my own childhood in comparison to my children's: assessing my existing issues seemed to be dredging up my former issues. I felt as if I was perpetrating as much damage onto Rylee and Lucas as my own mother had on my brothers and me. Did loving, adoring and selflessly placing your children foremost in your life not contribute in some diminutive degree to their formation? Could the outcome of a childhood be the same despite the rearing and environments exposed to in life?

From the time I was expecting Rylee, my objective was to raise her with an effectively different upbringing from what I had been subjected to. I felt fundamental parenting was teaching her the principles that mattered in life, and strived to do just that with as much love, kindness and tolerance possible. My goal was to teach her the importance of using discretion in life because choices ultimately carried consequences, the end results ultimately good consequences...or bad consequences.

Either way, you live with the end results, so it's imperative to respectfully contemplate making them beforehand.

I was compelled to relay the importance of counting the little things in life, because the little things indubitably bestow the greatest impact for us and for those around us. Though I considered it pertinent to teach her that and so much more, I'd one day realize what I didn't comprehend at the time; that somewhere deep inside I wanted her to live her life through my lessons. After years of parenting, that would become a lesson in itself.

Though self-doubting to be competently raising my children, I did recognize the fact that I was doing everything conceivable to do best by them. A prime example of my infamous parenting techniques was the fact that I never spanked Rylee and Lucas because I elected educational dialog and guidance over physical and emotional abuse. My astute viewpoint concerning parenting was from absolute determination that my children's upbringing be dissimilar of mine.

Confident of methodical my approach, I knew the precise moment my daughter first tested my concept. It was approximately the same moment I also reverted back to the Proverbs verse in the bible "spare the rod, spoil the child". I was standing at the kitchen sink, and glanced up to find Rylee looking at me while standing within a few feet of the TV screen. It was as if she was consciously waiting for me to catch her, waiting for the moment to make her move. As I looked at her, I could see the gleam of mischief on her little face. Then ever so subtly, she slowly moved forward a few steps at a time. Game on! I raised my eyebrows as if saying to her, "Don't go there! You know better!" as she nonetheless inched forward. My eyebrows rose a bit higher with each deliberate step that she took, and I have no doubt that my eyebrows and hairline looked as if they had become one by the time she accomplished her mission!

"Rylee Page!" I said her name with stern conviction, certain her response would be to retreat and find something more entertaining to do. She was my sweet, innocent, well-behaved baby girl and would never disobey me! But the look in her eye as she stepped closer within touching range of the TV told me there was a slim chance that she might not reach her teen years. All I could say at that point was, *"Don't do it*!" in a calm but matter of fact "mom" voice. She took the final step and plunged her finger at the TV screen with assertive conviction as if to retort, "So there!"

Like a cat pouncing on a mouse, I moved toward her so aggressively that I don't think she really had time to be afraid. She simply stood there and removed her finger as if she had never touched the TV at all. I grabbed her tiny wrist and faintly slapped at the back of her hand as if slapping at a butterfly, thereupon dropping to my knees to her level so that she could stare into my eyes. She stood there staring back at me with her blue eyes wide open, bottom lip pouting as it commenced to trembling as the gates opened and the tears began to flow. You would have thought I had beaten her!

I took her to her room to let her cry and muse over her mishap, standing outside the room until I opened the door and went to her. Dropping to my knees again I took her hands in mine and keenly gazed into her eyes: "Do you know why you are in trouble, Rylee?" Still pouting but with not a tear in her eye, she nodded yes. "Then why didn't you listen to me?" I calmly asked. She stood there looking at me as though she didn't understand what had just happened, but self-assured that she could come up with something to get a reprieve. I repeated the question, and this time her response was to say yes while she shook her head no.

Once I explained why she was being admonished, I hugged her and let her out of her room. It was a plausible assumption that I would be given the same mixed response numerous times throughout the years to come...little did I know!! I do know that I felt guilty enough afterward that I could never bring myself to reprimand by swatting her, let alone spank her.

I discovered disciplining a boy was unlike that of a girl a few years after he was born. The first time I elected to spank my son was in response to his behavior in school, and it was the last option I had left. Lucas had an extroverted personality and even at a young age he had an innate charisma and ability to make people laugh, constantly the life of the party. But being the life of the party at home and with his friends was one thing, being the class comedian was another. As the notifications accrued and were notoriously documented in his folder as a warning by his teacher, I took the "philosophical" approach as I had with his sister. "If you don't stop disrupting your classroom and you get another mark in your folder, there will be *consequences*." He was old enough to comprehend what was happening as we discussed the need for self-control in his classroom.

By the third warning after my threat, I started taking away his video games, followed by other privileges such as after-school activity and playtime with his friends. There is a limit as to what you can confiscate and deprive from a seven-year-old child, and so I threatened that if it happened *one more time* there'd definitely be a spanking. I was counting on the fact that my using the "S" word would scare him into meeting my demands. Nevertheless, when he came home with the same mark in his folder the following afternoon, I had to follow through with my warning.

Rylee followed behind Lucas as I led him to his room, and stood just outside his bedroom door as if assured I'd never spank her brother in a million years, since I had never spanked either of them before. I calmly instructed Lucas to select a belt from the two he possessed and bring it to me, his expression nothing less than hilarious under different circumstances. Where had I seen that expression before? Rylee remained standing at the bedroom door, and looked at me with those big blue eyes now filled with disbelief, watching as I forced her brother to bend over in preparation for his beating.

I took a deep breath, then made the slightest swat that I could bring myself to make, the cloth belt barely even grazing his pants. The belt hadn't even left his butt when he began to cry, Rylee began to cry, and tears filled my own eyes. The most logical thing I could muster at that moment was, "Do you want to go get some ice cream?" I grabbed one of his hands as Rylee came across the room and grabbed the other, both nodding yes to my question. Ice cream would never be the same.

Though I prudently affirm taking the necessary actions to discipline children, for my brothers and me discipline was about control, antagonism, and ridicule--there was no love or guidance. I had little respect for my mother growing up, and even less as an adult. Ironically,

I've concluded we oftentimes obsessively fear becoming what we despise and unconsciously become that which we scorn. Though unintentional, my methodology of parenting possibly contributed to decisions that, ultimately, may not have been in my children's best interests. There were times that I was blindly naïve and made excuses for things when I should have been stricter. The daunting reality is that the more I attempted to make their lives healthier and happier; I may have adversely accomplished the opposite.

***

Derek and I never disagreed on the fact that family was important, and with my job at Paragon Air it allowed us travel opportunities to many glorious places and provided us with unforgettable memories. The sights and experiences of traveling were priceless, but some of the memories created remain some of the most treasured within our hearts. And they are irreplaceable memories we endlessly share.

To this day, one of the favored memories reminisced between us was our trip to Aruba when Rylee was about thirteen and Lucas nine. The beaches there are incredible and the waters some of the most splendid, but touring throughout Aruba you find yourself astonished at the different way of life that they live. We had checked out the sandy beaches, the rolling sea and all of the pictorial scenery in-between, then opted to check out the surrounding mountains via horseback ride. All of us were waiting on our horses so that we could mount up and prepare to ride out, when one of the employees walked up with a mule. Derek began laughing hysterically, as he pointed to the mule and boisterously told Lucas, "That's your horse!" The local worker pointed to the mule and then enthusiastically began motioning with his hands to come over. Lucas contracted a look of disappointment, but nevertheless began walking over.

The boy grasping the bridle began pointing his finger again, waving it as if his life depended on it. Derek turned in the direction of Rylee and me still laughing, before turning back toward the mule to find it standing right in front of him. The hired hand spoke in broken English:

"This you ride, Mista. You get on ass. He carry heavy load, you ride Mista!" First, we laughed at the look on Derek's face, and then we laughed even harder at the sight of his legs wrapped around the mule, as his entire body bobbed up and down on a mule that was at least two sizes too small for him. It was especially funny when we looked ahead and saw Lucas on a horse three times his own size! We grinned and chuckled all the way up the mountain and back. You had to be there...

Because I collected lighthouses, throughout the years it became a ritual for us to locate a lighthouse each trip we took. So another treasured memory is a particular trip we spent half a day looking for a lighthouse, to discover it was merely a big black box with a light, not a traditional Fresnel lens. It was debatable if it could have genuinely shed any light, even across the trifling portion of ground it sat on. We must have driven past that thing ten or twenty times looking for a towering, traditional lighthouse and questioning how the darn thing could vanish into thin air.

Once we located a traditional lighthouse and had cautiously climbed our way to the top, Rylee did not want to risk moving away from the wall's parameters to look out over the rails. The perceptible horror across her face conveyed the "you're not going to make me go out there" expression, was nothing short of comical. Derek captured the priceless moment with his camera, and the moment he captured visibly speaks for itself: I'm standing in front of Rylee and looking at the camera as the wind is blowing so hard that my hair is all over my face, trying to coax her out on the walkway of the lighthouse. Rylee is standing to the side and slightly behind me, her sweet face filled with unambiguous terror, eyes bulging with visible apprehension, as she appears to be melted into the outside wall of the lighthouse. Behind both of us, you see Lucas in the background laughing with a hint of mockery and glee in his eyes as he's pointing at Rylee. It looked as if he should be in an entirely different picture.

There were an infinite number of memories that captured and chronicled our life together as a family. Some were funny, some were filled with tenderness, and some were simply timeless. But the tragedy of most relationships essentially falls to the incidents that are not all-encompassing of those memories, and as much as we'd like to forget specific fragments of time, those cannot be forgotten either. Too many fights, too much pain, too many broken promises and disappointments, too much deceit, and six counselors later, Derek's and my relationship of twenty-five years came to an end.

Perhaps because I'd loved him a little bit too much all along, it took me a considerable amount of time to acknowledge the end of our relationship inevitable, and any chance of it surviving had vanished. I came to the conclusion upon leaving the marriage that I had little control over myself when it came to Derek. I ignored things I shouldn't have and was exceedingly tolerable when typically I wouldn't have been.

The day I ultimately headed out the door, it was trailing a lengthy battle of fighting for the man I'd loved right from the moment he'd walked into my life. When it became transparently indisputable that I had no choice but to leave, I didn't walk out…I ran. I was tired of the fighting, and even worse I no longer wanted to fight for our relationship.

As someone that had never been a quitter, at every opportune occasion I'd make the statement to my children that people didn't leave a relationship because it got too hard, they left because they no longer wanted to try. While I may have known it to be true, that self-made hypothesis was hard for me to swallow.

By the time Derek realized that I was at that point, I had already emotionally detached from our marriage long before I really left. I slept on the couch, went out on the weekends when the kids were with Lance, and had little or no communication with him unless absolutely necessary. We had become roommates, and it had been that way for some time. After years of desiring to be with him and putting forth the fight to stay with him, I packed my bags, hired a moving truck, and had the divorce papers served to him in the driveway of our home.

I took Rylee and Lucas from the home they had grown up in, from the family they had been a part of throughout their lives and placed them in a town where nothing was familiar to them. I moved us to a town called Addison, thinking at the time it smart to move closer to Lance. The location would be close enough to Rylee's school in Richland Hills that she could manage the drive and finish her senior year, and Lucas's new school was literally across the street from the new house and within walking distance. The neighborhood itself was quaint and on the traditional side, with accessible parks and walking trails close by.

I worked diligently to make the move and transition as easy as possible for them, while trying to minimally change our lifestyle. Taking distributions from my 401K-retirement account I purchased furniture and whatever else was needed to accomplish that, fully furnishing the house so there wouldn't be one empty room, all in the hopes that our hearts would not feel empty either. While I believed at the time I knew what emptiness was, I had no idea, even though I thought that I did. I was in for an emptiness that I never knew existed, and it was fast around the corner.

Chapter 16

In my mind, I can see both of them as if they are sitting in front of me, Rylee on the couch and Lucas next to her on the floor. I was on an ottoman just across from them, and my grave expression unmistakably forewarned them that something was amiss, because they had seen the look before. In my head I was saying one thing, and in my heart, somewhere deep within, I was feeling something disconcertingly different. I hadn't spoken with Derek since we had moved out three months earlier, but he had called moments before to break the unsuspecting news that Lance planned to counteract my child support suit with his own custody suit. Anticipating an increase in child support, I'd be challenged by Lance filing for primary custody instead, and going into court caught off guard and unprepared for his petition.

As I'd listened to Derek disclosing the information to me, I was in absolute disbelief that Lance would contemplate doing that kind of thing to our children. I had been the primary custodian of them since we had divorced over fifteen years ago. Exhausted from the workweek or not, I was the parent up every night when they were sick, the one that rushed them to the emergency room or stayed home when required. I was the parent who took them to the practices and their games when they participated in sports. I was the one who bandaged their scrapes and mended their hearts. I was the one in the middle of the night that chased away the ghosts when nightmares haunted them. I was the parent who had taken care of our children while he was pursuing and developing his high-power, high-income career. I'd done it throughout our marriage and after we divorced.

Always having candid interaction with my children no matter what, I began my sentence with a sigh, trying to find the right words before I spoke. "Listen, I know you guys are aware that I plan on taking your dad to court for additional child support now that we are on our own, but there's a chance he may be petitioning for you to live with him in Plano and pursue custody. I want you both to be reassured that will never happen, and everything will be okay."

I waited for the "We'd never leave you, Mom," or the "I can't believe Dad would try and do that to us!" but the next words out of my daughter's mouth were words that I knew with certainty would change our lives forever. "Mom, it will be so much easier on you if we moved in and lived with Daddy. You really can't afford for us to be here, it will be best for everyone."

My jaw must have hit my knees, and tears filled my eyes. I could feel my heart's rhythm accelerating and calmed myself not to overreact. I became aware of the increasing warmth on my back from the sun's rays that filtered through the window, yet I could sense in front of me the clouds that were gathering on the horizon. A pain went through my heart incomparable to any I had ever felt, and I shivered in spite of the warmth.

What had just happened? Were they seriously thinking about leaving? I took a deep breath and began talking to them as reasonably possible. "Rylee, we will be fine. You guys don't need to worry, your dad and I will work this out, and there is no place you need to be but here with me."

As if afraid to speak my son didn't utter a word, his eyes focused on me with a look of bewilderment and anxiety. Rylee looked at me as if she was an adult with all of the answers, and confident she had all of the right answers. Details began to unfold of the conspired scheme during the past two weeks to live with their father, including the fact that they had already signed the agreement and presented it to Lance's attorney. They hadn't consulted me or felt that my role or feelings were worth considering, and they were going. I recognized that I had been incontrovertibly betrayed and I was grateful that Derek had given me the heads-up. I could not imagine entering court expecting something to be given, and instead everything arbitrarily taken.

But sitting there in that moment and listening to my daughter, I was flabbergasted by the decision they'd irresponsibly made. I couldn't even begin to retaliate with a sane response. That night and many that followed Derek's phone call I sat in isolation, thinking how others could so markedly spawn the most significant alterations in the course of our lives.

It was June 25, and the next day was my daughter's seventeenth birthday. We had originally intended to have her friends over for a cookout to celebrate the occasion, but by the next morning I could hardly function, and I couldn't pretend or behave as if the anarchy hadn't occurred. They were both expected to go to Plano later that evening, but due to the indifferences prevailing between us I felt that they should leave to spend the day with their dad earlier than planned. I could not resume the façade that everything was fine let alone sustain a smile, and I didn't want to spoil her birthday.

As soon as I made this suggestion to Rylee she sneered at me like "Whatever!" as she belligerently turned to rush up the stairs. Shortly afterward she returned with Lucas, and both walked out the front door without saying a word, leaving me alone and in silence. They did not close the door behind them, and I stood inside the doorway watching them go.

Any sunshine that had brightened yesterday was completely gone, making it seem much cooler outside than normal for the month of June. The wind blew the rain in various directions as if contradicting which way to blow, causing some of the rain to sporadically fall and mix with the tears streaming down my face. A coldness invaded my body that had nothing to do with the weather as I watched them drive away until I could no longer see the car, hoping they would turn around--if nothing else but to say goodbye.

Once they were out of my sight I turned to go back inside, shutting the door behind me, but powerless to shut out the pain. There was no one I could talk to or count on to rescue me, and there was nowhere I could run for consolation or encouragement.

I started up the stairs, barely making it halfway before falling to my knees. The cry that came from me probably sounded as if someone had ripped my heart out, and head bowed I hugged myself begging God to help me get through that moment, uncertain I'd be able to. There and then I grasped the desperation of people when they've hit rock bottom and felt there's nothing more. I understood that moment when they contemplated taking their life or decisively did so. Without question, the only way I endured that day, was nothing less than the strength and mercy of God.

As time came and went I'd realize the pain had diminished but never altogether left, and looking back later on, I would be amazed that I did in fact get back up on my feet and somehow climb the remainder of the stairs. I did get up each day to shower, eat, and go to work. Every night I cried. Every night I prayed. There wasn't a single second that I didn't miss my children or ache for them to be with me, compulsively recreating the moment they walked out the door as if they were merely going to visit friends for the afternoon.

Additional anguish was inflicted by the fact that they alienated themselves from me in the months that followed, without calling or coming around. I began to relive the loss of my brothers as if intermingling the past with this present turmoil, no end and no beginning. As much as the pain had overwhelmed me at the time, I never could begin to fathom the pain my mother must have experienced when we lost them.

But the consolation of losing someone through death is that although you won't see that person again in this life, death is not chosen. The majority of the time you have the comfort of knowing that the person you loved, loved you in return. Whenever someone decides to walk away and leave by his or her own choice, you continuously ask yourself, "Why? What did I do wrong? What could I have done differently? What can I do now?" Sadly enough, you seldom come to know those answers, and soon discover that it doesn't really matter. Time ultimately fades into the oblivion and life does continue, even when you think it might not...or that it should not.

I had the entire house packed up and was moved out by the following week that they left, no longer requiring a three-bedroom, three bathroom, and two dining room home. As I began trying to reestablish my life, I learned through the grapevine that Rylee was no longer living in Plano with her dad, but had moved back to Richland Hills and was living with her stepmom's parents. Her expeditious move from Plano to Richland Hills gave cause to suspect that the living arrangements must have been an integral part of their plot from the beginning. Plans have a way of falling apart in the smallest of ways.

Chapter 17

I was able to find a one-bedroom studio conveniently close to work that allowed easy access to Plano. Though it wasn't spacious, it was warm and cozy with lots of natural light streaming in from the windows. The new furniture I had purchased to fill the house in Addison was either sold or placed in storage since there wasn't room for it. With the new accommodations, whenever Lucas came for his visits one of us slept on my bed, and the other either on the blow up mattress or couch. It was all I could afford at the time, but I remained mindful to live by my philosophy, "Make the best of the worst."

With the exception of Lucas coming to visit I was very much alone, and the next several months reminded me that I was capable of being alone and enduring it. Since the kids were of age to make the decision to live with Lance, there had been no justification to create astronomical legal fees fighting the inevitable. It never entered my thoughts that there might be an issue seeing my son, either on his behalf or his father's behalf.

His dad had moved to Plano after marrying Simone when Lucas was seven and had made it nearly impossible for Lance to attend or participate in their scheduled sports and practices, recitals or any other school functions. Even before the divorce, we had agreed that he should not be the "every other weekend" dad. Without the courts getting involved, we had agreed that Lance would pick them up on Thursdays, but on the Thursdays it was his weekend, he'd keep them overnight and be responsible for taking them back home or to school on Monday. I wanted the kids to live close enough to him that they could be with him whenever the opportunity or need arose.

Within a short timeframe of the kids leaving, I established the fact that Lance did not intend for me to be a part of our son's life nor did he feel the same regarding visitation rights. I was lucky if I had four days out of the month with Lucas, and his dad purposely attempted to keep him unavailable by sending him to his grandparents in Houston, and various summer camps throughout the summer. He didn't ask my permission or notify me concerning the arrangements, and I wasn't provided information on how or where I could reach Lucas.

Without any indication of the request, I finally gave in and called Lance to invite him to lunch. Whether he knew what was coming or not, he agreed. We had not spoken since the kids left, and though I had no desire to see him, I had no choice if I wanted to resolve my visitation rights. Those same visitation rights were on his mind too, but not in the same capacity.

He had arrived at the restaurant first and was already seated at the table, his cell phone directly in front of him, and his briefcase on the ground. I assumed he was working while he was waiting for me to arrive, and sat down opposite him without saying a word. His glass of tea was half empty, and the hosts that had escorted me to the table took my drink order and promised that the waitress would refill his glass. She turned to walk away, and as she did, Lances eyes met mine.

His eyes looked void and dark, not dark underneath the eyes from stress like mine, but deep into his soul dark. I had wanted to speak with him face to face and appeal to his waning rational integrity, but looking at him, all I wanted to do was get up and leave. He began speaking first, and within moments I wanted to use the knife that lay atop my napkin.

"I know you can't afford to pay me child support Autumn, and if you will give up your parental rights to the kids, I will get a court modification issued, mandating that you are no longer obligated to pay." At the end of his sentence, he pulled out some papers from an envelope and reached for his phone. "Are you recording this conversation on your phone?" I asked. Because I was hoping that he was. The audacity of his wretched proposition took any feelings that I may have had left for him, and obliterated them entirely. He shook his head to imply no at my question, and handed me the papers.

It seemed he had taken the liberty and already drawn up the agreement; all I had to do was sign at the bottom. Everything was so businesslike with him, and so controlling. But he was not going to control and manipulate me, like I summarily realized he had controlled and manipulated our own children! Those were the kindest of any thoughts in my head, as I began shredding the papers with my hands, hoping the next words I spoke would shred any hopes of his evil plan.

"Lance, you will _not_ take away my parental rights! And you will not interfere with the relationship between my son and me, or keep me from him so that you can control him!" Lance looked as if he was about to speak again, but I didn't give him the opportunity. "You have gone too far, and there is no amount of money I won't spend to make it right for Lucas!" I stood to go, and sprinkled some of the shredded remnants of the papers over his head, exclaiming as I walked away from the table, "Go to hell!" And I meant it. For the first time since our divorce, I no longer felt guilt over anything I'd done, or with anyone I'd done it with.

I would have given anything if I could have gone and picked Lucas up right then. I was afraid that his father was telling him that I did not want to see him, and I could not reach Lucas to set the record straight. After my meeting with Lance, no one answered or returned my phone calls, including Rylee. Weeks turned into months without any communication with my kids. I didn't have the money for an attorney, so my only option was to take out another loan against my retirement savings so that I could take Lance to court, to have my visitation rights enforced.

After the initial court summons, Lance realized that I would keep my word to do whatever had to be done to see my children, and made good on the court ordered visitation.

***

The first visit with Lucas was awkward and uncomfortable for both of us. Rylee was not a part of the initial visits and that left the two of us to carry on conversation and act as though nothing out of the ordinary had taken place. Each time he visited he came across aloof and put out for having to spend time with me, thus creating tension between us. Regardless, every time Lance picked him up and I watched as he walked away I felt hollow and lifeless, and the period in between his visits seemed to stand still. By the time a year had come and gone, it was hard to conceive that I'd come to terms with the realization my new life was the life I would have to live, permissive of the changes imposed. I joined a book club, started having friends over, went back to school and even began dating. But every time I overcame one challenge, before I could catch my breath and halfway recuperate, another loomed right around the corner.

Employed with Paragon Air Employee Credit Union for nine years at that point, the fact that I was a dedicated and hardworking employee was soon forgotten and seemed irrelevant, as my career was flushed down the toilet in a matter of weeks due to an incident that I was not aware of, or had any sort of control over. I could sense myself becoming overwhelmed with everything that had transpired throughout the previous year and felt it would be beneficial if I enjoyed some extended time out of the office to regroup and refresh. I decided to take two consecutive weeks of vacation, and unfortunately managed to get sick during the second week. I was on the couch recuperating when my phone rang, and though I customarily didn't rush to answer when I was off work, I saw that the call was from my office and answered.

I answered to hear Amanda, the credit union president and at that time one of my closest friends, saying hello. After nothing more than the initial greeting, she began questioning me about a mass defection in which the department's financial advisors all deserted the company without notice. Without hesitation she bluntly asked me if I was aware of anything to do with the incident, and I told her the truth...I did not. I wasn't sure what she had expected me to tell her, but I sensed that the response I provided her either wasn't a satisfactory answer, or she wasn't convinced that I didn't know. Rehashing the conversation in my head afterward, I was a little offended by the entire scenario.

The first day I returned to the workplace happened to be the day of our annual team-meeting event. When I walked in, there was no "we" in team, any more than there was an "I" in team. It was soon noticeable that no one wanted to acknowledge me or talk with me, let alone hug me as typically happened. I could not figure out what had occurred to create such unmerited belligerence toward me, until a coworker smarted off in a sarcastic tone, "What are you doing at work? We all thought you left with the others!" and grew perturbed as I made the gradual connection that everyone was assuming precisely that. I had taken a vacation, and now everyone including those who claimed to be my friends thought I had walked out on my job? My guarded reply was a dejected, "No, I'm afraid I didn't know anything about that conspiracy!" By the end of the day, I wished that I had left with the others.

The next day I made my way into the office as if nothing out of the ordinary had transpired the day before and had sat down at my desk to sort through my emails, when the vice president of the credit union walked up and asked me why I was there. I figured it was obvious--I was trying to work. A peculiarly baffled look crossed her face as she turned to walk away, and I then happened to notice a coworker I had trained prior to my departmental transfer was sitting in one of the private offices deliberately ignoring me.

As the vice president was leaving, the human resources manager walked up to my desk and informally instructed me to come with her. As she led the way, her insinuation was that I needed to feed them additional information other than what I had already provided during my vacation. Information that I still did not have. I was becoming irritated over the misconception that I was a participant in the treachery, and growing extremely uncomfortable with everyone's insolent ill-conceived theories that I was a spy, providing information to the enemy. I was simply trying to reclaim a normal life.

It became evident to me that their objective wasn't to acquire information, but to contrive some means of keeping me from pertinent client information of possible significance to the departed financial planners. They claimed it was in my best interest to stay out of the department, and placed me in Human Resources "temporarily" until things became stable. Six months later I was still there, making my way through every other department in HR, doing the tasks that experienced departmental employees were responsible for.

Everyone kept their distance and prejudged me guilty of the allegations, treating me as if I had the plague and should be quarantined. I was alone at home, and now I was alone at work. Even after applying within the credit union for several positions that I was as equally or more qualified for, the answer each time was unequivocally no.

After a nine-month period had passed, I was frustrated from working in a department where I was not officially employed and performing duties that I was not getting proportionately compensated to do. In my mind, it seemed reasonable to request that I either be moved officially into an HR position, or reinstated to my previous position. My appeal was wrongly interpreted as an ultimatum, and from then on it became their quest to find a way to legitimately terminate me, or make it unbearable for me to withstand their harassment. To their dismay, I consistently proved myself and tolerated their berating, and they had no choice but to accommodate my wishes and return me to the financial department.

I was resolute in my pursuit to move forward regardless of the circumstance that interfered with any normal existence for me. The most expedient way of accomplishing that goal was to seek alternate employment within a company that provided me a substantial pay increase and fresh opportunities. I began applying for various positions with Paragon Financial Advisors (PFA), located on the upper floor of the building and at the time under the same airline ownership as the credit union. The PFA manager I'd interviewed with in the past never felt the available positions a favorable career move, but an opportunity emerged that he felt would be a good fit, and after several interviews were conducted I was offered a position and eagerly accepted.

My career at Paragon Financial Advisors as an Executive Assistant to the Vice President of Sales began in September of 2008. The company strategically planned the onset of my new assignment prior to the sale and separation with Paragon Air. Employee benefits including insurance, vacation, and flight benefits would be carried over and grandfathered in without interruption. With the sale of the company, it was unbelievably hectic for both the current employees and any new employees. But it wasn't long before I discovered that the work ethics, expectations and the mindset within the company were unique to its culture, including the company's employees.

I'd been consistently adept at my previous vocation with the credit union and proficient in that particular industry, but now I was lost and trying to learn new computer programs, procedures, policies, and everything else mandatory to fulfill the obligation of my new profession. Concluding a week of insufficient training I was delegated responsibilities that would typically require months of extensive coaching, but informed would not be provided due to the sale of the company.

As fate would have it, my desk was next to a woman who had an antagonistic attitude toward me and made it clear she was out to sabotage me in any way she could. One of the utmost blatant incidents occurred after my incorrect submission of an expense report. Unversed in procedure and unaware of restrictions that anything over a thousand dollars was to remain at our office until approved, I accidentally sent the original items to the home office. I began calling the back office to attempt obtaining the receipts as immediately possible, and was curtly informed that it would require an unknown amount of time to trace and retrieve the information I was urgently in need of. In addition, they were unable to reimburse any incidental charges until the items were submitted as protocol. My rational thinking was: simply cut a company check to cover the outstanding expenses until the issue could be resolved. The person submitting the expense report was a company employee, so it seemed any discrepancies could easily be worked out. To me, it was idiotic to overreact and create such senseless issues.

At the culmination of my fruitless efforts, including countless phone calls and numerous faxes, by the end of the day I was ready to pull my hair out. As I walked past the assistant adjacent to my cubicle, her words stopped me dead in my tracks. "I just want you to know that was the most fucked up thing I have ever heard!" I stood there looking at her as if she was an alien. Who would vocalize that to anyone for any reason, and with such malicious vindictiveness? All I could muster in response and that I felt remotely work appropriate was, "Well then, why didn't you offer your assistance if you recognized that I needed it and you knew what to do?" When I heard her snippet reply, "You didn't ask me for my help!" I literally cringed at her smartass reply and dreaded the mere thought of having to work next to her every day, suspecting that it wasn't going to be pleasant. *"Really?"* was the glib response I imparted as I turned to go back to my desk. Regardless of the efforts, approach or actions taken to conciliate the rift between us, nothing seemed to improve.

Soon afterward my supervisor assigned me to create a PowerPoint in preparation for an upcoming scheduled Board meeting. I had never created nor had I insinuated that I could create a PowerPoint presentation, and once I enlightened my supervisor that I was unable to complete the task, he all but accused me of listing the experience on my resume, then agitatedly requested the same coworker I was at odds with to prepare it. Her smirk of contempt told me she wanted to reiterate the comment she had offensively thrown my way a few days ago about being "fucked up". That was okay, because I wanted to make the same statement to her.

It shouldn't have surprised me when the supervisor and the company's HR representative pulled me into a meeting behind closed doors three weeks later to discuss some issues that "I" was apparently having. The first issue presented implied that I was creating tension and stress in the office. I don't think I laughed or even smiled at how ridiculous the accusation was, but I know my jaw must have dropped to my knees. I sat before them chagrined and speechless while my supervisor told me that he was no longer confident I was right for the job he'd hired me for, and the company needed time to deliberate the most favorable solution before getting back with me. By then I wasn't even listening to a word he was saying. I was now living on my own with no one to assist with the financial burdens, and legally obligated to pay child support for my son on top of all my other debts. It would be devastating for me to become unemployed! Both stood and dismissed me without further ado, and my pride already obliterated, I was embarrassed even more by the sly looks thrown my way as I walked to my desk.

In the midst of trying to prove myself and maintain a positive outlook, I picked up the phone at work to hear a female voice asking for me in a curt, professional tone. It was October, and the stern voice on the other end responded to my, "This is she" with the information that she was Lucas's school counselor. Whenever you get a call from your child's school counselor your radar mechanism kicks in because you know they're not making a social call.

I was informed that Lucas was in her office, and that it was urgent I get to the school to meet with her before the end of the day. Remember two things: I had just started with the company, and the school he was now attending was over fifty miles away. I felt slightly panicked and inquired if everything was okay. She began with sharing that Lucas was having difficulties and that he had been for several months, so my first assumption was that it concerned his schoolwork. I assumed that living with his father hadn't changed the fact that he never liked doing it, and unable to reach Lance the school was contacting me to discuss concerns for his grades. But as she began explaining the reason for her call, I sensed unexpected trepidation in my heart.

In a brisk voice she informed me that Lucas had been visiting her office in need of someone to work through the overbearing emotions he had been experiencing since living with his dad. My brain seemed to freeze as she further elaborated how he had pleaded she not mention to anyone that he was seeking counseling, and had vowed to honor his request. But he seemed so depressed during his last visit that it caused her to be alarmed for his wellbeing, and she'd felt it crucial to intervene. It broke my heart that my son felt he could not share his heartache with anyone but the school counselor, who he had known for under a year. What kind of family had we become that our own child had to fight these feelings on his own, for fear of creating increased friction and animosity?

Feeling it was the right thing and possibly the best thing for Lucas, I called Lance. I judiciously informed him of the conversation with the counselor, and that I planned on picking Lucas up from the school to have dinner and find out what was going on. I further explained that once we had dinner, I would return him home and the two of us could discuss options. I resolved that I'd wish the same respect extended if the circumstances were reversed.

I was relatively certain the conflicts Lucas was trying to overcome encompassed the backlash from things he had no control over. He had been uprooted from the home he'd grown up in, lost the family he'd grown up with, along with the familiarity of his neighborhood and school. He had been catapulted into a scenario unprepared and unequipped to handle on his own. His sister left within a week subsequent going to live with their father and he no longer even had the security of his one "constant" in life. He was left fending for himself with a stepmom who didn't care for him, a new baby brother his dad catered to, and the absence of any friends whatsoever. The promises specified by their father about becoming one big happy family with bigger and better things, never happened. In both his mind and heart, he must have felt that he too had been betrayed, and on so many levels.

Unfortunately, Lance was not happy in the least with the counselor for contacting me and even less pleased with my arrangement to pick Lucas up from school. "What right do you have to do that?"--RIGHT? His implicit anger established that he resented any degree of involvement on my part. To me, his imprudent reaction caused suspicion that he must have known or had some hunch all had not been right with his son. But for the time being Lance was the last person I was worried about, and callously dismissed him before calling the counselor to let her know I had made the necessary arrangements to be there as soon as possible.

On a whim, I told her that I had also called Lance to apprise him of the situation, sharing my concern over his aggressive behavior and lack of support for me to remove Lucas from school. She informed me Lucas's phone would be taken from him until he left with me, preventing Lance from having any correspondence with him and possibly making alternate arrangements. Taking precautionary measures she had already made the necessary arrangements for his early dismissal in order to leave with me. Before hanging up, she emphasized the importance of visiting with me prior to her speaking with Lance, and my mind started racing uncontrollably, questioning what all Lucas could have possibly shared.

Having scarcely gotten into the car, my phone rang displaying Lance's name, and I answered the call expecting to hear his voice, but to my astonishment heard Lucas. "Dad has picked me up, Mom. You don't need to come and get me." I could sense the distress in my son's voice, and calmly asked to speak with his dad. Once he was on the phone my composure dissipated and I began indignantly questioning why he had picked Lucas up, knowing I was on my way to get him myself. Lance's response to me was bitter! "Why do you feel you need to pick him up and talk to him?" My first thought was, why are you afraid for me to pick him up and talk to him? Defiantly, I simply answered, "Because the school called *me*, and that was the arrangement!"

I could feel my aggravation begin to intensify and my frustration surfacing at the realization that he had my son and had no intention whatsoever of letting me communicate with him any further. Apparently, Lance hadn't even allowed Lucas to get his cell phone from the counselor before leaving, hence the call from his dad's phone. With a growing urgency and the anger in my voice escalating with every enunciated word, I told Lance I wanted to see my son without his manipulative postponements, and that he could either bring him to me, or he'd find me at his front door with the police. I'm not sure how much of what I said was heard by Lucas, but the response from his father conceding to meet me at a nearby restaurant came across unmistakably belligerent on my end.

Hanging up with Lance, I called the counselor to inquire if she was cognizant of the fact that he had managed to withdraw Lucas from school. Placing me on a brief hold, she returned to confirm that his dad had not registered or notified anyone that he was withdrawing him, and further disclosed that there was no documentation authorizing me to remove Lucas from school...for any reason. Lance had not notated that I was his mother or even listed me as an emergency contact, therefore legal documentation would be required that supported my parental rights.

For a moment I thought I misunderstood the issue, how had she managed to get my phone number and contact me if the school didn't have documentation that I was his mother? And why would she call me if that were the case? I conveyed my thoughts and concerns to her, trying to conclusively establish what the issue was and what the school needed me to provide. She reiterated that it was critical I expedite providing legal documentation stipulating my parental rights since there was nothing on record that authorized my parental rights. As if sensing my next question, she told me Lucas had provided her with my contact information himself, and that she had only reached out to me out of dire concern for him. Officially, until the matter was resolved she would be restrained from any further communication with me.

I was determined that Lance would not coerce me out of my son's life as he continuously and aggressively strived to do. I was comforted to a degree knowing I could resolve the issue by faxing the school my copy of the modification decree before the morning bell the next day. With that thought prevalent in the back of my mind, I turned my car from the direction of the school and instead to the restaurant Lance had chosen to meet at. Emotions would be running high for everyone, but I had to reassure my son everything would be ok and remain calm no matter how much I wanted to serve Lance up on a platter as the main course.

Entering the restaurant I saw them already seated at a table waiting for me, and the look on their faces confirmed my concerns. Approaching the table, I reached out to hug Lucas and offer him some degree of comfort, hoping the fact that I was there would provide that. I forced a smiled at the man who now seemed more like my enemy and not the father of my son, trying to remain civil if for no other reason than he was the father of my son. Unprepared where to start or who to start with, I restrained myself from taking Lucas's hand and simply walking out the door. Oddly, I became the meditator between the two and fought to restore what I could between them in the inadequate window of time that I had.

A couple of hours into trying to find a way to mend the broken and rebuild what had progressively been destroyed, we all agreed on the changes that needed to be implemented, which included Lucas and me spending extended time together. One of the chief complaints was Simone's reprehensible chastising and demeaning behavior toward Lucas. She'd throw his clothes in the trash if he happened to leave them in the washer or dryer, make him scrub the kitchen floor with a toothbrush if he spilled something on it, and go to bed without eating if he hadn't finished his homework by the time dinner was ready. Those were merely a few of the many injustices that had to stop, and there'd be no grace period bequeathed her. The list compiled was alarming, so much so that I wasn't sure it could possibly be advocated or accomplished with Simone's blessings, but I had no other choice than to trust that Lance would keep his word.

Pulling out of the parking lot after we'd all said goodbye, I mentally surveyed the list of the things I had to check off in order to keep my side of the agreement, which included transmitting the modification paperwork to the school. As easy as I thought rectifying that should be, a snag that I did not anticipate came up in my strategy. After faxing the forms, it was brought to my attention that there were no signatures on the paperwork. How did I have a copy of a legal document with no signatures on it? The school could not accept legal documentation without certified signatures. Now I had to approach Lance and solicit him to initiate and complete the process all over again. I anxiously made the call informing him of the constraints upon me and that the matter needed to be resolved to avoid additional obstacles. He argued repeatedly that he had taken care of it, and I repeatedly argued that he had not. Giving in if for no other reason than to shut me up, he said he would check into it.

Soon afterward I received a text from Lance saying I was correct and that he'd submit the signed papers, then provide me an updated copy. I questioned why I wasn't listed on the school's administrative correspondence since he had remained listed when I was primary custodian, and shouldn't be any different for me. I was stunned when he became argumentative, rationalizing that if anything happened to

Lucas there were five other people ahead of me that lived much closer and would be happy to accommodate, including the neighbors. How methodically devised and delightfully convenient that everyone seemed able to get to my son but me.

Indignation began to consume me, and I conveyed that he had better resolve it, or I would. I reminded him that I was already doing everything I could to mollify the strife between him and his son, yet he continued to ambush me with his unnecessary insolence. By the end of the next school day, my name had been added to the school's emergency contact list, and I wasn't in such a desperate need for the signed forms. All I had wanted to accomplish was to be able to get to Lucas if he needed me.

A few days after what I had believed to be a productive and beneficial discussion with Lance and Lucas, I received another phone call from the counselor requesting me to meet with her, informing me that Lucas was in her office and severely distraught. The sickness in my stomach literally went to my brain as I poked it into my supervisor's office to inform him that I was leaving due to some personal matters, briefly explaining the development. I grabbed my purse no longer caring of the contemptuous looks hurled my way, and all but ran out of the building and to my car. As I turned the key in the ignition and anxiously headed to his school, I hit the highway well over the speed limit. I was determined that I would be the one to reach Lucas first this time, and on that particular day I didn't bother to call his father.

Chapter 18

In all the time Lance lived in Plano, he never allowed me to pick the kids up or take them back to his house for visits even if suggested, so I had never seen his house let alone the school Lucas was now enrolled in. Driving up to the school, the building loomed in front of me. Right off the bat, I came to the conclusion that it was a prestigious school by any standard, and those attending belonged to privileged families. I pulled into the parking lot and sat there trying to breathe, reassuring myself that I was ready for anything or anyone, but feeling as if I was going into battle with a tremendous disadvantage.

My uncertainties were all the more amplified once I entered the school's front doors. Its vastness was comparable to walking through a university, and I realized my son existed in a world he had never known before. Regardless of how he'd gotten there, he was in a place filled with opportunities and possibilities that I'd be unable to provide him. What could be so wrong that he didn't want to be a part of this? Why were they calling me and not Lance?

I introduced myself to the front desk administrator and was escorted midway to the counselor's office, where I was received by the counselor with a partial smile that said there was no time for chatter. Once inside her office, she cut to the brunt of her concerns before she even closed the door behind us…and the information began to flow. Articulate and direct in her choice of words, she was obviously an extremely bright young woman, and the pictures on the credenza behind her reflected that she was also a mom. It gave me comfort to know that Lucas had been able to confide in someone that had children and a caring heart. Funny thing however, there was something that unnervingly reminded me of Simone. I wondered if he had noticed that himself.

For well over an hour she elaborated on the details of Lucas's frequent visits to her office the past nine months, concluding with what she had alluded to over the phone about his current stresses and conflicts. I'm not certain how I came across to her, but she carefully scrutinized me before interposing her question regarding the degree of my awareness about the situation. The distressing fact was that I had observed that there was something different about him, but unable to put my finger on it. I had been presumptuous in thinking he simply didn't like to visit me, not having a room of his own and being cramped in my infinitesimal living quarters in comparison to an expansive house with his own bedroom.

On top of the uncomfortable adjustments of living with his father, he no longer had friends that lived nearby when he came to visit, which I assumed made it awkward and boring for a teenage boy to be stuck hanging out with this mom. There had been so many wrongful conclusions that I'd established…why had I not seen it in his eyes or detected the turmoil he was suffering? How had a mother that once lived and breathed her children miss what was so astoundingly flagrant in looking back? Yet I had missed it, and missed it for some time it would seem.

The custody of our son was a bone of contention coming to a head, and I felt the need to elaborate on the unnerving incidents that had taken place. I later assessed that the counselor had undoubtedly heard the same details from Lucas, and my input was old news. But she listened without interrupting and seemed empathetic and supportive--of her student. This was not about choosing sides with parents: her alliance and concern was for my son and my son only, and she felt with certainty that prompt and aggressive actions needed to occur. I did not miss a thing in her eyes as she looked directly into mine…I could see it all. I wished that I could reassure her that everything was going to be fine, and assure myself at the same time. The sickness in my stomach was much worse than it had been earlier, but the sensation in my heart was what made me want to throw up. How could I fix this for my child and help him know it would all be okay, that *he* would be ok?

I hadn't mentioned to Lucas that I had met with anyone at his school or knew of his ongoing struggles. I wanted to keep the counselor's intercession private for the meantime so that he wouldn't recoil from her as well. As timing would have it, during the interim of his next visits with me I actually began getting text messages from Lucas that his stomach and head were hurting, each text message crying out for relief from his anguish. I was torn between wanting to run and take him from his father, and feeling it ultimately beneficial for him to reconcile with his dad. I didn't want him to practice the habit of making his first choice picking up and leaving whenever things weren't easy or going the way he fancied. However, when I received the call from his counselor informing me that she was requesting both Lance and I come in together, I had doubts that working it out with his father wasn't an option that would deliver the instantaneous results needed.

I was the first to arrive in her office and quick to observe the resolve and determination in her eyes that wasn't there the last time we had met. She briskly informed me that although she had called Lance and me both in, she hadn't mentioned to him that I would be included in the conference for fear he would not attend. She had purposely brought me in beforehand to acquaint me with the details of her agenda. As I took the seat provided, she summarized in one sentence the agenda and purpose for our meeting: Lucas wanted to live with me again. Although he loved his dad and did not want to upset him or disappoint him in any way, he could no longer handle the distress he was struggling to manage. The counselor was going to help him do what she felt would be in his best interest. She was going to help Lucas return back home with me.

Leaving me alone in her office while she went to the receptionist desk to greet Lance, I sat staring out the window at the school's parking lot, lost in my thoughts from the assorted emotions that inundated my mind. I became aware that Lance had arrived and was in the process of parking his car, observing him as he got out and removed a briefcase that looked like a piece of luggage he was about to load onto a plane.

He paused, then turned and headed to the car once more, placed the briefcase into the back seat, shut the door, and turned as if he'd resolved the quandary and the briefcase would stay. Not even two steps from the car, I watched him turn to open the door again and retrieve the briefcase before decisively heading into the building.

As I watched him, I felt a tug at my heart. I sensed that he knew what could happen, and was apprehensively more circumspect after having already lost his son once, years before. Even though I had moved around the corner from the home we had all shared as a family when we initially divorced, it might as well have been hundreds of miles. Omitting the tactics in which Lance had managed to get Lucas back, in his mind his son was home. Lance did not want to fail, and I could tell he felt as though he may have already done so. He looked as tired and drained as I shockingly felt right then, and wiping away my tears I remember saying to myself, "He doesn't even know what's coming." And for some reason…I thought I did.

***

Lance walked into her office and didn't fully recover from the surprise of me sitting there as speedily as he wanted. I had no doubt that in that brief moment, he anticipated some kind of conspiracy was awaiting him. Feeling the need to defend myself the first thing that came to mind and out of my mouth was, "I didn't know anything about this." The look he sent my way implied, "Do you think I am going to believe that?" mixed with, "If I could get away with killing you right now, I would." Frankly, all the way through the rest of the discussion he seemed to be calculating how he could do it and manage to get away with it.

The counselor began to speak profoundly and forcefully to Lance periodically looking my way, but the message was directed to Lance. The same story began to unfold that she had shared with me, and it ended on the same note: Lucas wanted to live with his mom. No matter how much time and effort he had spent the last nine months trying to work it out, to make his father happy, Lucas was definitely not okay, and we needed to be aggressive in implementing a resolution. She sent for Lucas so that he too could be a part of the meeting, and I had the urge to get up and run to find him so that I could tell him that he didn't need to be afraid. However I was afraid for him, afraid for me, and at the moment just as afraid for Lance.

When Lucas walked into the room, he looked unmistakably broken and as if he had aged twenty years overnight. His forehead and eyes held the lines and wrinkles from worry, hurt, and concern that typically took a lifetime of experience to acquire. His eyes conveyed immense stress and bewilderment, and I felt my own eyes begin to fill with tears and my throat contract as if being strangled, scarcely able to breathe. I looked at my son with endearing love and support, wishing I could whisk him home without further ado. His counselor instructed him to take a seat and then nodded in his direction, indicating that it was now his turn to speak and express what he wanted. I watched my son sitting angst-ridden before us, crying remorsefully as he attempted to convey those feelings to everyone, but most especially to his father.

The response he received from Lance was cold and acrimonious, his face exhibiting nothing but the guise of steel as he refrained from looking or speaking to our son. The oppression my son was combatting crushed me, and I felt protectively compelled to nudge his father and whisper underneath my breath, "Give him a hug!" with hopes he would comply.

At the touch of my elbowing he turned to send me a piercing stare, and I flinched at the darkness in his eyes, convinced that he had most likely decided how he would get rid of me: it was strangulation, and he was no longer concerned if he got caught doing it! Unresponsive to my appeal, he seemed only to recede even further from offering any degree of empathy.

When Lucas had finished expressing his feelings and could no longer go on, the counselor spoke up, requesting that Lance comply with Lucas's wishes and permit him to leave with me. Lance's quick-thinking response was that Lucas did not have a change of clothes with him for school the next day. Unruffled by his guileful rebuff, the levelheaded counselor turned toward me in contemplation; "You can wash his clothes for tomorrow until he can get extra clothes picked up…" It really wasn't an inquiry but a factual affirmation. My reply was, "Yes, of course! We can do whatever it takes."

The next rejoinder from Lance was intentionally and rancorously aimed at the counselor, not once looking my way as he spoke. "He has school tomorrow, and I don't want to disrupt school." The counselor then aimed her words specifically at me with absolute determination. "You can bring him to school and pick him up until he gets his transfer, right?" Because Lucas was scheduled to be with me that weekend and it was a holiday weekend, he would not have to be at school that Monday. Since it was already Thursday, having to get him to and from school only one day made it feasible for my schedule without creating complications at work.

Evidently she felt the arrangement necessary, and was avidly pursuing whatever measures to facilitate the process. I could not decide whether her insistence to have Lucas leave with me was out of her concern for him, or because she suspected a do-or-die situation as the likely consequence of Lance's defiant stance. She stood up from her chair as if affirming that our meeting was over and all the decisions satisfactorily agreed to, instructing Lucas to finish his last class before going home with me. I stood to leave her office along with Lance, turning to ask him if he would like to talk things over before leaving.

I should have known better; he was good at talking but not so much at listening, and it was apparent that he had no intention of listening to what I had to say this time. Yes, the meeting was definitely over, but his next statement gripped me and I knew what he was saying implied much more than his actual words. "No, I can't talk right now. I have to let my family know what's going on and take care of some things!" Without a goodbye, looking in anyone's direction or even pretending to be polite, he walked out the counselor's office door. I looked at the back of his head as he left, and turned utterly bewildered to ask the counselor, "You know what that means don't you?" With a foreboding look she curtly replied, "Yes, that means you're gonna need to get *your* ducks in a row. Fast!"

I have found that timing in life really is everything. I had approximately an hour before school was out and with no time to waste, I anxiously contacted my attorney. I had not spoken with him since losing custody to Lance, and while that outcome was ascetically unsuccessful, I was counting on him to counter with a win this time. A part of me had blamed the incident on him for recommending I take Lance back to court for an incremental child support increase in the first place. Nonetheless, what seemed important right now was the fact that he had history with the originating custody specifics, and so I fervently began dialing his number.

His assistant answered, informing me that he was on vacation and couldn't be reached. How could anyone in the world be on vacation right now? And how was I going to contact him? This was of unparalleled importance and nothing short of an emergency, to say the least! I figured she could hear my panic and frustration, but continued informing me that she was unable to reach him as if my emotions were a minor thing. She *could not* reach him, or *would not* reach him? I now had to advance to 'plan B', and it occurred to me that I did not have a 'plan B'. Unconcerned with who was nearby, I began calling friends in the middle of the school lobby to track down an available attorney.

I consider myself to have many friends, and out of the several I called that afternoon only one had the name of an attorney they could recommend for a custody case. I called the number, and explained the urgency of my request with hopes that this time it would get me somewhere. The attorney I'd been referred to wasn't available during the timeframe I needed, therefore the receptionist directed me to a junior partner who would be able to assist. After speaking briefly with him, he transferred me back to his assistant to schedule an appointment that would require both of us to attend. Lucas wouldn't have a problem coming with me the upcoming holiday Monday, so the appointment was scheduled for that day. I heard the school bell ring shortly afterward and stood at the door where Lucas had left me earlier to wait for him. It seemed like the past few hours had lasted for days as mixed feelings clouded my head. And then I became aware that I no longer had a headache.

The drive to Richland Hills from Plano took a good hour, and the entire way my son talked of nothing but what had happened in the recent months. He candidly shared the elements regarding the onset of his visits to the school counselor, entrusting me with intricate details of how he had escaped from his troubles and heartache with drugs. He divulged how one particular night he'd almost drowned after taking a tainted dose of drugs, which had thankfully scared him enough to steer clear from ever using drugs again. In its place he had taken up smoking and drinking, and his school grades had spiraled downward. I was angry and saddened, and to some degree I was in disbelief. But everything that he offered up made me even more thankful that he was sitting beside me, and that we were heading home together. Though his eyes looked swollen and tired, I was beginning to detect the thankfulness in his voice that he too, was feeling that moment.

He seemed entirely focused on permanently moving back in with me, and unwavering on his stance not to live with his Dad. There were lots of questions he wanted to discuss, the main one seemed to be how soon he could start school and where we would move. I explained that I was currently in Ft. Worth outside the Richland Hills city limits, and since there was not adequate room for us both to live there we would need to locate a larger place and in the Richland Hills school district. That would enable him to return to the school he had previously attended and be near familiar people and places.

I was aware that my son needed this transition to go as smoothly as possible, and I would have to move fast and furiously to make that happen. We needed to locate a place that would be a home and provide a healthy environment for him, so that when the judge inquired about his living arrangements I could provide substantial evidence supporting the move as favorable. That would validate that there wasn't any reason Lucas shouldn't be permitted to live where he wanted to live, since the courts had allowed him to make that decision once before.

Chapter 19

Lucas was as excited and anxious as I was about relocating back with me, and his eagerness was even greater when I told him he could help select the place we would live. Calling various apartment locators to assist in our search, we were steered toward several selective residential prospects. We ultimately located a townhome on the outskirts of Richland Hills but within the Richland Hills school district, and this would enable Lucas to take the bus to and from school. The first floor of the townhome had a bright kitchen, a half bath and good size living room with windows that extended floor to ceiling and overlooked a river and golf course. The upstairs had two bedrooms and two full baths with lots of extra storage.

It seemed to be a perfect setup for us, and my son's enthusiasm made me smile with pure joy. Not only did he seem enthusiastic about the townhome, he seemed especially eager to fish in the river, to have a swimming pool, a workout facility and a clubhouse where he and his friends could hang out. My goal from the beginning of this nightmare had been to make sure that he was happy, that he felt safe, and able to put the previous year behind him in any way possible.

Saturday and Sunday uneventfully came and went. It was wonderful that I didn't have to watch my son leaving for the first time in a long time. Even though a portion of our time was spent looking for a place to live and finagling all the details, we'd enjoyed a great weekend together. I hadn't experienced such contentment since he and Rylee had moved to Plano, and I was grateful that we would also have the day together after our meeting with the attorney! And as we drove into Dallas for our appointment that Monday, I wondered how Lucas would communicate to the attorney what he had already communicated with me.

All the way into Dallas we were filled with excitement and hope, but as we entered the elevator he clearly began to grow uneasy. I sensed his feelings had given way to conflicting emotions, and he was deep in thought about the path on which he was about to embark. As we rode the elevator up to the tenth floor, neither one of us spoke the entire way. I found my breath catching, nervously holding onto the belief that a sophisticated Dallas attorney was adequately equipped with the necessary knowledge to triumph over a custody battle, hands down. There was simply no way he would be unsuccessful in winning our case!

Unfortunately, when he came into the conference room where we had been escorted to wait for him, I couldn't really settle on my first impression. It wasn't that it was a bad first impression, but it wasn't exactly what I'd envisioned a Dallas attorney would resemble. He was a sizeable man, and his shirt looked as though he'd attempted at tucking it in, but he had done so in such a hurry that he hadn't altogether accomplished the task. His hair looked like he had just come in out of the wind, and he had brushed his hands through it to brush it from his eyes.

He shook my hand and without delay turned to shake Lucas's, sitting down in the chair across from us as he began his inquisition. Lucas expounded on the details in his own words and from his own perspective. I watched as the attorney took notes, and listened as if it was the first time I had heard the story. He was doing a phenomenal job of recounting everything, and I felt immensely proud and impressed knowing that I could not have delivered equivalent justice to his story of events as they unfolded.

Lucas finished and leaned back in his chair with nothing further to say, both of us waiting for the attorney to direct us to the shortest, quickest, and least costly way to get the matter resolved. Instead, the attorney looked my way and informed me matter-of-factly that he had never presided over a custody case. Red flag! I had no time to respond, as he began directing his next set of enquiries at me. "Is Lucas going to remain with you until after the hearing?" Yes. "Do you know if the agreement that was signed a week ago has been submitted for sure or not?" I replied I was not sure...and to myself questioned the importance. He scrawled notes, promised that he would research and follow up, requested a check for his retainer fee, and the appointment was over and we were out the door. Though I couldn't pinpoint it, the meeting hadn't come across as positive or hopeful as anticipated, and we left feeling more deflated than elated.

If you have ever driven in a large city, it really does take a skillful amount of knowing what to do and when to do it. A text message came across my phone and assuming it was the attorney with something he additionally needed, I made the mistake of reading it while driving down the highway going sixty-five miles an hour. It read; "Return Lucas home today, or you will be served with contempt of court and be subject to jail." I was thankful there was an off ramp ahead, and I exited going about ninety, knowing I had to pull over or I would end up killing both of us and possibly others.

As soon as the car came to a halt, I began dialing the number of the attorney and conveyed to his assistant that it was an emergency. Even with everything that was going on, somewhere amongst my scattered thoughts I was reflecting how I had handed him a substantial amount of money less than thirty minutes ago, and that he'd dang well better take my call!

Upon hearing his voice, I explained the text message I'd received and inquired what I needed to do or should do. He advised me to remain calm and cool, and internally questioned whether he was conversant with what he was doing or conscious of the atrocious feud he had gotten himself into. He informed me he would place the call to the Tarrant County Family Court Services and investigate if Lance had actually resubmitted the signed modification forms or not. As the conversation had continued between us, I noticed Lucas's facial expressions begin to emulate what I was feeling. I bravely flashed my son a reassuring smile, skeptical I was not fooling him in the least.

I had waited until after speaking with the attorney to reply to Lance, not certain if I was supposed to respond to him or not, and with one more reassuring glance in Lucas's direction, I began my text message: "What do you mean? We agreed that Lucas was to stay with me!" His rapid text back to me was filled with control and demand: "Yes, for the weekend. It was your weekend, but now you need to bring him home, or I will have you arrested!" As I read the words he had sent, it was as though I'd been hit in the gut and couldn't breathe, yet breathing was all that I was doing, and I was on the verge of hyperventilating right there on the side of the road.

Having heard the conversation with the attorney and seeing my expression to the text message, Lucas understood exactly what was going on. When I looked across the seat the terror visible across his entire face appalled me. Calm...I had to remain calm. I put the car into drive and cautiously merged onto the highway, afraid to reveal anything further. And though words were not spoken, it was apparent what had just transpired. His father had found a way to kill me and get away with it after all, and it was apparent that he did not give a damn what that meant for anyone.

***

I recalled several years before when Simone first became involved in our family. Lance and Simone were living together at the time but not engaged, and she had called me at work requesting to pick Rylee and Lucas up from daycare a little earlier than usual. It had been a part of their routine to say goodbye to me before heading to their dads for a visit, making it an easier transition when they went with their father for any extended period of time. It was a comfort to them and me to maintain that ritual before they left. They would leave on the Thursday of his scheduled visitations and return the Monday afterward. That arrangement was not in the divorce decree, but Lance and I had both felt it in the best interest of the kids to extend their visitations, thus allowing Lance to be intricately involved in their lives and daily routines. Therefore, when I received a call from Simone requesting she pick them up prior to our standard schedule my immediate question was, "Is anything wrong?"

At the time the kids were not quite six and two and I was steadfast in keeping with the routine, but I also wanted to confirm that an emergency had not arisen which would require a change in schedule without advance notice. Her reply to my question was short and abrasive. "No, nothing is wrong. I simply need to pick the kids up." I replied back, "I don't mind at all, if you would give me time to run home and let them know what is going on. Half an hour, tops."

Her response took me by surprise. "Why is that necessary? I am simply picking them up from daycare early!" I heard her condescending tone and took a deep breath before calmly responding to her. "First off, they are not at the daycare, they are at home with my grandmother who is in town for the month. I don't have a problem with you picking them up Simone, but I would appreciate the time to follow through with the established routine, especially since you are picking them up earlier than scheduled." I was about to imply that I would try to make it sooner, but heard a click on the other end of the phone. Really? Had she just hung up on me?

In that split second I made the calculated decision that it would be wise for me to call Lance and explain what had transpired, before he heard it from her. That way, he would know there wasn't an issue with Simone picking up the kids earlier than usual, and provide me the opportunity to discuss the particulars behind the misunderstanding. I called his cellphone twice and did not get an answer, but figured he'd call me as soon as he heard my message.

Perhaps trying to get my goat Simone called me again, and still unable to resolve anything she merely provoked more of the same insolent banter between us. By that time I could have been home and said goodbye to Rylee and Lucas at least three or four times! My frustration toward her intensified the longer she was flippant to me and wouldn't compromise, so I replied as calmly and politely as I could, "Look, since this has become such an issue, I'd prefer to discuss the itinerary with Lance."

As soon as I told her I wanted to speak with Lance, she quipped in a snide tone that he was not in town and would not be home until the following week! My thoughts were unrestrained. Where was he? Why had he not corresponded with me before leaving? Why was she picking up the kids if he wasn't going to be in town for the weekend? But my solitary, inquisitive remark was "Where is he?" For all I knew, she had hit him over the head, hidden his body, and now wanted to take my children and do the same.

I managed to remain cool and collected, until her next inimical response. "You don't need to know where he is, Amber! What difference does it make?" My list was short and to the point. "First off, Simone, my name is *Autumn*. Secondly, because he is the father of my children it is my right to know how to reach him, particularly when it concerns our children."

I had respectfully practiced making a point of staying at a distance from Lance, and anyone he was in a relationship with. If at all possible, I made certain the kids called him concerning any minor communications required, and schedules pertaining to school, doctor visits, etc., were placed into their weekend suitcases. But the respect couldn't be one-sided, and at present, it was absolutely lop-sided as far as I was concerned.

When I heard the sound of another click, my first instinct was to drive over to the house and shake her until her teeth fell out, and afterward shove that dang phone where the sun didn't shine! That was all I could tolerate, and I'd had enough! I called my grandmother to let her know that if anyone came to the door she shouldn't open it, briefly explaining what had occurred. Later that afternoon my grandmother would inform me that she did come by the house, tenaciously banging on the door for several minutes before leaving.

The majority of the day had come and gone without a resolution, and I had yet to hear from Lance. I was beginning to believe he must be dead somewhere and decided to stop by the house to investigate what was going on. Maybe if Simone and I spoke in person, it would circumvent the worsening of any further dialogue. I pulled in the driveway where Lance habitually parked, leaving the other side accessible whenever she arrived. The garage door opened just as I was getting out of my car, and as she pulled in I began walking in to greet her.

"Hi, Simone! I thought it might be good for us to talk and explain my concerns of not knowing where Lance is." She turned to me with a look that caused me to envision running for my life, and had me convinced that she had indeed buried Lance in the backyard. I physically took a step backwards before she began grinding her teeth and speaking through them. "We will *not* be a tribe like you hope we will be! Lance does not want to have anything to do with you, he's forced to tolerate you for the sake of the kids, so leave before I call the police!" It seemed there was nothing else to discuss, and she turned to go into the house.

The house had remained in both Lance's and my name and therefore, my logical deduction was that at the moment it was as much my house as hers. With the intent to prove that she couldn't intimidate me or make me leave against my will, I sat down on a cooler inside the garage speculating where the father of my children was or why I had not heard from him all day. In the middle of my thoughts, I was spooked hearing the door to the house unexpectedly open, and without uttering a word Simone firmly hit the garage door button to close it. For a moment I was imagining that not only would they find Lance buried in the backyard, but also find me dead in the garage from lack of air when they finally opened it! It took me a good five minutes before common sense kicked in and I realized that if I just pushed the same button that closed the garage door in the first place, it would reopen.

Sitting inside it with the door now open, I noticed a police car slowly pulling into a driveway down the street. At least if I needed reinforcement while I was haggling with Simone, they would be in close proximity! Then I watched as the police car turned onto the street and began driving in the direction of the house, when it suddenly registered that they were approaching the house. Pulling up at the curb, two women in uniform made their way toward the garage as Simone opened the front door, closely observing the scene unfold from inside. One officer stood behind the other, as I was advised that I had to evacuate the premises or be arrested, however if I chose to vacate

215

without further dispute, the incident would be reported merely as a domestic disturbance.

I got into my car to show that I would respectfully comply with their request, explaining that I was the ex-wife, whose name remained on the mortgage. Still not impressing them with my reasoning, I began defending my predicament to them, explaining my bewilderment over Rylee, Lucas and the father of my children, finishing on a faint sob. As I wiped my tears and my nose and tried to compose myself, one of the police officers moved closer to my car door, leaned in, and directed her next sentence to me underneath her breath: "There would have been nothing she could do if you had parked across the street and not in the driveway." I smiled my acknowledgment through the tears spilling onto my cheeks before backing out onto the street, watching Simone's look of satisfaction as I pulled onto the road. If she wanted war, she now had one!

Praying I would reach him this time I rushed home to call Lance, but was immediately connected to his voicemail. Discounting that I loathed the mere thought of any interaction with Simone but virtually frantic with concern, I begrudgingly put aside the latest incident and contacted her. To my chagrin, she was no longer answering my calls and the most rational and sensible thing left to do was leave Lance a message. Hopefully he would return my call with an explanation that would clarify what the hell was going on and end this entire charade.

I had to get a result of some kind so I became the monstrous, ex-wife I generally scorned and dialed the house to leave a message on the answering machine: "Lance, I have attempted to contact you all day and have been unsuccessful in reaching you. Your girlfriend has tried to put me in jail because I requested to know where you were since you didn't communicate to me that you wanted *her* to pick the kids up from daycare, or to get them earlier than typically scheduled. It is your weekend visitation, and I do not know where you are or how to reach you! If I have not heard from you by 11:00 this evening, you will be in breach of contract and contempt of court and the next phone call will be from my attorney to yours!"

Leaving the message on the answering machine ensured me that Simone would hear it and realize that I meant business. I hung up and dialed Lance's cell to leave the same assertive message, convinced that if he did not call me back after that, he was dead and buried for sure.

My phone rang soon afterward, and the moment I answered Lance ruthlessly began yelling and screaming at me. He sounded frantic himself as he told me that Simone was hysterical over my message and asking me in a pompous manner what the hell was going on. I replied yelling at the top of my own lungs! "She *should* be hysterical! The nerve of her trying to pick our kids up and not telling me where you are when I asked!" I then began to relay the story of the day's calamity.

My grandmother heard, my kids heard, and I was reasonably positive the neighbors heard my entire side of the conversation. Nonetheless, I hoped that they both got my message loud and clear. It would become one of many detrimental battles fought between us, and though I relentlessly pressed the concept of joint parenting, Simone would eventually be proven right. We would never be a "tribe"--for we would barely be a family.

Breach of contract...indeed. I sat beside my son in the car speculating just how long Lance had waited to repeat those same words to me. I'd now substantiated that the "ducks in a row" he had been talking about were all lined up.

The court would not release any information to my attorney, and he called requesting I contact them at once. I held my breath as I called the courthouse, and after several exchanges with various people I was eventually informed that Lance had submitted the signed modification papers, the same afternoon we were called into the school. The very day Lucas had bared his heart and soul, begging his dad to understand that his attempt to move back home with his mom was nothing personal against him. But Lance had taken it very personally, and he was making sure that what he wanted was going to happen one way or another.

***

Psalm 34:18 (NIV)

*"The Lord is close to the brokenhearted and saves those who
are crushed in spirit."*

Not only are there moments that change who we are or who we
will become, there are moments in our lives that we know we will never
forget where we were when it happened. Trying to escape the afternoon
sun shining down on us Lucas and I sat in the car underneath a tree
in the parking lot where I worked, as the shadows from the tree cast
a gloomy gray inside the car. I can still recall the sky's incredible hues
all blending with subtle traces of brilliant oranges and muted touches
of reds and yellows, the fluffy white clouds a contrast to the palette of
colors. The air was a little on the cool side, as October often is, and
if you hadn't known it was autumn you would have thought it would
soon be spring.

I remember everything because it was one of those moments I
recognized would irrefutably change both me and my son, and I knew
it as soon as I called my attorney to relay the same information the court
had confirmed. Now submitted, the modification form was a binding
and legal contract by the court of law, and would temporarily put a
kink in things. If I didn't comply with the court order, he could have
me placed in jail, therefore losing any chance of ever getting custody
of Lucas again. I had no choice but to return him to his dad's. In my
moment of vexation and strife, I repeated what the attorney had just said
as if his reply wasn't a legitimate response or I had misunderstood him.

I realized Lucas had overheard the conversation when I heard his
heart-wrenching response before I saw his reaction. I turned toward
him as he grabbed his head and slumped into the car seat, shamelessly
crying out like a man on death row. "No! Don't make me go back! You
can't make me go back there, Mom. Please, please..." The look in his
eyes scared me, and yet they were a reflection of my own desperation!

The attorney was as dismayed over the ordeal as much as anyone,
and began apologizing upon hearing the same devastation from my
son. I couldn't help but echo the same thing Lucas was saying. "I can't

take him back, *please* don't make me! There must be something we can do!" No amount of praying, fighting, crying, or begging was going to change the outcome. Lance would not have had to kill me if he hadn't already pretty much done so, but I would have gladly given up my life at that moment if it would impede my son from going someplace he'd rather die himself than return.

I began the drive to Plano, both of us crying and not even trying to hide the fact that we were. I reassured him it would not be too long before he would be home where he wanted to be, but we had to be courageous in the meantime. It was growing dark and much colder, but there was no darkness compared to that in my heart, and there was no cold like the cold inside my soul. I was telling my son to be strong, and I wasn't sure at that instant I could accomplish doing it myself.

For the weeks that followed I would do what I could to communicate with Lucas in-between his visitations, but from the time I had taken him back to his dad's, he seemed to be spiraling downward. I could see the sadness and emptiness in his eyes, could hear the apathy in his voice. Lance now conformed to the designated visitations, but whenever Lucas was there it was hard for both of us, especially on the cusp of his departure. I had already signed a contract on the townhome we had picked and moved into it in preparation for him to live with me, but without him there it didn't feel like home, merely a reminder that Lucas was not living with me but in Plano with Lance and Simone.

With no other option, I had already spoken with the property owner concerning the issue of unavoidably breaking my lease. Even though I had only lived there shy of two months, I could no longer afford to live there due to temporary hardships. I would have to seek a less expensive place, proportionate to my budget. My credit was already damaged from breaking my previous lease by a few months, so I was trying to do whatever I could to sidestep any collateral damage. The amount they wanted in order for me to break the lease could easily have made a down payment on a small house, and if I could have paid that amount I would not have had the need to break the lease in the first place! Troubles seemed to be multiplying by the day, and my options dwindling before me.

I was in trouble and losing focus as I began succumbing to the perils of what I believed was now my hell on earth. I was unable to sleep, eat, and had absolutely no inclination to be with anyone or talk to anyone. After work I would drive around, sometimes all the way to Plano just to be near Lucas. I didn't want to be in the townhome without him, returning from my drives late into the night for the mere sake of going directly to bed. The view that once looked inviting and comforting to me now appeared ominous.

The stories Lucas had told me before all of this had taken place were all I could think about. What must it be like for him at that house *now*? I could feel the anguish he must be experiencing every moment that I could not bring him home with me. He had counted on the system to protect him: he had counted on me. As resilient as I considered myself, I experienced a weakness that I had never faced before. I now understood how parents took their children and fled, never looking backwards or caring what the law ordained as right or wrong, never caring about repercussions. I could relate to the gut wrenching helplessness they withstood when incapable of safeguarding the emotional and physical wellbeing of their children. I grasped every bit of it, because I had been living all of it, ever since Lucas was returned to his dad's.

Counting on my faith to lift me up for the zillionth time, searching and praying for answers that seemed to elude me, only gave me cause to become bitter as I began retaliating and cursing the very faith that had sustained me throughout my life. I hesitated asking anyone for anything, but at the rate I was going there would need to be an immediate intervention from someone that knew all of that without me having to convey the fact. It seemed just when I no longer had the will to fight, Colin called to tell me he was on his way, intuitively sensing I was at my breaking point and should not be alone. He already knew I had fallen to my knees, and this time I could not muster the strength to stand again.

Colin arrived late on a Friday evening, and together we looked at my options hoping to find a solution that would make me feel I had some inkling of control over my life. We discussed me moving somewhere close to work, perhaps even returning to the previous apartment studio where I'd lived prior to everything happening. He then posed another option he reasoned might be worth keeping in mind: pack up my things and move to Austin with him and his wife, Hannah. I could stay in his daughter Elsa's room, which would allow adequate time for me to rebuild my resources and later provide alternatives that I currently didn't have. But as much as I wanted to run and hide from my troubles, I did not want to run further from my kids, and there were no plans I would consider that didn't involve getting Lucas returned home.

My brother planned to leave on Sunday, and piled boxes of my belongings into his truck that I would not have room for or need once I moved. I no longer had storage because I had closed it and moved everything inside the storage to the attached garage at the townhome. While that had worked perfectly at the time, extra storage was no longer going to be available or a feasible option.

Before leaving that Sunday afternoon, we sat in the living room together both dreading the moment he would have to leave me alone. Looking around the living room I cynically commented that it felt to me as if someone had died there, or that something tragic had taken place. My brother hit at his leg exclaiming, "That is *just* what I was thinking!" That didn't help anything, but at least I knew I wasn't going completely psycho.

I stood watching my brother leave, waiving goodbye until he was gone, and then, taking a slow and steady breath, turned to go back inside. Dusk had fallen, and shadows lay across the backside of the golf course and the riverbed. The night air made me shiver, and I hurriedly shut the door behind me, not knowing where to go or what to do. I had the urge to call out for someone as if someone might be there to answer, as if Lucas might be there. It dawned on me what should have been so transparent to me all along: there had been a death there. It was the death of hopefulness, the death of a family for Lucas and me with new beginnings and anticipated happiness. Yes, there had been a death there, and it felt like mine.

Chapter 20

I actively attempted being as much of Lucas's life as I possibly could, finding ways to be with him as often as I could, but realized it was not enough. I wasn't sure what I was going to do, but painstakingly aware that drastic measures needed to be taken to get us through. When you have broken two leases during a two-month period, it is almost impossible to find someone who will let you sign a lease. My brother was trying to sign or co-sign a lease for me so that I could relinquish my current lease and move to a place I could afford. There were no available properties that seemed inclined to negotiate or overlook my predicament. But things happen for a reason...

Sitting at my desk one day at the office I overheard the conversation of a coworker finding something they needed on an Internet site called Craig's List. It seemed to come to me out of the blue: if I had to move again, and Lucas could not move where I was, why not move to Plano where he was? Maybe I could find a sublease or some type of rental where they would be empathetic of my misfortune and lenient with their policies. It was the end of November by then, and I'd determined a strategy that restored my hope and dissipated my despondent feelings. I began a diligent search for residential listings within my price range, and came across something that seemed doable.

I didn't realize the listing was an apartment locator, but it proved to be the best thing that could have happened. The real-estate agent assisting me was unbeatable, incredibly pinpointing two places that fit both requirements, which was my price range and to be located within the same school district Lucas was attending. I received a call later that very afternoon that a two bedroom had become available, after the person they had been holding it for changed her mind. Additionally, they worked with me concerning the broken leases by accepting a co-signer along with a deposit and the first month's rent. I took it without even looking at it and arranged to sign the paperwork, give them my deposit, and close the deal the following day.

I was about to make Plano my home. It would be well over a hundred miles round trip for work each day, but only the distance of a golf course between where Lucas was living with his dad, and not even two miles from his school. If he needed me, he could get to me by merely walking across the golf course that ran between my new home and Lance's house. I could not have planned it more perfectly if I had tried. If there had been any reservations remaining, they diminished the second I walked into the apartment. Strangely enough, it already felt like home.

It consisted of two bedrooms with two full-size baths, a kitchen and sizable living and dining area. Each room was painted in a warm off white color, and I had chosen a rustic paint for the living room and kitchen. It had several windows alongside the patio and an accessible sidewalk with a couple of trees that provided privacy. It included an attached storage closet, and a separate storage that was almost as big as the garage at the townhome, which meant that I wouldn't have to pay storage fees!

I could afford it, even if it meant deferring my child support on a consistent basis. I could catch-up on the payments at a later time if I should end up having to 'rob Peter to pay Paul' as the saying went, for now getting near my son was all that mattered to me. Being near him would allow him to have a part-time job, go to school, and maintain his friendships without any interruption.

I could not wait to tell him! Better yet, I could not wait for Lance to know that his scheme to eradicate me from my son's life was about to backfire. It had all come together so effortlessly that I knew it was truly a blessing orchestrated by God's hand. I was ecstatic to be making a move now that it was in a constructive direction, and submitted my prayers of thanks that it had come together with no further hassles, concerns, or efforts. Admittedly, I welcomed a blessing or two my way.

By December, I had the movers hired, the lease in hand, and the utilities scheduled for connection. All that was left was to tell Lucas, and I was a bit apprehensive about how he might feel. Partly because I'd recently driven to Plano to watch the school's holiday parade of lights Lucas was participating in, and we'd planned on meeting up at some point. That point never came. I made it to the parade, but never managed to locate Lucas. Standing alone in the midst of families smiling and waving as the floats passed by triggered hurt feelings and uncertainty that I had made the right decision to attend the parade, and mulling over the fact that I'd been better off staying at home. Though I called and texted Lucas unceasingly throughout the evening, I never saw or heard from him. Once the final float disappeared and almost everyone had departed I left as well, cautious not to speculate what had happened, my mind nonetheless filled with irrepressible conclusions. Did he not have his phone? Had something happened and he wasn't even there? Did he not want to see me?

When we finally spoke the next day I was a little aggravated and a tad peeved, questioning why he hadn't responded to my text or phone calls. He explained that the students were not allowed to have their cell phones with them and he had left his behind, but never saw a message or a missed phone call from me. He seemed to doubt I had really been there, questioning how I could not find him at the school's float if I was there. I wanted to question how it was that he had never received my texts or phone calls? Due to his lack of appreciation for me being there and his trivializing attitude, my first notion was that things had improved with his dad and he'd perhaps changed his mind about moving back with me. That's why I was second-guessing my strategy to move to Plano, or surprising him with the news.

What if the sacrifices it would take to do it didn't mean as much to him to justify those sacrifices? What if he didn't want me to live in Plano or wanted to stay with his Dad after all, but feared telling me? Even though I believed the latter couldn't possibly be true my mind gave way to hesitation, but I pushed aside my negativity and concentrated on the two prized gifts that I anticipated sharing with Lucas during Christmas. I had nothing to lose.

Even though I couldn't afford them, I purchased two tickets to the Trans-Siberian Orchestra concert, which he had wished to attend their concert for years. I made copies of the new apartments diagram and I put both into his Christmas card, and arranged to take him to lunch on the last Saturday of November. The card inside my purse, I couldn't wait past the time it took for our drink orders to be placed before I leaned forward to unveil my plan. "I have a couple of early Christmas gifts for you Sweetie, and I hope you like them." His face lit up and I was barely able to pull the card from my purse before he grabbed it, eagerly ripping at the envelope.

The tickets fell to the table, and as he picked them up he shouted with delight as he read the concert name, his second gift unnoticed. With a serene smile I pointed to it, "Lucas, there's something else in there for you." I had not seen him filled with such joy in so long that it literally brought tears to my eyes. Maybe I should have saved the other gift, but he was holding it in his hand and looking at it like he wasn't sure what he was looking at, let alone what it inferred. I gathered by his expression that he was questioning why on earth would I give him a piece of paper with a floor plan? He didn't seem to fully comprehend what was going on, so I took a deep breath and commenced explaining my well rehearsed plan, and that he was holding what would soon be our new home when he came over to stay. He would have his own room and even his own bathroom, right down the street from his dad's!

At long last I could see the excitement flash across he face when he finally understood what I was attempting to tell him! His mother was going to move to Plano and would be near him. The tears came to his eyes, and I was not sure whether he was happy, scared, or sad, but his next words made me exhale deeply and gratefully. "Can we go see it now?" followed by "When are you moving? Can I stay over?" We both laughed and could not even finish our lunch, asking the waitress for our ticket so that I could take him to check it out it and show him how close I would be if he needed me--for anything, for any reason.

He absolutely loved it, and ran throughout the apartment acting as if he was six years old! He loved his room, he loved his bathroom, and when he'd finished checking everything with a fine-toothed comb he gleefully asked me to drive to and from the school and Lance's to check the distances. Dropping him off at his dad's afterward, he was genuinely smiling and looked as if the weight of the world had already been lifted off his sunken shoulders. I knew I had done the right thing, no matter what happened in the end.

Though both of us were delighted about my move to Plano I wasn't enthusiastic toward sharing the news with Lance, or even Rylee. Lance would presume I was doing it to infringe upon his parental rights, while Rylee would feel I had deserted her and chosen sides. I discussed the matter with Lucas, and we both agreed that neither of us would share the news with *anyone* until it was closer to the moving date. A part of me could hardly wait, but a part of me seemed reserved in what the future was going to render. The night of the concert I coerced Lance into meeting me at their local Target to drop Lucas off, explaining that Plano was on the way to the concert and therefore the most logical and practical arrangement.

It wasn't until afterward that evening when Lance met me to pick Lucas up, that I informed him I had rented a place in Plano and would be moving nearby. I watched his response closely as he valiantly tried feigning his endorsement of the news. But I knew him all too well, and Lucas later shared an entirely different version of Lance's feelings once they got home that evening, which was quite contradictory to his reaction in the parking lot. I must admit I enjoyed that version over the one displayed.

As virtually the entire world was celebrating 'out with the old and in with the new' on New Years Eve, I was packing and moving as much as I could before the movers came the next day. I made the move alone, feeling that I couldn't possibly solicit the help of friends when the majority of them had assisted in helping me move twice, if not a third time, in a matter of months. I worked tirelessly on the apartment for the next three days to complete the unpacking, decorating and grocery shopping, lastly removing all remnants of the move with hopes of removing remnants of the past few disappointing months.

On my next scheduled visitation weekend, I arranged to get Lucas from school and take him home with me. From that weekend on, we began a ritual. Each Thursday of the week I would get him overnight, feed him breakfast on Friday morning, then take him to Lance's house so that he could catch a much later scheduled school bus from there. My drive from that point typically took, at minimum, an hour to work, and even longer to get home in the evenings. Major road construction often added time to my drive wherever I was going or whatever day I was going. What didn't take a lengthy amount of time was the drive to and from Lucas's school, his dad's or his friends, avoiding any disruptions to his activities just as I'd intended.

Disappointingly, my devotion to be near my son and spend time with him was importunately manipulated into what I could do for him and his friends, instead. In addition to the mileage from driving to and from work each day I was now a taxi driver, the single mom with nothing better to do and thus deemed their on-call chauffeur. I'd take them where they needed or wanted to be, pick them up, get each of them home and then end up at home alone, which was how the bulk of my time was spent throughout the week and weekends.

Lucas's room wasn't getting used as much as I'd intended, since he'd usually end up staying over at his friend's house more weekends than I began to be able to keep track of. Even on the weekends that weren't stipulated visits, he would call to request I accommodate their transportation needs due to the fact that the other parents always managed to become unavailable for the task. After my frustrations had escalated I quizzed Lucas, "Why is it that I am a single parent, and I am the one doing all the chauffeuring for you guys?" His response was to shrug, laugh, and reply, "Oh, Mom, you're the greatest! You know you love it!"

As much as I loved my son, I had the urge to express just how little I was enjoying anything that was happening and to yell at the top of my lungs "No, I don't love this. I don't love that I came here to Plano see you more and be here for you, and yet I see you less and you don't even seem to need me for the reasons I moved here. I don't love that it seems you take advantage of me, making me feel unappreciated, used and unloved!"

But I did not smack my son, nor did I mention to him the way I was feeling. I could not place excessive stress on him inflicted by me, and it was key that nothing should prevent him from feeling the apartment was home away from home, and a haven of comfort. I was contingent upon the fact that with some patience and a little bit of time, inevitably it would all be resolved. I couldn't bring myself to imagine otherwise. This was only the beginning of my new living experience in Plano, and I had a lengthy period of time before the custody trial took place.

I came to the conclusion that I wasn't only stressed, but a tad bit emotional due to the challenging adversities of recent months. I reminded myself not to be shortsighted over temporary snags, and that the main strategy remained true of the original, and that was to be the mother Lucas needed me to be barring custody or not. But I was so focused on making sure he was taken care of, it seemed I had managed to neglect my daughter and her troubles. Evidently, my concerns for moving closer to her brother and further from her were indeed warranted. Living with her step-grandparents Rylee had been allowed to come and go whenever she fancied, and no one ever questioned or seemed to care about her comings or goings.

Regrettably, while focusing entirely on Lucas and trying to make certain he graduated, I let Rylee slip through the cracks. She squandered her own senior school year detached from her family, including me. She was working three part-time jobs, paying her own bills, and barely seeing anyone or doing anything. Living as if she was already an adult and not a carefree teenage girl, she missed out on enjoyable activities that theoretically high school is all about: attending pep rallies and football games, Friday night dates and weekend shopping at the mall with friends.

She was so lost in being independent and grown up her last year of school that so many memories passed her by. So did the time to plan for college. Her Dad did not assist her with gas money, car or health insurance, money for food or any other necessities she incurred. As time passed she began seeing her father less and less, when she needed him most. It would be the beginning of a bitter downfall of their relationship.

Although I was clueless of the falling out she and her father were undergoing at the time, I had become acutely aware of the dissention between her and her brother. The resentment Lucas was targeting at his sister broke my heart above anything else. He was incensed beyond endurance over the "betrayal" of her convincing him to move to Plano to live with their father, then leaving him there after reassuring him that would never happen. Lucas would argue that she had used him to bargain for what she must have allegedly wanted all along and now seemed to have, and he was the one enduring a living nightmare. She should have been there with him as she had promised, but rarely saw or spoke with him, staying away because of the growing hostility between the two. An interminable and troubled estrangement was created between them that seemed only to accelerate instead of dissipate.

She kept her distance from me as much if not more, than anyone else. No matter how persistently I reached out to her in hopes she would respond, she remained emotionally detached. I wasn't sure if the wall she had created was due to the guilt she might be harboring, the disappointment she was experiencing, or the animosity she'd incurred. The live-in arrangement with her step-grandparents only seemed to aid in promoting tension and disharmony within the family, and she was feeling less and less like a part of the family. Fed up with the endless array of conflicts she and a friend moved in together, which provided her with some degree of relief from dealing with Lucas, her father and Simone, and Simone's parents.

Only a few months into her lease, I received a panicked call from Rylee one evening while sitting in my car waiting on Lucas at his friend's house. I was already tired and frustrated from work and had been waiting for him longer than I'd estimated, and adding the fact that dinner had to be cooked before driving him back to Lance's wasn't helping. I was thrilled to see her name come across my phone, and I smiled as I answered in anticipation of hearing her voice. But her usually calm, sweet voice sounded flustered and I instinctively perceived something was dreadfully wrong from her tone. I hadn't even uttered my usual "Hello Sweetheart!" when she began telling me that her roommate had left abruptly, leaving her portion of the bills behind, and questioning what she was going to do now? I became a little panicked myself, since all I currently had was a two-bedroom apartment and barely able take care of her brother and myself. Nonetheless, she was seeking my help and entrusting me to make every effort on her behalf, just as Lucas had.

When you're a mother, you would like to imagine there could never be a day your child wouldn't relish the idea of living with you regardless of their age, especially in a moment of dire necessity. But as an adult, you know that day will predictably happen, because that is the circle of life. So that evening when I suggested to my daughter that she live with me until she got on her feet, her immediate laughter expressed that her feelings were nothing like the night I had tucked her into bed as a little girl. She had looked up at me in innocence and unadulterated love saying, "Mommy, I never want to leave you. I want to live with you forever!"

I had looked into her blue eyes and momentarily wished that she could live with me forever, but smiled a melancholy smile and replied, "That is a lovely thought Sweetheart! But believe it or not, the day will come when you will hate the mere thought of living with me, and laugh whenever you remember this conversation!" It seemed she had discovered that day…and as I was recovering from reminiscing, it hit me that I didn't know what to suggest or how I could help her. She quickly alluded to the fact that she wasn't looking for my problem solving tactics or financial contribution, and already had an idea in mind. As she began telling me, I wasn't sure how to feel or what to think, and she was shrewdly aware of that. I did know one thing, it would probably be the smartest thing she had done since all of this had taken place. Rylee wanted to return to the home she'd grown up in and live with her stepdad.

Before I replied, I took a moment to consider exactly how I wanted to respond to her tentative solution. I found it slightly peculiar that that she had laughed at the notion of moving in with me yet was so keen on the idea of living with Derek. It took short of an instant before I seized some tidbit of insight into my own question. My daughter was convinced that if she chose to move in with me, that would be failure in her eyes. More significantly, she would feel increased guilt being with me while Lucas remained in the abysmal situation she had helped put him in. Not to mention, Lance had threatened that if she moved back with me he would never see or speak to her again, convinced that if she returned, Lucas would follow. Cautious of the unresolved clashes between her and her father, she could not risk completely losing him.

I suspected what my daughter was going to propose even before she asked: she wanted me to call Derek for her and scope out his thoughts of her temporarily moving in with him until she could get on her feet. I was hesitant to get in the middle, not to mention I hated even the forethought of communicating with him. If my calculations were correct, there'd be a 50/50 chance he'd agree to her moving back, and it could go either way. He would either be open and supportive to her living there, or he would feel it best she didn't, explaining every reason under the sun why it wasn't a good option. But this was a pressing matter, and due to my limited resources the only feasible way I could help my daughter was to call him.

In the midst of working out the most strategic angle to submit her proposal to Derek, it dawned on me as to why Rylee sought to live with him; she longed for things to be like they were before all this mess took place. She had rushed into growing up and now wanted someone to be there for her, take care of her, offer guidance and encouragement. And she wanted something familiar and comforting that could fill the emptiness. Sadly, I was apprehensive that her living alone with Derek wouldn't last, and in the end create an even greater void for her. Nevertheless…she had to move, and she didn't have any other pragmatic choice in front of her. I knew I had to make the call, if not that moment, then the next day.

By then Lucas had come out to the car and we finally made it home, and realized as I began cooking dinner that it would be much later than usual for us to eat. I called Lance to ask if there would be a problem with Lucas staying for the evening, explaining that he had returned late from a friend's house and dinner was running behind. As I began talking with Lance, his tone was abrasive and rude as he began questioning why it was necessary he spend the night. He went on to imply that he was doing me a favor to let him be there at all, making innuendoes that implied Lucas would be reprimanded for having me ask if he could stay the night. In the interim of listening to his derogatory comments, Lucas had jumped in front of me grabbing at his head, shaking it profusely as tears filled his eyes. I grew even more frustrated, not sure which one I wanted to address first, my overwrought son or his lunatic father. I began with his father, using the same voice he was now using: yelling. I rambled off all of the things I could think of to put him in his place, reminding him lastly of the impending custody trial and ending by me inquiring if the same condescension and treatment in return appealed to him once I won custody of our son?

His rage coming across the phone was unmistakable, mine equally comparable! He began to threaten having me arrested due to breach of contract, reminding me that I had limited rights and that I would never get Lucas on a permanent basis. Hanging up on him I turned toward the stove and away from my son, knowing he had heard everything, including his father's threats. I was prepared for any anger and resentment that he felt aimed toward his father, but not at me! His own voice began to rise as if panicked, questioning why I had bothered to call Lance in the first place. What was going on? How could a simple request create that amount of grief for everyone? I turned the stove off and moved closer to my son, reaching for his arms to place them by his side, gently shaking him, and directing him to stop behaving in such a way. It reminded me of the day my attorney had relayed to us that he would have to go back to Lance's house. Despondent.

Insistently asking him a second time to tell me why he was becoming so unraveled, he frantically began explaining. I listened in exasperation, trying to comprehend what was going on as he desperately attempted to make me fully aware of the damage it seemed I had caused. Evidently, by calling Lance and implying that Lucas had been at a friend's house and not spending time with me like he had conveyed to his dad, I had instantly destroyed all of the trust and any progress with his father he'd been working toward. With all that had taken place over the prior months, Lance had stated to Lucas that he felt betrayed by him and no longer trusted him. Lucas was doing everything possible to regain that trust.

I countered by questioning why his dad would care or think he had lied because he went to a friend's house from school until I could pick him up after work? How could that lead to his father believing he had lied and cause him to get so suspicious and bad-tempered? It seemed ridiculous to me, and stupefied I stood there not knowing what to say, but knowing what I had to do.

It seemed dinner tonight would consist of crow for me, and dialed Lance to tell him that Lucas would be home as soon as we ate. I also offered that at the last minute I had to work late, which was the reason he'd been with his friends. I could only hope that my explanation would calm them both and minimize the damage my son was convinced I might have caused and avert any accusations when he got home. By the time I took Lucas back that evening I was completely bewildered, and watching him until he got inside the house merely magnified the regret created by the deep sorrow in my heart.

The next day I called Derek as promised Rylee the night before, and I could tell he was surprised to hear from me. And when I mentioned Rylee wanting to move back with him, he seemed to have mixed emotions and his own concerns about her proposal. He did not mind her moving back, but speculated that she had been on her own for too long and wouldn't adhere to any boundaries het set for her. Derek was always about boundaries and rules for the kids, and conveyed that he expected me to communicate and enforce the stipulations of her moving in. He began with how he wanted her to either attend school and work part-time, or work full time enabling her to provide for herself. She would have a curfew, even though she would be paying him $150.00 a month for rent. Did I hear him mention he wanted her to pay him rent? For a moment, I began to hear not only his rambling in my ear, but the screaming inside my head to hang up! It was a perceptible deduction that one of Derek's goals was for Rylee to become a self-sufficient, responsible adult if she moved back. While I could appreciate his thought process, I knew all too well that Rylee had grown up and had pretty much been all on her own and responsible for some time.

Sensing Derek was waiting for some sort of definitive answer, I told him I would revisit with Rylee and try to let him know within the next few days. I wasn't sure what I wanted to revisit with her about, and ventured to presume that if she'd heard the little chat I'd just had with Derek, there might be a remote possibility she'd reconsider *my* proposition.

My son was with his father but didn't want to be there, and now my daughter wanted to be with her stepfather and I wasn't sure he wanted her there. I'd never imagined I could inflict such heartache and grief upon my children. I'd hoped only to move forward and make amends for the choices I had made in the past, but that concept kept biting me in the butt, one mistake at a time.

Chapter 21

Even though I didn't present it to her in a very optimistic light, Rylee accepted Derek's offer and moved back into the house. If she worried her father would have a problem with her moving back with me, it was nothing in comparison to her moving back with her stepfather. It created an even greater division between her and her father and with her brother. Worse, it didn't take long before the battle of wills clashed in full force between her and her step-father, any hopes for a more calm and settled life short-lived.

The final straw for Rylee happened on a weekend Lucas wasn't with me, and she seemed so disturbed that I called Derek to meet with him in hopes of smoothing things over and get him to lighten up on his grip. She was paying rent to live there and had been on her own plenty enough that she was used to coming and going as she pleased, yet Derek overbearingly treated her like a child. His fight was to maintain control of her, all the while she fought to make sure Derek was aware of the fact that he wasn't. It seemed she had not come home one night when he thought that she should and gave her a curfew, in addition to threatening her with having to move out if she didn't follow his rules.

He agreed to meet me at a little burger shop down the street from him, and I reluctantly agreed to pay. I thought about how amusing it was for me to foot the bill, since it seemed I typically paid for both of us, no matter when, where, or why. Even the child support check received each month from Lance had been deposited into a joint checking account and applied to our bills during the time we were married. Yet anytime I purchased necessities for the kids I had to account for every nickel and dime, recurrently berated over the purchase of something as petty as a coke. The first thing I did when I sat down at the restaurant was order a coke…

We began our conversation by going over what had caused the conflict with him and Rylee, which led into my issues and struggles with Lucas. Since there had been no one to talk with about Lucas and the frustrations I was experiencing to keep afloat, it was nice to converse with someone familiar with the difficulties. He nodded as he sat listening, inserting a few thoughts and opinions here and there, subsequently moving off the topic of the kids to what was left – us. Funny thing is, no matter how many times I attempted to explain why I left, he could never understand or fathom that I left for flagrant reasons that only he seemed unaware of. We sat there talking until the burger shop closed, rehashing the past as if it would make a difference to the conclusion of our story.

The weather began to change as we were leaving, and storms began to move through Richland Hills with increasing lightning and winds. Not only did I now have to drive home the fifty something miles, but in the midst of a major storm. Saying a quick goodbye and giving Derek an impersonal hug, I jumped into my car and headed back to Plano. Pulling onto the highway I called Lucas to make sure he was safe from the storm, and learned that he would be staying at a friend's house for the night. I then called Rylee to learn that she was safely located at a friend's house, and would not be at Derek's that evening. They were both doing their own thing, and in that split second all I could think about was the ability to drive right down the street where home used to be, and where my children should be. The water in front of me was no longer the rain falling, but tears brimming over onto my cheeks. Barely able to see in front of me, I wiped my face and turned the wipers up a notch on the car with the realization that the storm was becoming even more hazardous as I drove.

As the intensity of the storm grew I pulled underneath an overpass at the airport to call Derek, afraid to stay under it and just as afraid not to. He hurriedly viewed the weather radar to check the forecast and informed me that the worst of the storm was predicted to depart the area within the next thirty minutes. Before I could respond, he asked if I wanted to come to the house to wait for the storm to pass, or go ahead and attempt driving to Plano? One storm for the night was enough, and I decided it best to remain underneath the overpass and resist his tempting offer. Over two grueling hours later, I managed to reach my apartment in Plano. I barely had the energy to crawl into bed and underneath the covers, pulling them over my head to block out the remainder of the storm and the evening that I had been through.

One storm behind me didn't change anything in the upcoming months. Offering to meet with Derek to help resolve issues with Rylee was to no avail, and as I had presumed, it was shortly afterward that they both acknowledged it had been a mistake for her to move back. For the next couple of weeks I stayed in touch daily with both Rylee and Derek even though a solicited mediator, I tired to be an unbiased mediator. Sometimes one or both were kept apprised that I spoke with the other, sometimes not. But no matter the situation between them or how much I tried to stay out of the middle, I managed to be lured in. I thoroughly enjoyed talking with my daughter on a daily basis, but deliberated if I shouldn't be so hands-on for her sake and mine, especially since I was now speaking daily to Derek.

I was counting down the days and hours approaching the deadline for which I could petition custody for my son again. I was also counting the days that Rylee would move from the house and away from Derek. If I wasn't already drained from everything I'd been dealing with beforehand, the chaos was beginning to make me feel as though I'd collapse from unmitigated exhaustion. The longer I dealt with office controversies, negotiations between Derek and Rylee, and the legal and emotional barriers between Lucas and Lance, the breakdown I was due seemed fast approaching.

With the idea to keep peace in the family, Derek and I met for dinner on a regular basis, to discuss "Rylee and Lucas" and as the weeks passed I was spending a humongous amount of time in Richland Hills. Within a few months, Derek and I started dating again. Dating is an extremely broad term if you've previously been married to the person. Oddly enough, it was almost as if we were trying to start afresh and somehow repair the damage we'd not only inflicted onto ourselves, but also the kids.

Reconciliation leaves one teeny, inescapable problem at the end of the day: the reasons you left in the first place, will be the same reasons you can't go back in the second place. I had not learned that lesson yet, and continued with moving forward--by going backwards. I was further impelled to recreate history when Derek called me on a Friday evening to inform me that he had lost his job. My heart sank. It had seemed a career that yielded so much potential for his future, what had happened to change that?

That evening as we sat in the living room, Derek informed me he could not sustain the house mortgage with only the unemployment income. I knew what he was hinting at, but I didn't want to volunteer moving into the house, I wanted him to have to ask. By the end of the evening he did ask me to return and we executed a tentative plan, which included paying fees to break my lease. Since we would be living together but not married, we'd split the household debts between us and approach the arrangement like roommates. Hadn't I left and divorced him because we had become roommates? I foolishly pushed that terrifying connotation out of my mind, and thought about the fact that I didn't want to lose the house the kids had grown up in. And maybe, just maybe, since I had left him he would be attentively more conscious to the reasons I'd originally left.

Lucas had not seen or spoken with his step-dad in over a year, and when I told him I was occasionally seeing Derek, asked with unconstrained excitement if we could stop by for a visit. The hug exchanged between them warmed my heart as much as it did their own, and we stayed until it was time to take Lucas back to Plano. Maybe the happiness and the hope enveloping Lucas would comfort him and grant him strength. As his mother that gave me comfort, yet telling him we were seeing each other and telling him I was returning to Richland Hills was two totally different things. As much as I had been hopeful Lucas would be thrilled at the idea, talking to him about it wasn't greeted with the enthusiasm I'd anticipated.

I could sense the same concerns that I had, even though he did not speak any of them aloud to me. Knowing that I would not be near him if he should need me was not a pleasing thought, and I couldn't help but second-guess my decision after everything we had all been through. Regardless if he wanted Derek to be a part of his life, he had been witness to the discord between us that had originally ended our relationship and ultimately made me leave, and that fact was in the back of both our minds. With tears in our eyes we agreed it would be a financially beneficial resolution, and in six months we would attempt another custody hearing and bring him home, too. And even though I should have been happy, it was with a heavy-laden spirit that I took him back to his dad's house.

The process of me moving back with Derek was an uncomfortable and uncertain undertaking. Rylee was already in the process of making arrangement to move, and as soon as she learned of our plans wasted no further time in doing so before I was scheduled to move in. I was relieved that she had volunteered to leave on her own, because I didn't want all of us living in the house without Lucas being there. Nevertheless I packed up the apartment, hired the movers again, and tried to assure Lucas that even though I would no longer be as close in proximity, if he needed me I would be there.

I spent the last portion of my savings buying new furniture, getting carpets cleaned and re-stretched, painting rooms that had not been painted since I had last painted them, and decorating. What had once been his sister's room became Lucas's room, giving him additional space and a much larger closet. We replaced the single bunk bed with a full-size bed, hung up some of his personal things, and added a TV so that he could watch his own shows and play his video games. Eyeing the completed project I had mixed emotions. Would he feel like this was his room? Or would he feel as if he was a visitor? There would be only one way to find out.

To safeguard against Lance learning that I had returned to Richland Hills with Derek or of the plans to acquire custody of him, I asked

Lucas not mention either to his dad. Therefore, each weekend he was scheduled to be with me I would drive to Plano to pick him up after school, and on Monday take him to Lance's house in order for him to catch the school bus. The ritual aided in the facade of me residing in Plano, and each time I left him was one week closer to Lucas returning home and the charade ending.

Living at the house saved me money on gas and commute toll fees, but it seemed I was paying more toward expenses than when I lived independently in Plano. I had put a tremendous amount of money into the house and was now paying for most of "his" bills, but needed to prepare for the large chunk of money required to pay the attorney and court fees before going to trial. I discussed this with Derek, and he offered to let me put the fees on his credit card as long as I reimbursed him. Repay him? I didn't want to argue or negate, I just needed to make sure that when the time came I had the money to take care of what needed to be taken care of.

By Christmas I was pretty much settled into the house again, and Lucas was getting excited about the fact that he would soon be home too. After the holidays, I hired another attorney local to the area to meet with us before I took him back to his dad's, so that he could participate in the initial consultation. The attorney's questions and thoughts were specifically directed toward Lucas, and it quickly became evident that my son was no longer the juvenile boy that had left me, but a young man adept at answering them on his own.

The lawyer was precise and matter of fact, assiduously informing us the course of action we would pursue, and didn't waste time implying it anything less daunting than what it was. As soon as possible I was to provide an official letter to Lance asking for my summer visitation, giving him ample notice would award him plenty of time to arrange his summer schedule with Lucas, and less opportunity to decline. I was to "inform" Lance that I would pick Lucas up the last day of school and return him to Plano in thirty days. Lucas wasn't to comment to *anyone* concerning leaving Plano or coming to live with me. The plan was for him to leave with me from school the last day of his classes, and not return to live with his dad. He was to bring no clothes, no toiletries: nothing of his personal items.

Then he turned to speak to me as if we were the only two people in the room, his tone somewhere between fact and dread. Due to the volatile history created between Lance and the kids, he recommended we place a restraining order on Lance. The action would avert disruptive or threatening phone calls and text messages from Lance, and prevent him from being able to approach Lucas for the time being, ceasing any contact between them whatsoever. My eyebrows rose in surprise and I turned to look at Lucas, sitting there looking as dumbfounded as I felt.

No matter what, this was his father we were talking about! How could I--*we*--do such a thing? My heart began to pound a little faster, and I could tell by the look on my son's face he was the one who didn't know what to say, and I could tell by the face of the attorney there was nothing either of us could say. He wasn't asking our permission, he was informing us. It was part of the strategy, and he wanted nothing at all to jeopardize the objective. We simply had to follow his advice, and everything would end well. Hindsight...

After we left the office, I discussed the meeting with Lucas, asking if he had any relevant questions or concerns he felt we needed to address. He did not mention the restraining order or the fact that he would be walking away from his father and his life in Plano, leaving everything he owned behind him for who knew how long, possibly even forever. The only item he beseeched me to bring with him was the two soccer balls that his teammates had given to him when he was going through his heart evaluation. With everything he once owned but had lost for one reason or the other, it was the only thing in his possession that meant anything to him. I was fearful his father would question him if he left with them in hand, but Lucas had proactively plotted his getaway. He would tell his father it was for show-and-tell for the last day of school. Although frantic of the risk, I could not find it in my heart to tell him he should leave them behind.

My own excitement steadily grew with anticipation that soon everything would be back to "normal". With that hope in mind, the last day of school arrived and I made the necessary arrangements to pick

Lucas up. The attorney had called to inform me that the restraining order would be hand delivered to Lance on the last day of school and that his normal visitation rights, including weekend visits, would cease. The tactic would protect Lucas from being subjected to any sort of dilemma if he accidently exposed the truth to his dad by giving up our game plan. My son would stay with me until the court hearing and wouldn't be allowed to visit or speak with his father pending the official change of guardianship. At that point we would all be together and Lance would be over the fact that he had been deceived. Surely he would understand that we had to use the tactic we used because of his own ruthless deeds, which had inadvertently created this mess!

Pulling up in front of the school gave me a sudden reminder of all that had taken place, and the look on Lance's face as he'd left the counselor's office that afternoon to "get his ducks in a row." I now had mine in a row, a far cry from the last time I was there. In the time it would take for me to pick Lucas up from school and get him to Richland Hills, Lance would be served the restraining order. While a part of me believed he was getting what he deserved, another part of me cringed at the image of him answering the door to a stranger, then being handed paperwork informing him that his son would not be returning at the end of his visitation with me. For a moment I deliberated calling him to perchance work through our unresolved issues, when I spotted Lucas almost running out of the building with the grandest smile displayed from ear to ear…and two soccer balls in his arms. There was no turning back. I was taking my son home.

***

As we pulled up to the house a number came across my phone that I did not recognize, but almost instinctively knew I needed to answer. It was the constable attempting to serve Lance with the custody petition. She had witnessed Simone leaving, but had seen no one returning and was unable to get anyone to come to the door. It was imperative Lance be served by the end of the day, and therefore she would wait as long as needed. After what felt like an eternity the phone rang, and I answered the number I now identified with deflected reservations as the constable promptly began describing the person pulling into the driveway, confirming it was Lance before she approached.

From her abrupt mannerisms it was apparent there wasn't time to waste and minimal time for me to respond, so I hastily acknowledged that it was. Remaining on the phone with me she relayed her every move, sounding breathless as she apparently hurdled the bushes in the front yard to get to him before he made it to the door, doubtful he would open it to her once inside.

My own breath caught when I heard her speaking to Lance, informing him that he was being officially petitioned for a custody trial. I listened as he calmly queried what he needed to do, and she informed him that the instructions were detailed in the paperwork she had presented him. From his tone, I noticed that he didn't sound the least bit shocked, and for some reason that surprised me. The next thing I heard was the constable telling me Lance had officially been served, as she drove away from his house. Lucas had been sitting next to me and I knew he had heard the entire incident. Our moment of glory seemed to fade, as did the evening with yet another chapter in our lives.

Even though Lance was determined to maintain custody of his son, his attorney had apprised him in a rather contentious tone that he could spend all of the time and money in the world, but it would do no good. As summer came to an end the hearing was definitively concluded, in my favor. Unlike the last time, this time Lucas would be with me. Afterward, Lance and his family pretty much severed their relationship with both of his children, theoretically disowning them. They had absolutely no contact of any kind, and it would take years and the death of Lance's mother, their grandmother, to mitigate the strife created. If ever I doubted the consequences of divorce before, from that moment on I concluded there was no reprieve from the heartache it impinged upon everyone involved.

Chapter 22

    I would like to believe that things really do happen for a reason, and whatever the reason, it renders us a bit of comfort to believe whatever is destined to be in the end will be. But in my mind and most frequently in my heart, I do debate as to why things occur. I once felt the need to know why things happened, and why anyone or anything subsisted as an intricate part of this tapestry called my life. The one thing that I conclusively figured out is that there are rarely palpable answers in life, and that life is not intended to be methodical.

    I focused on putting everything in the former year behind me, including the numerous moves, Lucas's custody battle, a new occupation, my hospital episode and my brother's troubles. All I wanted to do was to get to a place that didn't have so much drama and difficulties. The kids were now old enough to recognize that Derek and I were experiencing friction, and I even shared with Rylee about my thoughts to move from the house once Lucas graduated. Rylee was supportive, and immensely encouraging considering the numerous ordeals previously faced. Whenever the opportunity arose and I needed her input, she would willingly discuss my options and render suggestions.

    The topic of my world-wind options was the conversation over breakfast one Saturday morning between Rylee and her boyfriend Dean. They were high school sweethearts, looking for their own place to move in together, and collectively grew enthused about some new homes being built that they also wanted me to explore.

But while the intent had been simply to survey the neighborhood and houses, by the time we'd left the model, two mortgage applications had been completed. I withheld saying anything to Derek or Lucas, it didn't seem necessary until I knew if I qualified for the purchase of a house or not. Oddly, the response was conveyed across the phone via text while we were all sitting in church that following Sunday. Rylee's cell dinged first, informing her their loan was approved and that they could begin selecting amenities in preparation for building their new house. As she placed her phone in front of me so that I could read the information, a text appeared on my phone with the same approval. The three of us had smiles from ear to ear, while Derek looked on with a curious expression, sensing that he was missing out on something and hoping that we would take it upon ourselves to include him.

Weeks went by, and with the loan approval in mind I wrestled with my inward deliberation to leave Derek and sever our relationship once and for all. Meanwhile, Dean and Rylee excitedly moved forward with their own plans in great anticipation. Learning that their house might be built and available in six months or less, leasing in the interim would be preposterous. As their plans became more concrete and their current lease came to the end, I figured it highly probable that Rylee would ask to move in with us temporarily. Though that would be the most simple and logical solution for them, Rylee was a bit apprehensive to ask. She hadn't forgotten the clashes that had occurred the last time, and I wasn't sure if me living there would be a plus or generate additional hindrances. We casually approached the subject with Derek while we were all having lunch together after church, and by the end of our meal the three of us believed he was perfectly ok with the short-term plan. Feeling the arrangement was in place, the kids rented a moving truck, packed up their possessions, and moved their furniture inside the garage.

Sadly, antagonism reared its ugly head even before the kids moved in, Derek blatantly not happy about the agreement. The second bedroom had been changed into an office when we moved Lucas into the larger room, which minimized the space available to use. Derek didn't want to convert the office into a makeshift bedroom so the den became Lucas's room, which meant he would be sleeping on the couch again.

I wasn't exactly thrilled with the prospect, but Derek pitched such a fit that I became defensive and worried that Rylee and Dean would feel unwelcomed.

I'm not sure if the situation was as bad the first time Derek and I married, or if the distance and time apart made me conscious of his unacceptable behavior. He complained constantly: if the lights and TV were on, if someone took a shower and it was longer than he thought they should, or even what time someone washed a load of clothes.

Hershey, which was Dean and Rylee's new, untrained puppy, had moved in with them. Hershey was used to being a housedog, but because we had left the kid's childhood dog Bailey outside for years, that did not sit well with Derek--or Bailey. He was explicit in his demands that Hershey be kept on a leash and prevented from romping around the house, including anytime she was in the living room with us. I don't think she could have caused much further damage running loose. The leash rubbed the tables, the couch, and the love seat. She whined every night, wanting to be set free while we were all sitting around watching TV. The absurdity that she be constantly tied up in the evenings and left in a cage all day aggravated me to no end, and I hated it for her.

A few weeks into the insanity, I made the mistake of tying the dog up in the bedroom with me until I was dressed for work. Coincidently that mistake wasn't my last for the day, making the impetuous decision to leave her tied up in the bedroom opposed to leaving her in the cage while we were away. Derek blew his top when he came home and discovered that Hershey had gnawed at the carpet seam by the door. If it hadn't been for a few fiber strands scattered across the floor, it would have gone unnoticed. Derek called Rylee about the incident first, livid and pugnacious, yelling at her to get rid of the dog. She called me ten times desperate to reach me and tell me not to go home because of Derek's outlandish temper. I assured her it would all be okay, but inside I was afraid that it probably wouldn't be for a very long time to come. The dog was merely one more issue we wouldn't be able to compromise on.

Added to the existing quandaries the master shower broke, and we had to hire a contractor to dig a gigantic hole in the bedroom floor to get to the pipes. Forget the fact that we had one bathroom for five people to use, but the amount of dust everywhere could have filled the Holland tunnel! With that cataclysmic destruction around us, the tattered rug a few days beforehand didn't look so bad. I contemplated mentioning that point, but my better judgment determined that would not be a wise thing to do, unless I wanted to find myself buried beneath the new bathroom tile currently in the process of being laid.

Like any other juncture in life, a day could sometimes feel like an eternity, but others came and went in a blur. The funny thing is, through it all I was thankful. How many times had I prayed for another opportunity to have both Rylee and Lucas living with me again? How many times had I pined for our family life and all we had taken for granted? And yes, even in the moments I couldn't wait to get Lucas into his bedroom again, I combated a sadness that soon it would end, and this would probably be the last opportunity for all of us to live together as a family.

***

It seems to me that struggles in life will do one or two things: (1) they will make you a stronger, better person, or (2) they will bring out your true character, revealing any obscured flaws! I had the challenge of comprehending that the man I loved and kept finding my way back to somehow, to be equally selfish and self-centered as anyone could be. But I was fast learning that such traits were inherent in his mom, so why would his characteristic imperfections surprise me in the least? And yet it did. It also broke my heart for Rylee and Lucas. They had not spoken with Lance in over a year, and now they were dealing with a stepfather who made them feel like they had to walk on eggshells to guarantee having a roof over their heads.

Two months had not quite passed when the Dean and Rylee were informed that they would be able to move into their new home sooner than originally calculated. I was torn between holding on and letting go, and the closer it came time for their move, the more melancholy I became. Apparently, I wasn't alone in dealing with mixed emotions. I came home early from work one night to find Rylee having a meltdown... about a refrigerator. Of all the things they had for the house, they didn't have a black refrigerator. She'd wanted one to match the black appliances in the new house, and not the temporary white one that she demanded go into the garage because it *didn't* match. It was almost as if she'd forgotten about the white refrigerator, and had completely lost her mind. "Mom!" she exclaimed. "We are moving, and Dean's birthday party is next week and I won't have anywhere to put the food or the cake for his party if we don't have a black refrigerator! How can I have a party for him if I don't have a place for the food and cake?" She was certainly my daughter.

I looked at her, and for a moment quietly surveyed the room. I was years older than her before purchasing my first home, and there was a chance that before long I would be walking away from the only home my children had ever really known. Lucas was standing in front of the fireplace where almost every event, holiday, gift, and friend had been lovingly photographed the majority of their childhood. His hands were on his hips, looking at me as if I needed to smack some sense into his sister because she had irrevocably lost it. Dean was sitting on the couch next to her with a look of panic, because nothing he had already said would calm her down. His eyebrows rose, and he was looking at me as if to implore my assistance, his eyes signifying the words "Help me! I am in way over my head!"

The TV was on, and Hershey was yelping and running around because...well, she was a dog and had been alone all day, so it was time to play. Thankfully Derek had not arrived home, and I plopped onto the love seat taking in the situation before me. My daughter was scared. I reached out to give her a consoling hug, and began my speech by emphasizing the accomplishments she and Dean had achieved at an incredibly young age. Dean had recently acquired a great job and a "new" used car, she had received an increase in pay which would help with their monthly bills, and they were moving into a new, practically furnished home, with the exception of the black refrigerator. I almost laughed at the sheer lunacy of her worries over a matching refrigerator. But I didn't. I opted to remind her that when her father and I had moved

to our first house, we didn't have blinds, a second car, or a refrigerator-
-period. And we had a four-year-old and a newborn.

A lighthearted giggle and twinkle in her eyes let me know she really was thankful for everything, and in the back of my mind, I was thinking how easy it was for us to look at what we don't have, and lose sight of what we do have. I surmised that the issue for my daughter was partly due to her tentative move and dreading the inevitable, and though I didn't look forward to her leaving, we both had to face it. Rylee would soon be leaving home, and in all likelihood it would be the last time she lived there. She now had to tackle the real world, pay real bills, and be a responsible adult. Even more overwhelming than anything else was the fact that she and Dean were about to make a lifetime commitment together. My daughter had to grow up.

Expressing those same sentiments to her, the twinkle in her eyes vanished and tears instantaneously filled them. "But I don't want to grow up!" I wanted to cry with her and tell her that I didn't want her to grow up, either. I wanted to tell her that I wished she could be there with Lucas and me and that I could shelter her from harm. I wanted to greet her each morning and see that she had breakfast and ate lunch and dinner. I wanted to hear about her day when she came home, kiss her goodnight before she went to bed, and tell her that I loved her. Instead, I looked at my daughter and informed her that she had to grow up, that was simply the indubitable evolution of life. I lovingly reminded her that no matter where she was or what she was doing, I would be there for her...come hell or high water.

It was as if the air had physically left her body and she went limp, a smile erupting on her face as if she had secretly known that fact, and was merely obtaining permission to do what she needed to do. Almost hesitantly, Dean asked her if she was okay, and she jumped off the couch and with a celebratory grin declared, "Yes!" That seemed to be the sought answer, and Dean and Lucas both stood up to follow Rylee out the front door for church.

As she was leaving, Rylee turned and gave me a grateful hug with a solemn, "Thanks, Mom." against my cheek. I felt my voice catch and couldn't speak. I could only give her a hug in return, and held onto her for a few extra seconds longer than I normally would. Then I knew I had to let go.

Along the Way

———— ⧲⧲⧲⧲⧲ ————

Autumn Carpentier

Their baby came before they had time to blink,
dressed to go home in pretty pinks,
Tiny comb to comb her hair, every shoe wanted, at least one or two pairs.

Simple lace and cotton dresses, small nightshirts, diapers for messes,
No matter the time, the time drew closer, when
she'd have let go instead of hold her.

Late night calls made from boys, they've now
replaced her childhood toys…
Soft makeup and sweet perfumes—the newest fad decorates her room.

But deep inside her mother held on, knowing all
too soon her daughter would be gone,
college classes and then graduation, a new young love and infatuation…

She became a woman her mother was proud of,
finding faith and someone to love,
Cascading veil and the dress she chose, the diamond
he gave her the night he proposed.

Counting down to the day they'd marry, it
came too fast and was a little scary.

Would he hold her, love and protect her? Walk
hand in hand as they both grew older?

As time would pass she'd become a mother,
holding the tiny bundle closely to her,
their baby came before they had time to blink,
dressed to go home in pretty pinks.

Footnote: I wrote this after reflecting on how fleetingly the time had come and gone since Rylee was just a little girl, and knowing she was well on her way to moving on and living her life. It is hard to imagine your children grown when they are little, and once they are grown, it's harder to remember them when they were little. I knew that while I was presently experiencing all of those thoughts, one day she would experience the same with her own daughter.

***

I do think that pivotal moments are oftentimes created in fragments throughout our lives that go unnoticed as to how extraordinary they really are, or to the degree they touch us. Pictures, words, thoughts, hopes, and dreams build us up, tear us down, give us insight, and make our journeys our own. Then there are those moments that without question, we know there is unassuming love, and nothing or no one can take it from us.

With Rylee and Dean now gone from the house it was only Lucas, Derek and I living there again. I still wanted to hang on to the idea of being a family and making sure Lucas was okay, all the while covertly wondering if he regretted his decision to live with me again. Was he unsatisfied with his choice now that he was apparently withstanding as much crap living with me as he had when he lived with his father? I had asked myself that question hundreds of times, but hadn't once asked Lucas that question since he had come back to live with me. Was I afraid of the answer? Or was I justifiably terrified of the disappointment that I'd most likely hear in his voice or see in his eyes? Would I ever be able to adequately express how crucial his happiness and wellbeing was to me? Amazingly enough I discovered the answer to my question and concerns, in a roundabout manner.

It was on a school night that Lucas called me to the bathroom, asking me to check his fresh shaved head to make sure it was a clean shave. He had shaved it before, and I knew precisely why he was doing it again. Each year there was a cancer awareness benefit at the schools, and the guys shaved their heads in honor of someone that had either died of cancer or survived cancer. The first year he did it, I was taken by surprise and so touched that I couldn't prevent the tears from falling. He wasn't even born at the time I was diagnosed with cancer, but he was acutely aware of the fact that I had gone through that experience. I kissed the top of his bent head once I finished checking out the shave and turned to leave the bathroom, as he followed behind me and requested I go to the den. Directing me toward the couch and pointing for me to sit across from his laptop on the coffee table, he opened his Facebook site where he had written on his wall and wanted me to read it:

A little late in honoring, but I just wanted to thank God for not taking my mom when she had cancer and that she is still here for me. I love you Momma!

I sat on the couch next to my son, consumed by the invincible love between us that could never be diminished by anyone, or anything. Unable to conceal my emotions I briefly closed my eyes to seize the moment, then opening them reached to embrace him. In the years forward he would combat his own battles, overcome his own trials and tribulations, oftentimes despite the odds. But for now he was sharing his gratitude for my personal conquest, and I was inexpressibly touched. His love solidified my one inspiration to stay with Derek and try to keep us a family.

She Stayed

Autumn Carpentier

She wanted nothing more than to go,
find a different way of life from the one she came to know.
Tried hard to move on a million times or two,
not always knowing what it was she should do.
So she stayed…
For one reason or another, they never quite got it right,
tried as they might to work past the fights.
He wanted it his way and never heard a word she said,
left her alone and crying, never holding her to him instead.
Yet she stayed…
Left kneeling on the floor, she felt as though she'd died,
trying her best to be strong, trying her best to survive.
No one will ever know the price her soul had to pay,
hanging on to the promises he had once made
So she stayed…
Stayed in a world she never found peace of mind,
stayed in a dream of something she once left behind,
No point in wishing, there was nowhere to run
All that mattered at the time was providing for her son

So she stayed…she stayed…
She stayed for all he needed and what she knew he deserved,
there's nothing like a mother's love on this earth.
And when the time came that he walked away,
she wished all the while that he might turn and say,
"Let me stay…"

Footnote: I woke up thinking about how much I love my children and everything that has happened in the last few years. I do not want to put them in the middle again, whether they were living with me or not! After all that Lucas has been through, he still has so much love in his heart. As much as I love him and desire to protect and provide for him, I know that even if I stay in this situation for him, one day that he will eventually leave, and at the end of the day I will be alone, and everyone else will have moved on.

Chapter 23

I have frequently been astounded at the lives I've witnessed disrupted and shattered by the results of those decisions both made or not made, and observed that evil is usually disguised within our heart's desires. I'm the first to confess that I am no exception, and my greatest challenge remains habitually pursuing those desires heedless of the outcome, tossing caution to the wind with hope of being beyond reproach. There should be something that hits us over our noggin when heading in the wrong direction and puts up a guardrail with blinking lights, pretty much like there is at a railroad crossing when the locomotive goes barreling through. Regardless of how slow or how fast that train is heading in your direction, if you don't observe those frantically blinking lights, you are going to be in trouble.

The first time I met Marcus my reunion with Derek was in the optimistic stages that we could rebuild and rekindle, and I had no intention of jeopardizing anything between us after everything we'd gone through. Well known at the credit union from the years I had worked there, he'd apparently inquired about me and came to visit me at my office. Though I declined his entreating invitation on that visit and many times afterward, he was determined to get what he sought and fearless in his quest to obtain. Even after I compellingly explained my current dilemma to keep him at bay, he remained steadfast in his quest.

He was an extremely handsome man who said and did all the right things. For most people, that would have been the moment they saw the blinking lights and the guardrail going down warning of danger. Did I stop at the guardrail knowing better than to keep going? Yes, I did know better, but as Derek and I began our pernicious spiral downward, it was inevitable that sooner or later Marcus would breakdown the barrier I had placed against him. Tired of my moral reasoning or tired of saying no to him, I recklessly agreed to dinner at his place, convincing myself that it was an opportunity to persuade him to keep his distance. More flashing lights, but I recklessly plowed ahead as if I were blind as a bat.

The evening was intended to be dinner and drinks at his apartment, but Marcus hadn't started dinner when I arrived and began making cocktails for us the moment I walked in the door. I appeared to be in complete control at the beginning of the evening, but I had been so nervous about meeting him I hadn't even had lunch or grabbed a snack. Consequently, I should have stopped at the second drink, especially since each drink he made me was stout enough to be equivalent to that of five. By the end of the second drink I was already plastered…and we never did have dinner.

My guard had thoroughly dissipated when he made his move and reached for me. I pulled away preventing the kiss he was fixated on taking, feeling his desire as he pressed his body harder against mine, yearning for the passion I was unwilling to surrender. Sensing he would carry me to a place I had not been since with Derek, I longed to experience that passion with him if only for a brief moment. As the night went on he wanted me to stay, but I knew I had to go.

We never made love and I never relinquished a single kiss, but we held each other and talked into the night as if we were lovers spent from lovemaking. Driving home much later that evening I opened the window attempting to expunge the smell of him from my skin, fully aware that his scent would convey the intimacy between us much more than words.

What was I doing? Even more bewildering, what was I thinking? I incurred tremendous guilt as I fantasized about all that had happened, and wishful of what hadn't happened, rationalizing my feelings as if that made it ok. I don't know what kept me from letting him seduce me that evening. My insightful conclusion in the days that followed was that

I'd learned a few fundamental lessons from my former wrongdoings, and didn't want to repeat the same mistakes. That didn't stop me from frequently reliving that night, and how I'd deliberated doing just about anything to have even a scrawny taste of what I lacked in my life.

Lucas called to me as he heard me come in a short time later and I made my way into his bedroom, self-conscious that he could smell the alcohol on my breath and the man's cologne that lingered on my skin and in my hair. His concern was genuine, and I felt even guiltier that he had been worrying about me. He had called and texted me several times at Marcus's and I had responded only once, telling him I would be home later. I kissed the top of his head, thanked him for waiting up, and said that I was sorry it was so late, kissing him once more before turning to leave and closing the door behind me.

I headed to my own bedroom wondering whether Derek was going to greet me with his disquiet or suspicions, and discovered the bedroom light off. I automatically went to the bathroom where I halfheartedly stripped my clothes before carefully crawling into bed, clinging to the edge as I did each night at that point. Arriving home to find that Derek had gone to bed, but my son impatiently waiting up for me, made the loneliness and emptiness inside feel that much stronger. I didn't utter a word or act like coming in after midnight was anything out of the norm, in case he did roll over. I pulled the covers up over my shoulders and turned onto my side as if going to sleep, and if he was awake he never spoke a word, not that night or even the next day.

The following afternoon, Marcus called me from work, curious if Derek had been waiting up for me or quarrelsome upon my arrival. When I told him neither, I heard him mutter underneath his breath; "He's a damn fool!" before slamming the receiver down. To be honest, I wasn't convinced which of the three amongst us was the crowning fool, but in all fairness it was a close race for the unworthy title. The days would come and go with increasing repentance over two relationships that created havoc in my heart, and unquestionable emptiness in my future.

Marcus tried to keep his distance from me, but a week before Christmas he called with the news that his company had transferred him and he would be moving to San Antonio. Two weeks later when the time came for his going-away happy hour, he called to personally invite me so that we could say our goodbyes. Both of us knew that if I made it to the happy hour it might be the difference of a night we finally shared…or one that would never come to fruition. I still desired him as much as I had the night at his apartment, but as desperately as I wanted to be with him I wasn't going to. There were too many variables that didn't make sense, no matter how much we might wish for the outcome to be different. I was at a different segment of my life, and the enormous age difference between us only magnified the milestones he had yet to reach in his own life. The life that we both knew would be a valley between us as the years passed, no matter the passion that emanated between us now.

The next day he came to my office with one relevant question, "Why didn't you come?" I knew he knew: we both knew. His yearning to have me was straightforward, even up to the moment before he turned and walked out of my life. The relationship that never really was, was over. Most would have deduced that my grieving was due to the end of the relationship between Derek and me, not from someone I didn't know that well and had so little time with. My world was once again empty, and the man that had yearned to give me the moon was as distant as the stars.

Self-Defeat

Autumn Carpentier

Cradle in the day, cradle deep into the night,
secret wishful longing that this could be right.
Saying with the eyes what can't be said with words,
trying day by day not to feel the hurt.
Completely out of reach, reaching for his love,
oh, the story's sad, the one that never was.
Traces of a dream that used to be so warm,
now more like a rose that only has the thorns.
Distance kept between them, nothing left to say,
pushing past the feelings that won't go away.
Laughing on the outside for all those passing by,
no one could imagine how many times she's cried.
Softly her heart treads, each moment that she goes,
empty are the hours, every minute slow.
One day at a time is all she can survive,
do not ask for answers, she couldn't tell you why.

> *But as the sun rises and the moon finds peace of sleep,*
> *It simply is the cycle of life's own self-defeat,*
> *of things we think we can control but find it isn't true,*
> *the choices that are made; the things that we do.*

Footnote: I wrote this after meeting someone who made me feel like I wanted to feel, but I knew it was not good timing or the right thing to do. I thought about how the more we long to control our hearts, the more we lose the control, all the while suffering the consequences.

Sacrificed Love

Autumn Carpentier

She went back to the place she had left behind,
the only home he had ever really known,
feeling certain it was for the best, even though it still felt wrong.

She tried to do what was right by him, so that
he didn't pay for her mistakes...
the consequences would be immeasurable, and
it was a risk she could not take.

She smiled at those around her; they would never know her pain,
the choices that she'd made were now too late to change.

The thought of hurting anyone or bringing such great sorrow,
kept her from moving on or looking toward more for tomorrow.

She knew the art of make-believe...how well she could pretend,
and though she could only dream, it was a place she could be with him.

At night she'd lay on her side of the bed, the
tears rolling slowly down her face,
but in the light when she saw her son, she knew it was the place;

The place he could become a man, learn to grow strong and good,
where he'd have a man to teach him things a mother never could.

She wouldn't regret her choices, or doing what she had to do,
he'd never know the price paid, giving up a love she never knew.

Footnote: I wrote this poem after I experienced the feelings of covetousness for something and someone that I couldn't have, because if I made the choice to be with him I'd have to leave Derek and jeopardize what I was trying so hard to give my son.

Chapter 24

———∿∽◦◖◗◦◍◦◖◗◦∿∿———

I was both saddened and relieved that Marcus had left, and kept myself busy shopping and filling the house with gifts wrapped in beautiful paper and bows. But without any notice, one gift came unwrapped that year. Derek and I had been watching TV when Lucas, Dean and his best friend Paul all walked into the house together with a gleeful, mischievous demeanor about them. I sat up straight, sliding my body to the edge of the couch as I watched Paul and Lucas rush past us and toward the den, both giggling but covering their mouths as if to contain their laughter.

Observing the two of them, I missed Dean taking a seat on the couch, but turned to see him looking at me with an awkward look on his face intuitively aware something was up. I held my breath knowing we were about to find out, and without much further ado Dean ecstatically requested, "Can I have Rylee's hand in marriage?" I'm not sure if Dean realized that my breath caught, or if it just felt like it, but I could feel the disapproval from Derek as well as detect it on his face. Dean would not understand that look, the look that mirrored my own concerns.

As two adults that had experienced the challenges of marriage, we both recognized that in youth they were oblivious of the road ahead, of the obstacles that awaited them. It crossed my mind that I had delayed marriage for years, and it had not prevented any less hurdles or heartache. All of those thoughts were circulating in my head when I realized I hadn't responded to Dean's nervous question, and jumped up to respond with one heartfelt word; "Yes!" giving him a huge hug and a reassuring smile that I--no *we* were excited for them.

Two nights later, Dean would pop the question to Rylee in the youth building of their church that we helped decorate in preparation for the evening. His proposal was well planned, romantic and filled with love. Music softly played in the background to greet her upon entrance, tossed rose petals throughout the room like a carpet beneath her feet. Lit candles glimmered across the room and a lace tablecloth covered the elegantly set table for two, the dinner Dean had prepared ready to be served by Lucas and Paul, both dressed in their Sunday best. With champagne on ice and her engagement ring in the pocket of his jacket, I remember the anticipation in his eyes and the smile on his face as I turned to leave him after helping decorate the room.

My heart soared with sheer happiness for my daughter, knowing she was about to embark on a spectacular venture with someone that loved her so much, and I was reminded what being in love was all about. I wish that I could have witnessed her face as she realized the same...

With the proposal behind them and Christmas ahead, the excitement grew as they all watched gifts pile up underneath the Christmas tree conjecturing as to which was theirs, knowing not to snoop or touch any of them. Rylee was already in the pre-wedding mode, but nevertheless Christmas Eve came and the kids baked a cake for Jesus, which we had not done in the past two years. I think it had come to mean more to each of us because we now appreciated that tradition was something in which we all played an intricate part in creating.

We later attended the candlelight service, returning home to read *Twas the Night Before Christmas* in front of the fireplace and drinking my infamous homemade hot chocolate. Santa came that night, as he had done every year since they were born, regardless of age or circumstances. Lucas woke us up bright and early Christmas morning by jumping on the beds as if the clock had turned back time, jubilantly running about the living room instructing us to commence passing out the presents. And on that Christmas morning, it was as if none of us had ever left, as if the last two years had never happened.

Unfortunately, Christmas was the only time we remotely had that feeling again. I had hoped things would transform and we would be able to move forward if I returned. Sadly, the more we attempted moving forward we inescapably managed to accomplish doing just the opposite. The remnants of our life before haunted and inflicted us as if we had never been apart. The endless arguments, lack of communication, and all the problems concerning his mom and friends progressively picked up exactly where we left off. We also had the same problem with our sex life: there was none.

I became extremely vigilant about the fact that needs required deep within our hearts and souls will ultimately find a way to be attained sooner or later…one way or another. I didn't want the rapacity of my needs attained from looking outside of our relationship, and I did not want to hurt Derek nor waste another twenty-five years. With those thoughts and feelings upfront in my mind, I was switching back and forth evaluating what the right thing was--for everyone.

There wasn't anyone that I could share my concerns with and I had no desire to further encumber my children. A faithful believer in prayer, as much as I prayed, I was missing something somewhere, until the end of February when I stood up from my desk at work and knew that something was terribly wrong. My heart began palpitating out of control and I could barely breathe, my palms sweating as much as my upper brow. I quickly called a coworker, Merissa, requesting that she drive me to the nearest emergency room.

If you've ever had to go to the emergency room, you know that unless you have blood spouting from your veins or something protruding from your body, chances are you will be waiting for several hours. Merissa calmly relayed to the nurse attendant that I was having chest pains, and the attendant nonchalantly pushed us the paperwork required to begin the process of admitting me. I turned toward the hospital attendant and took two steps forward before I grasped at my chest, certain I was experiencing a heart attack. Merissa saw me grab my chest and was suddenly not as composed and tolerant as when we arrived, announcing to the entire ER staff that she demanded someone accommodate us! As riled as she was, everything and everyone seemed to be moving in slow motion, and my heart beating faster and faster. I figured the fact that it was beating faster was better than not beating at all!

I was eventually taken to a waiting room where a nurse began documenting all applicable information, as another nurse began attaching sensors onto my body that would retrieve vital signs. With every attachment applied, red lights started blinking and warning signals began to sound. My blood pressure, which was normally 117 over 78, had shot up so high I was on the verge of a cardiac arrest. Nurses began running from every direction, as several of them rushed me onto a hospital bed and into one of the emergency rooms, Merissa close behind. While some of the staff hooked me up to various attachments and gave me shots and pills, others wheeled in an X-ray machine to examine my chest, giving me multiple medications and shots.

I was then admitted into the hospital to run additional tests, and though Derek would have been the last person I elected to call, it became necessary someone be informed. A short time later Derek came in with Rylee and the youth pastor, followed soon afterward by Lucas, his best friend and the church pastor himself. Apparently I was going to need prayers.

Two days later I was released after having everything from an Echocardiogram, MRI, CT and various blood work to help the doctors establish the cause of my incident. Thousands of dollars later, what they established was…absolutely nothing. I recalled hearing the same diagnoses years before with Lucas, and then later learned that wasn't the case. Frustrated, I was ready to draw blood. And not mine. It was inscrutable how all of that had taken place and the diagnosis was: "nothing." Diagnosis or not, the stress of trying to do the right thing was taking a dangerous toll on me. My deteriorating health was evidence that it was a matter of time before I had to make changes or it would be too late. I knew it, the kids knew it, and Derek knew it. The unspoken question that hung in the air, was how much longer would it take before I did what sooner or later had to be done?

I went home from the hospital feeling drained, but with a new strategy that pretty much epitomized the longstanding plan I had used so much I should have been awarded "frequent flyer" points. New plan, old plan, same plan…as time would have it another year had passed and the month of July arrived, as did another birthday. Several people from the office took me to lunch that afternoon followed by a happy hour that evening. I was ready for some rest and relaxation, and looking forward to forgetting anything other than being right where I was for the moment.

Shortly into the celebration and a few drinks downed by everyone, I saw that I had missed a text message from my brother in addition to several phone calls. I deciphered from the text message he sent that it was not going to be good: "PLEASE, PLEASE, PLEASE call." I had no choice but to return his call, hoping it wasn't as bad as I feared. As soon as I heard his voice, I realized neither was true.

He and Hannah had separated a few weeks before, after ten years of marriage, and now she wanted a divorce. I didn't even blink an eye, hearing the desperation in his voice I knew I had to go to Austin and do whatever I could to help in any way that I could. I walked outside in order for us to better hear each other, and seeing the pang in my eyes, my best friend Gayle trailed close behind. I took a few seconds to tell her what was going on after we were outside, and positive that she could appease him, she grabbed the phone from me. The look that sprang across her face told me she also heard the same desperation, and we both knew I no choice but to go.

I called Derek to tell him where I was going and why, and took him up on his offer to drive because I had been drinking and had no idea what I would find when I arrived. I hurried inside the restaurant to retrieve my purse and explain to the group that I had a family emergency and headed to the house to get Derek. My mind was crammed with the mental notes I was making in my head as I began to think of ways I could fix what would most probably take an immeasurable amount of time, in a limited timeframe.

I reached home in record time and after packing a few items that I would need, Derek and I left for Austin. I called Colin to let him know I was coming and attempted to block any thoughts of him alone or the pain he was going through. Hanging up, I began thinking of a couple of scenarios we might encounter when we reached him, and as much as I attempted to formulate even a glimmer of hope, it eluded me. The night became longer and longer and I was unable to remain awake, thankful that Derek had suggested driving. By the time we arrived I knew I would have had slim to none chances of making it if I had been driving, but all of that was forgotten when Colin opened the door to let us in. As I reached to hug him, my heart sank like a rock in water as I looked over his shoulder at the apartment that mirrored his heartache, both equally dismal and cold.

It didn't take long before he began sharing details of what had transpired, pouring his heart out as the tears unreservedly poured along with his words. It was late when he led us upstairs to sleep on the air mattress that he had been sleeping on the past few nights. I noticed that Colin had already placed a twin mattress on the floor for his daughter to sleep on during her visits, and it was there he lay down to sleep as we crawled into bed.

My heart was touched by how sweet it was that he had placed her things on one side of the room, to create a personal space for her. Already grown, his son had come to stay with him as well and was downstairs asleep on the pullout couch. Derek and I had nowhere we could really talk, but I took his hand to let him know I was glad he was there. I empathized with my brother's pain and thought about how I did not want to experience those same horrible emotions and heavy uncertainty. More than ever before, I didn't want to displace my son again.

Waking up in a bedroom that had a streetlight shining through the window the entire night boosted my determination to make his apartment feel like a home, and not a hotel. Using my car payment for the month, I went shopping for things that would provide warmth and make it halfway inviting--anything to offset the coldness he was feeling in his heart. I purchased pictures, dishes, knick-knacks, a comforter, and drapes to cover his windows and guard against the light that had shined into my eyes nonstop the night before.

Before beginning anything else, I went with him to the office to check on something a bit larger in the complex so that he could have a bedroom for his son Kyle, since he had decided to intermittently remain with his father. With nothing currently available we placed him on the two-month waiting list, then headed back to the apartment again to clean, hang, arrange, and make the bed with the day's purchases. Worried he'd lose even more weight, we shopped for enough groceries to last for at least a week, and fixed enough dinners so that he would have prepared meals to eat once we left. After dinner that night we sat together and collaborated ways he could accomplish paying his bills, after we helped him figure out the bills he was actually responsible for.

Our final mission before leaving was to help my nephew find a local job, hoping that he could contribute toward the household finances and take some of the burden off of his father. The last thing I did before we left was put away the bottle of wine he promised that he wouldn't drink until he could drink it without feeling the need to drown in it. I was uneasy about leaving Colin, I had grown up with him and knew all too well the emptiness he needed to fill, and skeptical that he was capable of being alone. He loved Hannah and wanted to be with her, and everything related to making that dream evolve had been taken along with her. Loving someone who doesn't return your love is almost intolerable, and at the end of the day any motive insignificant.

I hugged him before leaving, hoping what we had accomplished was enough to prevent him from sinking. I cried and prayed for my brother all the way home, then cried and prayed for myself and for so many others who repeatedly fought that desperate, sinking feeling but remained incessantly determined to stay afloat. Mercifully, engrossed in Colin's misfortunes I had no omen of the troublous storms of my own soon to undergo...

When

Autumn Carpentier

It is a strength that is given when you have none alone,
  when the worst seems so hard that you can't go on.
When the weariness feels like hurt beyond any pain,
  and you feel as though your life will never be the same.
When the day's sunshine doesn't make you warm,
  the cold inside has left you feeling battered and torn.
When words can't convey the thoughts of what's inside,
  and you feel as though your heart and soul has died.
When it's hard to pretend, even for just a little while,
  behind the mask of your courageous, empty smile.
When you need arms wide open and to hold you up,
  need someone else to be strong, someone else to be tough.

In that moment, know I am there right by your side,
no one could keep me from you, even if they tried.
I will be your soft place to fall and help you move on,
be the somewhere you are safe, until again you are strong.

Footnote: I wrote this after leaving my brother in his heartache and after a friend of mine lost her high school sweetheart and husband of fifteen years unexpectedly to death. They had three young children together. Another friend's husband was terminally ill, and she was with him, waiting for the inevitable. As death and endings surrounded our hearts, I think any one of us could have used that soft place to fall.

Chapter 25

The following Friday after our trip to Austin, I took the initiative and called to meet Derek for dinner since we had not spent much time together. I hadn't had the opportunity to mention to him that I was going to Houston to attend the funeral for Gayle's stepfather, who had passed during the week after being in the hospital for almost a month. While she would have her family with her, she wasn't married and wasn't currently in a relationship with anyone. She was my dearest friend and distraught, nothing was going to stop me from being there for her. Though she wasn't aware that I'd be attending the funeral, I anticipated staying the night and following her home, which would place me back in town late that Sunday evening. Knowing I had to share that bit of news and theorizing I'd have some degree of control over the evening's outcome if I had my own car, I requested Derek meet me at a restaurant down the street from the house.

Being the first to arrive at the restaurant I got a table and ordered our drinks, planning to have a glass of wine before he got there. Even with a few sips, I noticed that my breathing had become shallow the more anxious I grew. My health had continued spiraling erratically downward, and my legs were breaking out in a severe rash that looked as if they were rotting. The doctors were stumped and unable to diagnose what was wrong, since nothing substantial showed up on any tests. I was somewhat apprehensive that the next time I was admitted to the hospital, might conceivably be less fortunate.

I saw Derek from across the room and motioned to him as he made his way to the table. Before I could even get a "Hello" spoken, the first word out of his mouth was, "Smile!" snarled in a demeaning, mocking tone along with a fake smile displayed across his own face. I immediately knew that it had been a mistake to meet him for dinner. He wasted no time before confronting me regarding Lucas's absence from school the previous day, questioning if I had called to have him excused for his last two classes. "Yes." I quietly responded. His response, "Why?" was vocalized with harshness and anger. I didn't feel that I should have to explain but did so anyway, defensively reminding him that Lucas had been in the emergency room the night before with his heart racing and not feeling well.

Exhausted from the ordeal, he had managed to make it up to his last two classes and had called to ask my permission to go home. What was wrong with that? In a harsh voice he began emphatically telling me what he thought was wrong with the incident, by accusing me of not caring about the grades required for Lucas to graduate on time. He angrily began pounding his fork at his food and holding his knife as if intending to slit my throat, and not the food on his plate.

My heart pounding harder inside my chest and my head beginning to ache, I sat there without saying a word and guardedly put up my barriers. Why could he not put as much effort into our relationship as he was willing to put into everything else? But at that point I no longer cared to speculate on anything concerning our relationship; it didn't matter anymore--and I realized that for the first time. His voice continued to raise, his manner increasingly aggressive as he angrily slammed everything he touched before him on the table. "Why can't you talk? Is this the way you responded when you got in trouble with your mom? You once said that your parents never got involved with your schoolwork and did not care, and you are doing the same thing with Lucas by letting him do whatever he wants and not parenting him! I'm not mad at him, I'm mad at *you* for the way you are dealing with all of this. It is *your* fault, and you will not let me do anything to change it!"

Before I could stop myself, the words erupted from my mouth. "You can't just parent Lucas when you want to discipline him or complain to him! It takes more than that to be a parent!" His disconcerted response to me was, "I have been making every effort to be nice to him! I scarcely say anything to him unless it's to make him clean the bathroom or keep his bedroom floor picked up. And I really haven't even confronted him about that lately!"

The only two words I heard vented in his belligerent exchange were "effort" and "nice." I don't know what I felt or why those words stuck, but what I did know was that his choice of words bothered me. Nice? He was making an effort to be *nice*? Did it take so much effort to be nice to either of us? I was tired of the scene he was making, and determined it was time for me to leave. I asked the server if she would bring me a to-go box for my uneaten food, pulled out the money to pay my portion of the check and handed it to him. He all but threw it in my direction with a smirk, and when I shoved it toward him a second time he placed the money in the center of the table.

Trying to control myself, I pulled out my checkbook to write a check for my half of the rent due at the first of the month, and when I offered it to him he shoved it into his shirt pocket, leaving the cash on the table. What a nice tip the waitress was apparently going to get from us! I didn't care, and once he signed and put the credit card in his wallet, I stood to leave.

Without uttering a word we walked toward our own cars, and then drove off in opposite directions without glancing each other's way even once. The reality of our grievances hit me, and I knew I could not live another four to six months under the same roof with Derek until after Lucas graduated, whether he graduated on time or not. Feeling intolerably bewildered, I drove down the street to the playground and parked underneath the streetlight. I sat there asking myself the question to which I repeatedly implored to know lately, "How did I get here?" I bowed my head against the steering wheel and began to cry. I was drained, exasperated, discouraged, and disappointed. It had to stop, now.

Dean had already prearranged to pick Lucas up from work and take him to their house for the weekend, so I called Rylee to confirm, unable to hide being upset from her. We briefly discussed the earlier incident before she shared her solution; move to Burleson and live with her and Dean. I could use their garage for storage rather than pay a monthly storage fee, and Lucas could drive the hour trip to and from school. It would mean that I would also make that time-consuming drive, but it was either move there with them or stay with Derek in Richland Hills. For me there was nothing further to contemplate.

After arguing with Derek I was anxious about going to the house alone and risking another altercation with him, but I had to get a few things for both Lucas and myself. I told Rylee I would go to the house and grab what I could if Derek wasn't there, and call her once I was headed her way. She was leery of me going to the house and fretfully stated as much, but I assured her it would be ok. Arriving outside the house it didn't appear he was home, so I rushed inside and began blindly grabbing and packing anything that Lucas or I would need and be most costly to replenish, knowing clothes would be the easiest of necessities to replace. My heart stopped several times thinking I heard Derek at the door, suspicious he would pull up behind me and block me from leaving.

Satisfied with what I'd packed, I pulled out of the driveway as quickly as possible, relieved he wouldn't be afforded the opportunity to impugn my motives if he so had the hankering. I had a couple of hours to squander and needed to shop for clothes to wear to the funeral on Saturday, so I headed to Kohl's after stopping at Ross and Target. Why is it that if you aren't looking for something, it seems liberally and readily available at your whim? But, when you're searching relentlessly for something, it is nowhere to be found regardless where or how hard you look? Hitting the Kohl's department store in Burleson was my last hope, and as late as it was I didn't have much time before they closed.

You know you are desperate when you begin looking at the store mannequins and envision undressing them, not caring what the ensemble would look like or how well the items might fit. The saddest part is, that as desperate as I was, that idea wasn't working either. Exasperated, I grabbed a pair of black slacks, a coordinated shirt and jacket with jewelry to accessorize, along with a pair of black high-heeled shoes to complete my outfit, finally heading to the checkout register with minutes to spare until closing time. One set of clothes...one day at a time.

The next day I drove to Houston for the funeral and stayed afterward with Gayle and her family until Sunday as I had planned. Gayle and I had stayed up late into the night with her mother, laughing and crying about life as one often does when death has plagued our existence. She and her mother had wanted me to meet one of her brothers *when* I left Derek, and we laughed about the fact that I ended up driving to the cemetery in the backseat of his car, while his girlfriend sat up front in "my" seat. We cried about the emptiness of losing someone to death at the hands of our Lord God, and the bereavement of a love lost toward someone or from someone we once held so closely within our hearts. It was no secret that we were all mourning our own loss, in our own way. Gayle knew that come the next day, I would have to choose to either sustain my relationship with Derek, or bury my past.

Driving behind her that next evening, the closer we got to our destination the more I began to analyze which route to take. Apprehension gripped me as I got closer and closer to home, uncertain of my specific direction as I reached the divided highway with mere seconds to make my decision. The left lane headed down I-35 and was the direction to Rylee and Dean's, if I veered to the right it would keep me behind Gayle and ultimately to Derek. As I came upon the split, I steered the car to the left and headed down I-35, Gayle blinking her headlights in acknowledgement as she went the opposite direction. I was emphatically aware that I had just taken the road toward an altered path in my life.

There had been no further communication with Derek since we had parted ways the Friday night we'd met for dinner. I had merely informed him that I would be leaving from the kid's house to go to the funeral in Houston and I'd stay with the kids after I returned. Not once had he called to check on me or touch base, nor had I called him to check on him or touch base. Therefore, when he called me late Sunday evening to question where I was and when I intended on coming home, I simply told him that I wasn't. I could no longer imagine staying, and I could no longer imagine going.

We conceded that the relationship was undeniably finished, and established there was no logic in waiting until Lucas graduated in June. Why wait? We hung up the phone, and I fell backwards onto the bed closing my eyes, completely drained but to some degree relieved. I determined Lucas's spring break to be the most advantageous time to move and attempt to find him a car, so I took a week of vacation during that timeframe. There wasn't a need for secrecy anymore, so I let Derek know the details of my move, and ironically he gave the impression he was reasonably shocked that I actually intended to leave.

The movers were scheduled and the moving boxes packed and ready to head to Burleson, where everything would be stored in the garage until I moved. I had told Lucas to meet me at the house to pack his things, and he had me swear that we would be gone before Derek came home. However, right as we'd finished packing the last box and was loading a few items into the car, I noticed Derek driving down the street. Even though I had told him we were there packing and preparing to move, I felt like a thief caught in the act. I could hear the masked groan arise from Lucas, and with each "I told you, Mom!" that he spoke underneath his breath, Derek got closer to the house. I couldn't predict how assertive or compassionate Derek was going to be, so my own emotions were somewhat convoluted.

Pulling into the driveway, Derek got out of the car and made his way into the house exhibiting an apathetic mannerism, then stood inside the entryway looking about as if a typical day coming home from work. With an austere look crossing his face Lucas moved past him trying to avoid eye contact, as I explained that the movers would be coming the next day for the boxes we'd packed. As if it wasn't already awkward enough, Derek prolonged the conversation by discussing the possibility of renting a U-Haul truck and his assistance with loading and driving, to save on operating cost. An hour and a half later we determined it would be less costly to stick with my original plan and keep the movers previously scheduled.

Walking toward the front door to make our exit, the uncomfortable moment was there between all of us. There was no way to avoid it, especially when Derek reached to hug Lucas and told him not to be a stranger. Then Derek turned to me, and I hugged him goodbye as if I was leaving to go shopping for the day, and would be returning home later that evening. Tears filled my eyes, and while I could still manage it without falling apart, I turned and walked away. The previous months of stress and the fact that I was leaving again hit me hard, and I still had to return with the movers the following day and finish.

The next day the boxes I'd packed and the furniture I was taking were loaded onto the truck in record timing. I don't know if it was due to my compelling persuasion that I was on a major budget and had implored them to work as productively as possible, or the ominous dark clouds and the promise of rain that did the job. I went unaccompanied to the house to assist the movers, and felt immensely alone and maybe even slightly bitter for having to make yet another move without the assistance of the kids. It hadn't helped that they didn't once ask if there was anything I needed help with, or what they could do to make the transition smoother. Because of their lack of support I was now rushing around in attempts to beat the weather, fretful that what little possessions I was taking would get soaked and possibly ruined before the move was completed.

The clouds began to get darker and the winds stronger, so it was no surprise that as the truck was pulling out of the driveway, a few sprinkles began to fall on the car window. All the way to Rylee and Dean's, I kept praying that the downpour would postpone until everything was unloaded off the truck. The drive from one house to the other gave me plenty of time to relive the goodbye between Derek and I. How could it be that so much animosity, anger, and frustration endured between us for so long seem as if it was never there in the final separation? That in the concluding moments between us there seemed to be nothing less than bittersweet heartache and tears?

What little rain that had begun to fall onto the windshield earlier had completely dissolved, as I pulled up behind the moving truck just as the movers began the unloading process. Rylee and Dean came out of the house with Lucas following closely behind, all three watching as though observing a stranger moving in next door. Once the movers completed their task, I signed the invoice and turned to look at the garage now crammed with the last remnants of all that I possessed. The overflowing garage loomed before me as just one more abominable mess I had to clean up.

Without speaking a word to me, the kids turned to go back inside the house as the movers began pulling out from the driveway. Through cascading tears I watched the truck reach the stop sign down the road, barely noticing that the heavens had finally opened up to allow the rain to come pouring down as if shedding tears of sorrow, too.

The succeeding days were considerably bleak, and not exclusively due to the gray clouds and the endless rain. My dream of a new beginning all but dissipated before my eyes, and it felt as if I was retreating into some kind of anarchy. Whenever the offer was made to live with my daughter and son-in-law they had been receptive and supportive, but evidently the reality of me moving in had arrived and their impudence toward me triggered. I hadn't even completely settled in and Dean's domineering temperament had already emerged as if a switch had been flipped. It was evident that Rylee was feeling guarded and torn between her husband and mother, while Lucas evidently felt that he had gone from bad to even worse pandemonium. I held my tongue and my breath, mindful that everyone was tired and maybe a bit anxious, understandably so.

A few days after I'd moved in we decided to get out of the house for lunch, the gloom amongst us still prominent in more ways than one. Lucas and I took my car and Dean and Rylee took theirs because they had mentioned that they wanted to shop afterward. It was transparent that they didn't want us to tag along for the shopping, and even more obvious that the unresolved friction was creating futile hostility. I seized the opportunity to ask Lucas if he had any inkling what might be bothering Dean, and was informed that Dean had voiced "concerns" that I'd start decorating the house with my things and in my style, taking over their house as if it was mine.

I questioned Lucas as to why on earth Dean would imply or even think that? Not a single item had been brought in from the garage including my bed and TV, even my clothes remained unpacked in wardrobe boxes. He simply shrugged indifferently and stared outside the window without further response. I had moved from the house and in with my daughter for the primary objective of saving for their upcoming wedding and to give them a memorable day. I had no other choice but to live with them if I wanted to achieve that. I was suddenly feeling unappreciated for my sacrifices and offended at their behavior. I had the impression that I was being tremendously intrusive and they were helping *me,* not vice-versa.

Lucas became defensive as I questioned him, lashing out defensively that he knew he shouldn't have told me anything Dean had said. With that remark I quickly commented that we shouldn't have moved, even though my intentions had been to make things better for everyone, including him. Then he said something that suggested he had contemplated the confrontation at hand. "I'll just move back to Plano! I'm tired of this bullshit!" Of course as a mom, the foul language did not help my mood in any way, even though I felt the same. Not only was he talking about moving back to Plano after everything we had gone through, but he was also going to be cruel and disrespectful!

If I had not been driving, I think I may very well have slapped my son for the first time in his life, and for an instant contemplated pulling the car over and pushing him into the pouring rain to find his own way home, wherever home was to him. By the end of my response to his remark, he understood that he had gone to far. By the time we arrived at the restaurant, all I could do was sit in my car as he hopped out and ran inside, unconcerned about getting drenched and even less if I followed. My heart felt as if it was torn into shreds, and the very air I breathed being sucked from my lungs. My kids were grown and could now make decisions for themselves, and they had arbitrarily concluded I was to blame for everything, including the storms.

Nothing improved in the few days that followed, but regardless of the circumstance I had to accomplish getting Lucas a car for transportation to and from school, and pinpoint something affordable. My bonus check from work wasn't equivalent to the amount I had received the previous year and had been depending on this year. Unfortunately, the amount was hardly enough for dinner and a movie. I could have used both now. I calculated using it all toward a down payment for a new car, or purchasing a secondhand car minus monthly payments.

I was able to locate a Tahoe in the paper that was pretty close to my budget, and arranged to meet with the owner for a test-drive. The front window had a little crack in the corner, and the tags needed to be renewed, but compared to the other cars and trucks, it was exciting to find a vehicle that had a running motor and looked remotely like the picture posted. It was approximately three hundred dollars more than I could afford, and I wouldn't be able to get the money to him for another week, but boldly asked if I could pick it up at that time. The man explained that his father was the owner of the truck so he would have to check with him, but felt that the arrangement would not be a problem. I drove away feeling uplifted that I'd found a car, thankful it was one thing I could mark off my list.

I hadn't mentioned anything to Lucas about the truck, and he continued in his endeavors to find one. Within a few additional days of his constant pestering to search for cars and wasting his time and mine, I went ahead and told him I'd bought a truck. He was as excited as I hoped that he would be, and sincerely appreciative. Without wasting any more time, I texted the owners that following Monday morning to make the arrangements to take possession of the truck. There wasn't a response to my first text, nor the second text, and I presumed that he was unavailable and would call that evening.

But later that night when I hadn't heard from him, I became slightly panicked that he was not responding to my calls or my text messages. Around 10:30 Tuesday night his text finally came through: "Sorry, my dad sold the car to someone at his church for full price on Monday, as is." My dumbfounded response in return was a stunned "What?" but it didn't matter. I no longer had a vehicle for Lucas and had to tell him that he wasn't getting the vehicle I'd promised. Worse, during the interim of thinking I had found him one and learning that wasn't so, I'd managed to lose four days of prospective shopping. The last thing to cross my mind that night before going to sleep was an inappropriate but true thought; church people or not, they should go straight to hell for doing that to me.

By Thursday, I was ready to stand on a street corner and sell my soul to get my son a car. Nightmares of the previous week and the experience of looking for a car fresh in my mind, we embarked on a mission to find a half decent vehicle by Friday. I will never forget negotiating with the first car salesman and him asking me what amount of money I aimed to spend. When I told him $2,500.00, his facial expression looked as though he was certain I had been drinking. I could feel my blood pressure rising as well as my color, but one way or another, I was determined I was getting a car as intended. He showed us a "salvaged" car that made an outrageous noise from underneath the hood during the test drive, and looked like it was going to fall apart any minute.

Lucas wasn't concerned about either, eager to pursue the purchase and be done with the entire process. Sensing our desperation, the car dealer spoke up and vocalized that he would put his daughter in the car, at which point I debated telling him to go ahead and put her in it just to witness his expression. I didn't trust my son to be in it, and began thinking I was the only person logically weighing the situation at hand. Lucas had to be safe, and I was not putting money into a car that I'd spend indefinite amounts of money towing and fixing every other week.

After numerous attempts and disgruntled car salesmen, we sat at a local Honda dealership much later that day, both a bit cynical. We were by no means impressed with the dealership, but that didn't change the fact that two hours later we had test-driven a car and managed to walk away with keys in hand. My son hopped inside the car and drove off as if he was racing in the Indy 500, an ecstatic smile igniting across his entire face. I wasn't as thrilled…I now had an additional car loan that I would have to pay $230.00 a month with an increase in insurance and gas expenses to boot. My bills were increasing, despite the goal to decrease them in efforts to provide a wedding that I was beginning to doubt I'd be able to pay for. How had I managed to move in with my kids and live out of a tiny bedroom to help with my finances, yet end up more behind than ahead? If you have ever seen a monkey scratching its head, that's pretty much how I felt. Nevertheless, the animal that suitably described me right then would probably have been a jackass.

Chapter 26

Anytime you get a call from your children and the first thing you hear them say is, "I love you, Mom!" especially from that of a teenager, you should immediately take a deep, steady breath and prepare yourself for one of three things: (1) "I am dying, and I wanted your voice to be the last I heard before I die." (2) "I wanted to thank you for making me the amazing, responsible person that I am today." (3) "I need...I want..." Nine times out of ten your response isn't going to be the answer they called to hear from you, leading them to respond with a smart-alecky response along the lines of, "Whatever!" as you seriously debate ending their lives, all the while deliberating how on earth your child is the utmost irresponsible teenager in the world?

Lucas had called to inform me that a friend had invited him to the movies, adding a quick sales pitch that his friend would pay if he could go. I paused, wondering if he had any inclination of the money I'd recently paid and the expenditures that remained, and why his focus wasn't more on school at the moment. "Is he going to also pay for gas and food?" I replied. Need I even tell you the next words that sprang from his mouth at that response? The call to tell me he loved me dissipated into thin air, as he bitterly reinforced that he didn't have any friends close by, thanks to me. It was now moving on six weeks living with the kids, and it was wearing thin on all levels of sanity. Lucas was going to be eighteen in three days, and in his own mind he was now grown and self-sufficient.

For some intangible reason, I felt as though I'd unwillingly lost any parental rights or influence over my own children. When they were younger and had no direction, I was there to mentor. When they needed love and warmth, I provided love and warmth. When they needed protection, a listening ear, or someone to wipe away the tears, share the laughter and praise achievements, I was there. But while their needs had changed almost overnight, my impulse to provide and take care of them as I had throughout their lives, had not.

The reality was excruciatingly hard to admit, but my intention had not been to keep them dependent or make them feel obligated to me, I had simply wanted to do right by them and bequeath them the life and love I never had. I felt reprehensively unnerved that perhaps I had failed them more than I had failed anything else up to that point. Had it been a matter of weeks or months, or had it been from day one and I was realizing it years too late? Things were so chaotic and there was so much animosity between all of us that my guess was the latter. And it wasn't just about my relationship with them, but with Lance and Derek. Where Lance had all but deserted them, Derek had stuck it out and remained diligent in his efforts to be a dad to them, pushing them to be independent, to know right from wrong, he'd graciously become a devoted mentor to them. While he had been pushing them to grow up and persuading me to let go, had I been subconsciously pushing him away? Was I the one who had pushed him into his behavioral change and caused the problems between us? I was utterly mystified.

Numerous things crossed my mind following that unnerving conversation with Lucas and my quest for answers, none of which helped to clear my mind. I was facing an emotional meltdown brought on by the burdens that encumbered me. The conglomeration of kids, work, wedding, finances and divorce was slowly taxing upon my frayed emotions and I was beginning to feel overwhelmed more than ever. It was a perfect storm waiting to happen. It never failed that when I was in my uttermost fragile state of mind, Derek would manage to call. It seemed as if fate continuously pulled us together throughout most of our lives, and the phone calls he made to check on me turned into having dinner once a week. Our once a week dinner turned into dinner several times a week and then eventually to us eating in and me staying overnight.

My conceptualization about the relationship with Derek was that I kept winding up with him like a yo-yo on a string, so maybe we were meant to be together. I found myself assessing the scenario, and debating if things hadn't kept getting in the way or hadn't become problematic, would we have made it? The kids did not understand what was going on anymore than I did. They were baffled by the fact that I had left Derek but spending more time with him than when I lived at the house. Lucas was making the seventy-mile round trip from Burleson to school and his friends, while I was pretty much exactly where I had started...or ended.

It was asinine to be thinking of moving back in with Derek, but it seemed the only option at my disposal to get out of the hole I'd dug. With that frame of mind, I casually mentioned the idea of returning to Richland Hills to Lucas, rationalizing how he'd be closer to school and his friends again, making the arrangement practical for all purposes intended. I had concluded that he was in agreement with the idea, up until he exploded while were discussing a few details associated with the possibility.

His voice filled with tempestuous defiance, his expression with resentment and disdain: "If you go back to Derek, I'm not going with you this time!" Hearing the callous remark, I couldn't decide if I was angry toward him or if I admired him for his convictions, having none of my own at the moment. "You know what will happen! You will go back a third time and I will have to put up with the same shit, and not Grandmother or anything else will be different! Jason and Misty will not be different, Derek will not be different, and you will end up sleeping on the couch crying every night, talking about how much you are tired of dealing with it all."

I detested the fact that what he said was probably true, whether I wanted to believe it or not. Yet at the end of the day, Derek had been a constituent part of my life for almost thirty years. We had grappled through as many trials and tribulations as most, and married or unmarried he had been the singular, unremitting relationship in my life. As much as I wanted to reach a place of acceptance for what I had, and perhaps relinquish specific things I'd searched endlessly for but felt impossible to have, it was time I did one or the other concerning Derek. The resentment and defiance coming from Lucas wasn't just reflective of his own plight, but his roundabout way of looking out for my best interest and protecting me. He didn't want me to fail again, and he didn't want me to settle. Tormented by my indecisions, the clarification I was seeking came when I least expected, giving me insight that I had not had for some time.

I had prepared a pork loin for dinner and called Rylee to let her know that it was ready for the oven, surprised she wasn't home when she answered. She told me that she had stopped by the youth pastor's house to discuss something with him, and naturally inquisitive at her response, repeated "Something"? What was the something she had to discuss with him but didn't care to share with me? She came across vague, and I thought it might possibly be regarding some pre-wedding concern. I didn't want to pry too much, but the more we spoke, the more I realized the unspoken anguish she was trying to hide was because she didn't want to upset *me*. I didn't care if she disclosed anything to me or not, only that she was calm enough to make it home and her safety wasn't compromised. I was about to have her pull off the highway when she blurted out the cause of her distress. "Daddy is not coming to the wedding!" My response was a flabbergasted, "Why? What happened? Did he tell you that?"

She sorrowfully commenced informing me that Lance had been promoted to an executive position and would be relocating to San Diego with Simone and Zachary. After telling her that he was moving, he had coldheartedly told her he had no further intentions to be a part of her or Lucas's lives, and he definitely wasn't going to her wedding to be a "ceremonial dad". He further articulated his disapproval that she was getting married, and his discontent concerning the direction of her life, and the choices she had made overall. In closing, he had the gall to place blame on her for their relationship--or the lack of a relationship. At the end of the conversation, he had also accused her of placing a restraining order on him during the time Lucas had left to move back with me. She couldn't stop crying, and I could hear her emotions escalating as she agonizingly recapped the conversation.

I felt perplexed at the mention of a restraining order and a trifle unnerved by his allegation. What in the heck was he implying? Rylee was not the one that had placed a restraining order on him. Was he referring to the restraining order that I had issued during the custody battle for Lucas? There was no way he could pin that ordeal on his daughter. I opened my mouth to tell her so, when she commenced sharing the comeback she had to her father, which included a list of her efforts for their relationship and his lack of efforts. Her sorrow was amplified by the frustration that we were all struggling, and he didn't feel even marginally obliged to offer his assistance. He had not stepped up to the plate emotionally nor financially for them in a long time, yet he continually did so for Simone and Zachary. They would soon be living in a colossal house on a San Diego beach, none of them wanting or needing for anything.

She and Lucas had asked for nothing but his love, and he'd been unscrupulous in his tenacious indifference toward them, regardless of their attempts at developing a relationship with him. Why was he willing to toss them aside and do it so effortlessly? How could any of that be fair?

I took a long steady breath to collect myself and my thoughts before attempting to explain away the pointless shenanigans to my daughter in a way that might ease her turmoil, and help us both make some sort of sense out it all. Even though my own thoughts reflected hers, I could not let her know that. "I don't understand why some things are the way they are, or why your own father would tell you he wants nothing to do with you and your brother. But I do know one thing; though his life seems to emulate a fantastically successful one, no amount of money will dispel the emptiness he feels when he sits alone in his big house one day, void of the memories and laughter that he missed out on sharing with his children. He'll be haunted by disappointments and heartache from working away his life, and come face to face with his choices and regrets." I reminded her of the life and memories she had growing up and those still to come, full of unexpected treasures and unplanned dreams. She would have to make her life her own, and learn to embrace what she did have. She couldn't let someone else determine her happiness, or her success. What her father was doing was inexcusable, but it was her choice to renounce the encumbrance of that relationship and disappointment…or not.

She didn't say anything for a moment, but she had stopped crying. The realization that there was nothing she could do if her father chose not to be a part of her life was hard to accept, but it was a reality she had to concede. We both knew she had lost him long before, and though it would haunt her throughout her life she would eventually find a way to release that burden, allowing her the freedom to move forward. At that moment however, I sensed she needed time to mourn the loss that had held her captive for several years now. Finishing my viewpoint, I noticed her demeanor was much calmer because I could no longer hear the distress or sniffles penetrating her voice, as she informed me she was pulling into their driveway. The unpredicted storm that had developed wasn't creating any notable traffic delays, so I told her I'd be home right behind her.

Pulling up to the curb in front of the house I became conscious of how extremely tired I was, and dreaded what I was about to be subjected to. I sat for a few moments in hopes of mentally preparing myself for the proliferating emotions I'd face with my daughter, trying to remember to breathe and praying a brief prayer for guidance. As the rain began to fall even harder, I figured I might as well go into the house and deal with the inevitable rather than sit in my car procrastinating. Running to the house, I simultaneously began shaking some of the rain off as I reached for the door, looking up in surprise when I opened it to hear laughter greet me.

Standing in the doorway it appeared the laughter was coming from Rylee, who was sitting on the couch with Lucas seated directly across from her. Dean was in the kitchen with the pork loin in hand that I'd called to tell my daughter about, laughing along with them. It was apparent Rylee had been crying, but her brother had evidently been sharing one of his witty jokes or wise-crack remarks that had made them laugh, and made me smile just watching them.

Dean was the first to notice me, and seemed relieved that I was home as he hurried over to give me one of his bear hugs, Rylee close behind to do the same. In-between the hugs I heard Lucas's laughter still ringing from across the room at whatever they had been laughing about. Rylee stepped up to give me a hug as Dean inquired across his shoulder what the oven temperature should be for the pork loin, as he headed toward the kitchen. By the time Dean was back in the kitchen, my daughter had all but dismissed both of them and was intently focused on telling me about her wedding dress alterations.

I hadn't made it all the way inside the house but felt a tremendous weight fall from my shoulders, and relief lift my heart from the greeting I'd received, in lieu of what I had imagined. The hustle and bustle continued behind me as I turned to shut the door, stopping midway when I noticed that the rain had ceased and an enormous, bright rainbow now encompassed the sky. I could feel the sun's rays against my face and smiled to myself, before closing the door behind me. The storm was apparently over.

As the night came and went, I meditated on all we had risen above and the difference a few seconds, minutes, hours, or days can often make in our lives. Before I walked through the door that afternoon I'd anticipated the worst, but I had been given grace, bountiful love, and hope when least expected. Earlier, as we all sat at the table enjoying the pork loin Dean bragged about preparing, I had observed that the tears were gone and the smiles genuine. Whatever was to come, on that day it felt as though it was the beginning of the end for some of our challenges, and regardless of what the future held, I realized that the past wasn't our enemy. It was given to us to learn from, to guide us and bring us closer in our relationship with God. It could either provide us with faith, or take it away from us. Some referred to it as "free will," and it was our path to choose.

One of my favorite stories of faith in the Bible is located in *Matthew 14:22–33 (NIV)*

22 And straightaway Jesus constrained His disciples to get into a ship, and to go before Him unto the other side, while He sent the multitudes away.

23 And when He had sent the multitudes away, He went up into a mountain apart to pray: and when the evening was come, He was there alone.

24 But the ship was now in the midst of the sea, tossed with waves: for the wind was contrary.

25 And in the fourth watch of night Jesus went unto them, walking on the sea.

26 And when the disciples saw Him walking on the sea, they were troubled, saying, It is a spirit; and they cried out for fear.

27 But straightway Jesus spoke unto them, saying, be of good cheer; it is I; be not afraid.

28 And Peter answered Him and said, Lord, if it Be Thou, bid me come unto Thee on the water.

29 And He said, Come. And when Peter was come down out of the ship, he walked on the water, to go to Jesus.

30 But he saw the wind boisterous, he was afraid: and beginning to sink, he cried, saying, Lord, save me.

31 And immediately Jesus stretched forth His hand, and caught him, and said unto him, O thou of little faith, wherefore didst thou doubt?

32 And when they were come into the ship, the wind ceased.

33 They that were in the ship came and worshiped Him, saying, of a truth Thou art the Son of God.

Each time I read this biblical story, it emphatically reminds me how it illustrates that of my own life and so many others as well. When seeking the Lord, we arrogantly mandate validation that our faith in Him is deserved and forget the miracles He has already performed through us, for us, and around us. We forget that He has plans for us, and that we must trust in His timing. We have a tendency to overlook the infinite number of times He has aided and shielded us, unable to fathom His majestic grace and His tireless love.

***

Each of us has a story to share, none any less significant than the other. I simply chose to share mine. I make no excuses for the life I've lived up until now, but do wish that I could take away any sorrow or pain I inadvertently inflicted along the way. Most especially for my children...

I've written this book and risked becoming vulnerable simply to offer those suffering or bewildered the encouragement, hope, faith and even the spirit to always move forward with incessant determination. If you don't know what to do, don't do anything at all. Strive for an open mind and heart. The direction will come--perhaps not in the timeframe we've deemed relevant, but in the timeframe that eminently serves God's purpose. The most noteworthy lesson I would like those reading my story to carry with them is the fundamental lesson that I have learned: you must live life with resolve. Listen to the conviction of that inner voice, for it will guide you and bring hope and peace to your soul. Whatever struggles or ambiguities are involved, you will eventually transcend by way of God's amazing grace.

I have no idea what may await me, or how in the eleventh hour my story will conclude. I do know that so far it has always been better than what *I* had in mind, and I am grateful more times than I could conceivably count that God is the one in charge. Regardless of my improprieties, He has been gracious in allowing me countless chances, no matter the fighting and clawing to have my way, convinced my way gave me control. In the end I am thankful for the love He has given me, and the softness upon which He allows me to fall. Living a life filled with inexorable transgressions, I am grateful that my God reprimands with love, even when He has the need to be stern.

The Lord's promise is that He will always answer when we seek Him: He will never lead us into the storms or treacherous waters without the tools to stay afloat. Though we may not physically walk across stormy waters, it is inevitable that we will encounter arduous, faith-testing hardships. In those moments when we might feel submerged in despair, feel alone or unsure, the remedy is to look to Jesus and His miraculous power. He will provide us the strength we need in ways we could never begin to conceive! And in that moment when we feel that we may be sinking, He will be there to lift us, to save us from the drowning. In that moment when we think there is no hope to be found, we need only to look toward His light and reach for His outstretched hand, lifting us up to walk on water.

Epilogue

"See to it that no one misses the grace of God and that no bitter root grows up to cause trouble and defile many" (Heb. 12:15, NIV)

Jessica was never indicted for the murder of my brother, and remains sole custodian to all three of his sons. We haven't seen them since she was released from jail, and we no longer even know where they are. It is sometimes hard to believe that it all happened, and there are times I catch myself wanting to talk with both Billy and Corey, wondering where they would be and what we missed by them not being here with us. Their memories burn bright, and I count on the fact that spiritually they are both with me, and I know with certainty that one day we will all be together again.

My brother Colin divorced, and each day he strives to accomplish his own process of healing and closure. Part of that is coming to terms with the fact that it will take time to discover who he truly is, and realizing that he can be okay on his own. He recently purchased a two-acre lot with a house he's made into a home--complete with 5 dogs, 12 chickens, a rabbit and a fishpond. Trying to find his heart a home... he's dating. But the discovery of oneself is a never-ending journey, no matter where you are in life, or with whom you are going through it.

Lucas graduated high school a bit late, but I considered it simply a detour, and so many times the most marvelous part of any journey is found in detours. After years of sleeping on couches and being displaced, he eventually moved out and got his own apartment--and his own bed. To this day, given any opportunity to sleep anywhere else, he always wants to go home. His home. The ongoing heart and health conditions test his faith, but when I look at him my own heart swells with pride, and I believe that God's does as well. With continued prayer for his strength, I recognize it will be up to him to find and conquer his own voyage...to put efforts into triumphing good over evil, right over wrong...best over worst.

Rylee and Dean got married, though no one could have appreciated that the day was successfully pulled off any more than I could. Up until the Friday before their wedding day, I remained six thousand dollars short for the final payments on the wedding dress alterations, wedding cake, reception venue, hotel, photographer, and food. The saxophone I had previously listed online sold that Friday afternoon at 2:30 p.m., and six thousand dollars of cash was placed into my hands in time to deposit it that same business day, allowing me immediate available funds. Neither financial deterrents or the stormy weather was able to diminish from the wedding and reception, they were both were equally amazing.

They exchanged their vows as planned, but not quite under the circumstances we had originally rehearsed. Rylee was supposed to make her bridal walk in the Fuller Garden at the Ft. Worth Botanical Gardens, but the night before the wedding it began storming around 1:00 a.m. and never let up for two days. Improvising in the last minute of the last hour, we created a chapel inside the venue's Visitor Center located within the gardens. We started our creation by hanging a long, white satin fabric, which we draped from ceiling to floor to conceal the doors at the end of the hallway. The limited number of white chairs supplied was used to create the illusion of an aisle, and incandescent candles sitting in the windows shimmered against the rain, illuminating her pathway. It was almost ethereal. Because of the inadequate number of chairs, the majority of family and friends stood in waiting as Rylee made her walk amongst them, and remained standing as the bride and groom exchanged vows. She could not have looked more beautiful, and their love burned brighter than any sunshine might have burned that day. When I look at them and behold the love and the life they have together, it was all worth it. I earnestly wish that everyone could be so blessed, and I am grateful that they are.

Lance never moved to California like he originally told Rylee, but he didn't attend her wedding, didn't call her that day, or even send her a card wishing her happiness. As she walked toward the love of her life, I know she missed her first love being there. While disappointment, hurt and emptiness have been created between my children and their father, I know Rylee and Lucas both keep the hope that one day God will heal that relationship…just as I pray and hope for that. But until that time comes, they have begun to recognize and be comforted by the fact that they did all they could to be a part of his life: it simply is what it is. As we all do, they have to keep focused on the blessings given, which could be inclusive of some that are taken…

I completely adore my children, and have come to value the unique relationship we share. I wouldn't say that our family or our relationship is what most would call traditional, but it's ours. We recently watched a movie together depicting one of those traditional moms, whereas I jokingly commented to Rylee that I wasn't a traditional mom anymore. She grinned mischievously at me and replied, "No, but you were when you needed to be." Maybe being what we need to be in the moment is all we can do. One thing I know for certain, no matter what has happened, where we've been, or what choices we've made, the relationship with my children is solid: and filled with grace and love. Not a day passes that I don't pray for them, and count on God to sustain them when in the midst of their own perilous storms.

I moved into my own place soon after Rylee and Dean married. I never went back to Derek, and to this day we never see or speak with each other. The man I once thought I couldn't breathe without, never crosses my mind. While moving forward in just about every aspect of my life, I stuck it out with Paragon Financial Advisors and was tenacious in overcoming the various conflicts, discovering that the tribulations and changes withstood were a tremendous blessing in disguise. Not only were God given talents unveiled, I was provided the opportunity to write this book. Without the events being orchestrated by God's hand, it most probably would not have been written. I am far from being in the exact place I ultimately want to be, but venture to question that if I was, would I be at the end of my journey?

I don't waste my energy or sell myself short, incessantly rehashing "what-if" or wishful "what could have been". Whereas I once questioned the reasons for my emptiness and sought the world for my happiness, I have learned that the world cannot fill my emptiness or create my happiness. Both can only be rectified internally.

I trust that prayer does work, and in miraculous ways we sometimes don't even comprehend. The ongoing majority of my wars are the ones still fought within, and the resolutions are never revealed in the obvious, but discovered in the one constant of my life: my Lord and Savior. I'm learning that having faith in myself doesn't necessitate absolute control over everything or everybody, and that yielding to our higher power really is the epitome of faith. Perhaps because wisdom has come with time and experience, I eagerly and possibly a bit more cautiously, await and embrace the unknown before me. And somewhere, deep inside...I hold onto the belief and hope that this segment of my life might just happen to be magnificently extraordinary!

With that being said, did I mention that I eventually remarried years down the road? To that brother Gayle and her mom wanted me to date. I ride in the front seat now...but that's another story.

CPSIA information can be obtained
at www.ICGtesting.com
Printed in the USA
LVOW08s1501260717
542714LV00001BA/37/P

9 781496 965646